Other titles in this se

GW00676298

Taxation Simpl

A concise guide to all the basic forms of taxatio down-to-earth descriptions of all the principal a and packed with tips and advice for reducing or avoiding tax. Areas covered include: • income tax • corporation tax • capital allowances • capital gains tax • inheritance tax • value added tax • council tax • self-assessment.

Pensions Simplified

A complete guide to the current pensions system. The book includes a full description of current entitlements under the various types of pension scheme available, both from the State and privately, and gives detailed advice on how to set up a tax-efficient scheme to protect your own future. Areas covered include: • how to choose a pension, set it up and care for it • taking account of the tax implications • retirement planning • what choices are offered at retirement • transfers and opt-outs • dealing with divorce and mortgages • death before and after retirement.

Succession Planning Simplified

Succession planning – planning for the future ownership and management of a business after the death or departure of a key executive – is often left until the last minute – or not done at all. However, the benefits of advance planning can be enormous, not only in protecting the value of the business for the owner's heirs and successors, but also in ensuring a viable future for staff and employees. *Succession Planning Simplified* is a practical guide to the whole area, including a review of legal and taxation implications of the various alternative types of succession plan, and a thorough explanation of the planning methodology involved.

Business Protection Simplified

In uncertain economic times it is especially important to take whatever measures you can to protect the profitability of your business. This book covers the whole range of options, including "keyman" insurance, credit insurance, health and safety instruments, currency risk, life assurance, employment insurance, and much more. It also addresses tactical and strategic measures which managers can employ to protect their businesses, through sound financial planning, tax-efficient management, and properly constructed employee incentive schemes.

For further information on any of these books visit **www.mb2000.com**
or telephone Management Books 2000 on 01865 600738

The full list of titles in the "Simplified" series is:

Business Protection Simplified
Inheritance Tax Simplified
Long-Term Care Simplified
Pensions Simplified
School and University Fees Simplified
Succession Planning Simplified
Taxation Simplified
Tax-Efficient Investments Simplified
Tax-Efficient Wills Simplified

For further information on any of these titles,
or for a complete list of Management Books 2000 titles
visit our web-site, **www.mb2000.com**

INHERITANCE TAX SIMPLIFIED

Tony Granger

2000

This edition first published in 2020 by Management Books 2000 Ltd
36 Western Road
Oxford, OX1 4LG, UK
Tel: 0044 (0) 1865 600738
E-mail: info@mb2000.com
Web: **www.mb2000.com**

British Library Cataloguing in Publication Data is available

ISBN 9781852527877

About the Author

Tony Granger has been an inheritance tax and estate planning specialist and financial planner for more than 30 years. More recently he has established an independent trustee advisory service to assist trustees with investment trust compliance and to provide a workable inter-face for financial advisers and investment managers who plan and manage trust investments. He is the author of many publications and books, including *How to Finance Your Retirement* (Random House/Century), *Wealth Strategies for Your Business* (Random House/Century), *EIS and VCT Investors' Guide* (30 Day Publishing), *Independent Financial Advice and Fee-Based Financial Planning* and *The Retirement Planning Workstation* (30 Day Publishing), *School and University Fees Simplified* (Management Books 2000), *Pensions Simplified* (Management Books 2000), *Business Protection Simplified* (Management Books 2000), *Succession Planning Simplified* (Management Books 2000), *Tax Efficient Investments Simplified* (Management Books 2000), *Long-Term Care Simplified* (Management Books 2000), Elysium Bereavement Guide (*Practical Guide Series*), and numerous Tax Insider articles.

Inheritance Tax Simplified is aimed at consumers and financial advisers alike, and is most topical, affecting more than 10 million consumers, who should plan now to minimise their inheritance tax liabilities as house values begin to pick up, and the Chancellor continues to increase the tax take from estates and trusts.

Tony is a member of the Chartered Institute for Securities and Investment (CISI) and holds the certified financial planner certificate (CFP), as well as degrees in law and commerce. He is a past President of the Institute of Life and Pensions Advisers (Financial Planning Institute) of South Africa, and a member of the Personal Finance Society (PFS). He is past President of the Insurance Institute of Shropshire and Mid-Wales. He is Visiting Professor at London Guildhall Business and Law School.

Acknowledgements

I am indebted to Nick Dale-Harris of Management Books for his support and guidance in what is a most complex subject to write simply about.

Also, a special thank you to David Bertram FCA CTA for his editorial comment and technical insight. David is an experienced Chartered Accountant and Chartered Tax Adviser. He has worked mainly in tax including two years in Canada and as tax training manager to a major national firm. He is the author, co-author, or editor of a range of tax books, services and digests, a lecturer to professional and other audiences and a writer of articles in the professional press.

Thank you also to Zurich Life Assurance which sponsored earlier editions.

Contents

Forewords

Inheritance tax planning has become more and more complex with ongoing changes in regulation yet is as important as ever as demographics and property values in particular outpace the increases in the allowances. Never before has it been so important to seek the advice of a Certified Financial Planner professional to ensure that planning needs are taken care of. Books such as these can only serve to highlight the issues that consumers face as they plan for the future.

Nick Cann
Past CEO of the Institute of Financial Planning

I am delighted to be able to write a preface to this excellent publication. One of my aims as President of the Personal Finance Society is to seek to improve financial knowledge within the general public. It is essential that the consumer should seek advice from a suitably qualified Adviser and I would urge readers to seek out an Adviser who is a member of the Personal Finance Society. Such a person will be committed to maintaining a high level of knowledge and will adhere to a code of ethics. Consumers need access to well-written publications that explain financial concepts succinctly. This enables them, together with their Financial Adviser, to make informed decisions.

My hope is that after reading this publication you will feel better prepared to take decisions on your own inheritance tax needs.

Carole Nicholls FCII FPFS
President of the Personal Finance Society (2008)

Introduction

This book on inheritance tax and estate planning is timely and includes the latest update following the OTS Inheritance Tax Review published 5 July 2019. The groundswell of public opinion is unhappy about the many increasingly burdensome taxes affecting inherited and gifted property in the United Kingdom today. People who previously thought that they would not be burdened by inheritance taxes are now increasingly falling into the tax net, mostly because of increasing house prices along with the freezing of the inheritance tax exempt allowance of £325,000 (nil rate band) now to 2021, from when it will be indexed at the CPI. The introduction of the additional allowance with effect from April 2017 should begin to take more families out of the IHT net. However, until then we will continue to see more estates paying inheritance taxes. IHT receipts are currently £5.4 bn and expected to rise to £6.3bn in 2023/24 (Inheritance Tax Statistics HMRC).

Even those who have previously planned to leave assets to particular classes of beneficiaries will have to think again, as the effect of legislation affecting trusts and the safeguarding of trust assets, and the protection of beneficiaries, such as spouses and minors, mean that changes have to be made, and planning conducted to be more effective than ever before. Previous Governments were unable to give certainty and clarity to consumers in an area that affects them so acutely. We have seen this in pensions legislation, tax legislation and other areas, such as in trust legislation. Changes, often retrospective, bring a new perspective into planning, and consumers must be prepared to align their current thinking for financial and estate planning accordingly.

A summary of the significant changes affecting estates and inheritance in recent years is as follows (note that although some announced areas appear dated, planning for IHT goes back 7-14 years on trusts, longer on domicile etc.):

- **Loans to reduce inheritance tax:** after 6 April 2013, the amount of the loan must first be deducted from the value of the assets it was used to acquire, not the property it is secured on. The loan and the IHT-exempt assets cancel each other out in the IHT calculation and no tax is saved. (But see page 82 for more in this subject – this type of loan can still be a useful tax-planning tool.)

- **IHT Spouse exemption if non domiciled:** FA 2013 radically changes the IHT treatment where one spouse is UK domiciled and the other (recipient) is not. Up to 5 April 2013, such transfers were subject to a lifetime allowance of £55,000. After 6 April 2013 the IHT exempt amount that can be transferred from a UK domiciled spouse/civil partner to a non-UK domiciled spouse/civil partner is increased to the NRB amount, currently £325,000.

- **FA 2013 provided for an annual premium limit of £3,600 on life assurance policies.** Previously, there was no upper limit on investment premiums payable into a qualifying policy allowing individuals to obtain unlimited relief from higher and additional rates of income tax.

- **Domicile and residence statutory residence test:** There is now a statutory residence test for individuals from 6 April 2013.

- **Income arising in trusts that remains undistributed for 5 years or more:** is now treated as part of the trust capital when calculating the 10-year anniversary charge. See new section 64(1A) IHTA 1984 introduced by the Finance Bill 2014,

- **IHT nil rate band freeze:** the government will extend the freezing of the IHT threshold at £325,000 until April 2021.

- **Non-UK domiciled individuals** ("non-doms") who use the remittance basis and resident in the UK (at 2014)
  - 7 out of last 9 years charge unchanged at £30,000 per year.
  - 12 out of last 14 years to increase from £50,000 to £60,000 per year.
  - 17 out of last 20 years – a new charge of £90,000 to be introduced.
  - 2015 Budgets – permanent non-domiciled status abolished from 6 April 2017. If resident 15 of past 20 years will be domiciled.
  - £90,000 tax charge will become obsolete.

- **Deceased ISAs passing:** From 6 April 2015 a surviving spouse can invest as much into their own ISA as their spouse used to have on top of their usual allowance. The surviving spouse will then be given an additional one-off allowance equal to the amount the deceased had in their ISA, which would become available from 6 April 2015.

- **Pension benefits pass tax free:** From 6 April 2015 uncrystallised or drawdown defined contribution pension funds can pass to a beneficiary with no 55% death tax charge. Entirely tax free if below age 75, taxable at marginal rate over age 75.

- **Annuity benefits tax free on death:** From 6 April 2015 beneficiaries of individuals who die under age 75 with a joint life or guaranteed term annuity will be able to receive future payments from such policies tax free.

- **Joint life annuities can be passed to any beneficiary.** From April 2015, tax rules will be amended to allow people to set up joint-life annuities, which will maintain payments for any chosen beneficiary, after the original policyholder has died.

- **No tax relief for pension contributions if age over 75** confirmed (2014).

- **Multiple Trusts:** Government announces 3.12.14 that it will not now introduce a single nil-rate inheritance tax band across multiple trusts. (this would have applied from 6.6.2014 and to come in from 6.6.2015). HMRC consulted on this in August 2013.

- **Target Tax Avoidance:** The Government will introduce new rules to target avoidance through the use of multiple trusts. It will also simplify the trust calculation rules as suggested in the OFT Inheritance Tax Review 2019.

- **Armed Forces and Emergency Services:** The IHT exemption for members of the armed forces whose death is caused or hastened by injury while on active service has been extended to include members of the emergency services and humanitarian aid workers responding to emergency circumstances after 19 March 2014.

- **Intestacy Rules:** overhauled from 1 October 2014 (the Inheritance and Trustees' Powers Act 2014).

- **Multiple Trusts:** the new rules apply when property is added to more than one relevant property trust on the same day. (2015)

- **Relevant property trust:** calculation of trust changes will be simplified by removing the requirement to include non-relevant property in the computation.

- **Changes to trusts:** Periodic charge calculation changes remain in place. Legislation was to be introduced in Summer Finance Bill 2015 to remove the requirement to include non-relevant property in the calculation of the rate of tax under section 66 (the 10-year anniversary charge) and sections 68 and 69 (exit charges) for rate where appropriate for both sections.

- **Deeds of Variation:** Government to carry out review into IHT avoidance (Budget 2015) through deeds of variation. This was not proceeded with.

- **Extra NRB for Home:** From 6 April 2017, the RNRB was set at £100,000 but increases by £25,000 each year until it reaches £175,000 in April 2020. Just like the standard nil rate band, any unused RNRB on the first death of a married couple or civil partners has the potential to be transferable even if the first death occurred before 6 April 2017.

- **Proposed increase in Probate Fees** – still not passed by Parliament.

- **OTS (Office of Tax Simplification) Inheritance Tax Review – second report – Simplifying the design of Inheritance Tax 5 July 2019.**

Trust tax rates 2019/20

Discretionary Trusts and Bare Trusts

Income Tax rates
Where Trustees receive non-dividend income, 20% on income within the standard rate band (SRB) of £1,000. 45% on incomeover the standard band rate.

For dividend income, Trustees pay 7.5% on income within the SRB, and 38.1% on income above that.

Where Beneficiaries receive non-dividend trust income, tax is paid at their marginal rates of 0%,20%,40%,45%.

On dividend income, Beneficiaries pay tax at the rates of 0%,7.5%, 32.5%, 38.1%.

Capital Gains Tax Rates
Trustees pay 20% on capital gains, with a £6,000 annual exemption (shared equally by trusts with the same settlor to a minimum exemption of £1,200 for each trust).

Beneficiaries pay CGT at 10%,20% with an annual exemption of £12,000.

Trust investments and how they are made continue to be of importance, and reinforces the need for trustees to closely follow the criteria in the Trustee Act 2000 to diversify investments and take into account taxation.

Inheritance Tax 2019/20

The inheritance tax nil rate band for 2019/20 remains at £325,000 and is frozen at this level to 2020/21. Frozen since 2009, the nil rate band will remain the same until 2021, and not increase for inflation. The NRB rate is set to increase with inflation from 6 April 2021.

From 2017 if leaving the family home to direct descendants, a new nil rate band relief is added of £100,000 in that tax year, rising to £175,000 by 2020. More and more estates are growing in value and will be caught for IHT.

£425,000 each!

EIS and SEIS Investment Reliefs

For those using EIS qualifying investments where, after two years, the value of EIS qualifying shares is removed from your estate, with income tax relief of 30% limited to an amount of £1 million (or £2 million using carry-back); the Seed EIS (SEIS) provides income tax relief which can be carried back to a previous tax year at 50% for up to £100,000 invested and the value is fully out of your estate after two years. For 2019/20 the SEIS provides for CGT relief at 50% of the amount invested. This uplift could be significant for high net worth income earners, affected by the new rules on taxation and pension contributions, who desire income tax relief and a reduction of inheritance taxes.

Planning around inheritance taxes

Inheritance tax is usually a form of double taxation. People build up their assets from tax-paid income and investments in the main, only to have them taxed again on death. Later, when beneficiaries pass those assets on to others, it may again result in further inheritance taxes being due and payable. Add to this the possibility of going into long-term care at some stage (25% of those over the age of 80 will do so) and the costs associated with care (over 40,000 houses are dispossessed each year to pay for care fees once you have died, and a further 35,000 homes are sold to pay for care), and in many instances the chances of inheriting from parents and grandparents become slim. However, for the benefactor there is a choice. You can either write out a cheque to the Chancellor of the Exchequer for 40% of your wealth (after deductions for exempt assets) or you can elect to benefit your heirs or a charity. People go for the former option and planning is therefore essential.

Should you be concerned by inheritance taxes? The inheritance tax take is increasing over previous years, and in the last decade the highest collection years were 2018/19 at £5.4 billion. For the unmarried, cohabiting population, there is no nil rate band uplift for a deceased partner, and a great many households will still be affected.

There are many strategies available to reduce and minimise the incidence of inheritance and other taxes – some are simple, others more complex, depending on your personal circumstances. This book will indicate the best courses of action to follow, and should leave you with an action plan and a number of important questions to discuss with your professional advisers.

This edition is updated by the OFT Inheritance Tax Review 2nd Report of July 2019.

Much of what was announced in previous budgets has found its way into legislation or consultation for further study, or been rejected (such as the proposed tax changes to multiple trusts), and some of the other changes are as follows:

- The issue of non-domiciled spouses or civil partners has been improved.
- Simplifying the calculation of IHT periodic and exit charges for trusts.
- The Charity exemption for deaths after 6 April 2012, a lower rate of IHT at 36% will apply where 10% or more of a deceased's person net estate (after deduction of exemptions, reliefs and the nil rate band) is left to charity
- For all new life policies taken out after 6 April 2013 contributions are to be limited to £3,600 p.a.
- In the area of excluded property trusts and IHT avoidance, from 21 March 2012 new rules were announced in response to avoidance schemes which exploit the 'excluded property' rules. Under the schemes a UK-domiciled individual acquires an interest in settled property in an offshore trust, reducing the value of their estate that is subject to IHT. Assets which would otherwise be chargeable to IHT are converted, by a series of transactions, to excluded property which is not subject to IHT. The new legislation affects s.64 and s.65 of the *IHTA 1984*.

High personal taxation – an individual is taxed at 45% in 2019/20 with earnings above £150,000 with the loss of personal allowances between £100,000 and £125,000 on a 2-for-1 basis, with restrictions on pension contributions of £40,000 in 2019/20, and income and dividend taxes for trusts at 45% and 38.1% in 2019/20 – means that those with IHT issues will be engaged in redefining their financial planning and investment structuring to be more efficient. Income tax issues affect trusts and planning the least – costly routes for income to beneficiaries will become even more important.

Inheritance Tax and Wills planning remains a vital part of all estate planning. Yes, the aim is to reduce your estate as much as possible, so that as little tax is payable as possible. The Government has begun a process of evaluating all taxes, exemptions and allowances, as well, as tax evasion and tax avoidance measures. Some could yet be beneficial – such as the recently announced uplift of the NRB allowance for a non-domiciled spouse, and the new family home allowance, the residential nil rate band; but others will have severe impact – such as the exclusion of UK residents and/or UK-domiciled individuals from excluded property offshore trusts, the attack on multiple trusts, and the addition of undistributed income in trusts to capital to increase the periodic charge, and the ongoing attack on non-UK domiciled individuals as announced in previous Budgets, and the abortive attack on Deeds of Variation as a means to redistribute assets. 2014 saw positive reform to the intestacy rules, and pronouncements on trust tax charges, however inheritance tax will remain a burden for many as more deaths will bring increased IHT for estates.

Inheritance Tax Review – second report

Simplifying the design of Inheritance tax

The First Report published in November 2018 dealt largely with the administration of Inheritance Tax. This Report highlighted the fact that fewer than 25,000 deceased estates are liable to IHT each year. This is less than 5% of all deaths, yet 275,000 IHT forms need to be completed each year. Total deaths are around 590,000 annually. The administrative burden was seen to be too great for such a small number of taxable estates.

The Second Report investigated how to make IHT more understandable and clear to those dealing with it.

See: **https://www.gov.uk/government/publications/ots-inheritance-tax-review-simplifying-the-design-of-the-tax**

The Office for Tax Simplification (OTS) makes recommendations for the Government to follow. Following a consultation process into how inheritance tax works, the OTS reported on 5 July 2019 its 11 recommendations to make IHT more understandable and coherent. There were four main areas considered:

*   Taxation of lifetime gifts
*   Who pays tax when lifetime gifts are taxable
*   Simpler exemptions for lifetime gifts
*   Review of business exemptions

Taxation of Lifetime Gifts

Exemptions from IHT include the first £3,000 given away each year; individual gifts of up to £250; gifts in contemplation of marriage or entering a civil partnership; regular gifts out of someone's regular income.

It was recommended to replace all of these gift exemptions with a single personal gift allowance.

Recommended that the 7-year gift period (for gifts to be out of your estate after 7 years) be shortened to 5 years. Also, to abolish the tapered rate of IHT as the tax paid on gifts 6-7 years before death is low.

Options to simplify and clarify the rules on who pays the IHT on lifetime gifts and how the £325,000 NRB is allocated between different recipients.

Businesses, Farms and Capital Gains Tax

There is a high level of complexity in the interaction between Inheritance Tax and Capital Gains Tax, and the reliefs available for businesses and farms. Where families pass assets to the next generation, there are different tests applying to the same activity. The Report makes recommendations to reduce complexity, within the Government targets and policy objectives. Simplification of the administrative and technical aspects of tax are important to taxpayers and HMRC.

The whole issue of BPR, APR and other IHT reliefs (where trading businesses and farming assets may qualify for 100% relief from IHT) and BPR extends to certain companies trading on the Alternative Investment Market (AIM), is considered in the Report and the excellent commentary found at Market Update report **https://intelligent-partnership.com/br-industry-report-2019/**

The report fully covers the business reliefs within the IHT context.

Other Areas of IHT reported on include:

- Life assurance and pensions – the need for a life assurance trust
- Pre-owned asset tax – to review whether the POAT rules are necessary
- Residence nil rate band – the need for simplification on this additional nil rate band which is seen as complex
- Trusts – the IHT rules are seen as being too complex
- Charities – since 2012 if you leave 10% or more of your net estate to charity the IHT rate is reduced to 36%. This relief is not well understood and complicated as to when it applies

Any changes recommended would have to be legislated for in due course. The current position therefore remains as is until that time.

Disclaimer

Please do not act on strategies or information unless you have confirmed your proposed actions with a qualified financial or tax adviser, and taken the appropriate advice before acting, as the author, publisher, sponsor, and information providers in this book cannot be responsible for your actions and do not accept liability for them. The information given is based on tax and other legislation as at 1 October 2019, and this may change in the future. As is common, when discussing investments, the value of an investment may go down as well as up, and you may lose your capital.

If you take out loans or mortgages, be sure to service them, or your asset or home could be at risk.

Tony Granger

1

The Concepts

The concepts of estate planning and inheritance tax mitigation, and the importance of wills and liquidity planning

Inheritance tax planning is part of the general estate planning process. Once the estate assets and liabilities are known, these can be viewed against available exemptions and deductions, as well as dispositions made through a will and the setting up of trusts. Estate planning can occur before and after death. Whether you have made a will or not, your estate can be varied after you have died, so long as various criteria are met, and this is known as a Deed of Variation. Incredible though it may seem, your will can be rewritten up to two years after you have died, but you must have had one in the first place. If you did not, then you would die intestate. Intestate estates can also be varied in this way, but in the absence of a specific will to amend the process can be much more complicated.

Estate assets

During your lifetime you accumulate assets, either in your own name or in joint names, usually with a spouse or partner, but it can be jointly with an unrelated third party. You may have gifted assets to children or others, and if you die too soon after making a gift in this way, then those gifted assets will fall back into estate and may become taxable.

On your death, your assets are brought into account at fair market value, and are then available for distribution, after paying liabilities such as your share of the mortgage and your debts, and last expenses, such as medical and funeral costs, and any taxes such as outstanding income tax and inheritance taxes that may be payable.

Debts that die with you and those that don't

You will be happy to know that some debts and taxes may die with you and are not payable from your estate. Capital gains tax dies with you and does not become payable, so if you can defer a capital gain and the tax on it until you die, it need not be payable. If you are in an IVA (individual voluntary arrangement with your creditors), then this debt or commitment also dies with you. However, other debts that you may not be aware of that affect your estate position, would include salaries and amounts owing to employees, if you were a sole trader at the time of death – those employees would have a claim against your estate. Also, if divorced, with a contractual liability for maintenance payments to a former spouse, these do not necessarily end on your death, and there could be a claim against your estate for a lump sum payment.

Wills as core to estate planning

Once your estate has been settled, the assets that remain can pass to your beneficiaries either by will, or if you do not have a will, through what is known as intestacy. The will is the most important mechanism of estate planning and does a number of things.

1. The will directs where you wish your assets to go. Assets can devolve to anyone you name or a charity, or be directed into a will trust, to be administered by your trustees, for the benefit of the beneficiaries.

2. The will gives investment powers to executors and trustees. These are usually framed broadly and flexibly to take any contingency into consideration.

3. The will tells your executors whether you wish to be buried or cremated and whether you are an organ donor. It is important that an up-to-date will be immediately at hand on death so that your wishes may be carried out effectively. If you are leaving organs to science or for medical purposes, it would help to have a donor card.

4. Importantly, the will nominates a guardian for your minor children. This clause only comes into effect if both natural parents have died, and there are children under the age of 18. If you do not nominate a guardian for your minor children, by default the State is the upper guardian, and will do so. It is unwise to nominate the elderly (such as your parents), as bringing up youngsters may not be on their agenda for a happy retirement – choose someone your own age, if at all possible. I would encourage a monetary bequest to the nominated guardian (if the guardianship is accepted) as taking on a new brood of someone else's children can be an expensive business.

5. The will can deal with business assets, and should mention any shareholder or partner agreements that it is aligned with.

6. The will allows for fees and charges to be made against the estate for professional administration and executorship purposes.

7. The will must be in writing and witnessed by two independent witnesses who will not inherit from you and are aged over 18 and of sound mind.

8. Whilst you can change your will yourself at any time while you are alive, your heirs can also change it for you after death, through a deed of variation. Divorce and remarriage automatically revokes a will – so review your wills as often as possible.

9. To avoid will disputes at a later date, ensure that all bases are covered. If a will you have prepared is disputed you may be asked to disclose information about the circumstances surrounding its preparation and execution. Law Society advice on good practice on this issue was taken into account by the Court of Appeal in Larke v Nugus (1979) 123 SJ 337 (later reported in (2000) WTLR 1033) in relation to the issue of costs in a probate action: "When contesting a will, the first step is to make an application to the will draftsman for a Larke v Nugus statement requesting information such as how instructions were expressed by the deceased, whether the deceased showed any signs of confusion or loss of memory, the extent to which the deceased's earlier will was discussed and attempts made to discuss departures from his earlier will."

People often express doubts about making a will. 'I don't have anything to leave to anyone, so why should I have a will?' they sometimes ask – or, 'If I die intestate (without a will), the same people will inherit from me, so why bother with a will?' – or, 'If you can rewrite my will after I have died, what's the point in having one in the first place?' The big issue of costs also arises. Wills can be expensive, depending on where you go for one. Also consider a lasting power of attorney (LPA) to be done at the same time as your will. This enables someone to deal with your affairs should you be injured or sick or disabled or mentally incapable and unable to do so. From October 2007 you will have to apply to the Court of Protection to get an LPA, and this will be more expensive than the previous Enduring Power of Attorney (EPA) regime. If you have an EPA it remains valid.

To answer the above questions will give peace of mind to those currently without wills or whose wills may need to be changed due to changes in personal circumstances. The range of will-providers includes solicitors, wills companies specialising in drafting wills, and banks. You can also do it yourself through the internet or using a will form from a stationers. Wherever you go to have your wills drafted, wills are important as an estate planning mechanism. You may not have any assets now, but may inherit in the future; you may have a pension fund and wish to leave it to your heirs; you may have minor children and require guardians to be nominated; you may wish to set up a trust in your will to protect vulnerable beneficiaries who could squander assets if not protected. Above all, you have an opportunity to direct what assets you may have to your relatives or to a charity. Having a will is therefore most important.

For the estate planner advising you, a will can be effective in inheritance tax planning. For example, assets left to one spouse or civil partner by another are free of inheritance tax (the spouse exemption); you can make use of an additional 'nil rate band' exemption through leaving assets in trust to the value of the nil rate band. This effectively bypasses the spouse or civil partner estate for the benefit of the children, for example, thus currently saving £130,000 in inheritance taxes. Simple will clauses can save your estate a lot of money. Whilst the spouse exemption and nil rate band bypass trust can be accessed through a deed of variation after you have died at present, this may not always be the case in the future, and depending on where you get your advice, it may not even be mentioned that it is possible to do so. Therefore, plan as best you can, leaving nothing to chance. You may transfer your NRB to enable full use of both spouses' or civil partners' NRB. Also bear in mind the attack on multiple trusts in 2014 (where it was proposed that only one nil rate band may be available and divided for multiple trusts). This decision has been replaced with an anti-avoidance same day added property rule that specifically targets same day additions (aimed at asset-backed pilot and multiple trust strategies, but not the use of life assurance protection plans). Rysaffe Trustee Co (CI) v Inland Revenue Commissioners (2003) enforced the Rysaffe principle that under section 42 of the IHT Act 1984 a series of trusts set up on consecutive days reduces the impact of the 10-yearly periodic and exit charge through having a nil rate band for each trust.   Same settlor, different days are not related settlements.

Cohabitees

The will is one of the most important components of successful estate planning. It is also important if you are not married but cohabiting. It is likely that a significant proportion of the readers of this book will not be married, but living together. For them, there is no spouse or civil partner exemption. There may be a financial dependency to a claim of partner's assets on death, though, but this has to be proved. *The Inheritance (Provision for Family Dependants) Act 1975* allows the survivor in a cohabiting relationship to apply to the Court for reasonable maintenance from the estate. Also the *Law Reform (Succession) Act 1995* allows for an application for maintenance. As the surviving partner is not a spouse, there will not be any widow's or widower's benefits from a pension fund; nor will there normally be any death benefits distributable to them (although some pension funds do accommodate a letter of wishes, enabling certain payments to be made to financially dependant cohabitees). If at all possible nominate the non-spouse for death benefits. The new *Inheritance and Trustees' Powers Act 2014*, which came into force on 1 October 2014 did not make the expected changes for cohabiting spouses to inherit on intestacy.

The unfairness of the present system will affect many cohabitees who are not married or in a civil partnership, when it comes to inheriting assets from a partner. The intestacy laws will be particularly harsh, if you do not have a will, and you will not inherit at all. Only spouses and civil partners have that opportunity. Not being married or in a civil partnership is therefore severely penalised by legal restrictions, and where an unmarried partner (or one not in civil partnership) leaves assets to a partner, these assets will be subject to 40% inheritance tax above the nil rate band. A married or civil partner will have the spouse exemption and no inheritance tax is payable on the first death. Unfair? Yes, absolutely!

The legal case of the Burden sisters [*Burden v United Kingdom 2008 STC 1305*] featured a pair of elderly sisters living together who tried to get clarification on whether the Civil Partnership Act (introduced in November 2004) applied to them as living together and being of the same sex. At the appeal hearing at the European Court of Human Rights, 15 out of 17 judges stated the sisters had not faced unfair discrimination, on the basis that their relationship of co-habitation, despite its long duration, fundamentally differed from that of a married or civil partnership couple. IHT mitigation planning is essential and they, for example, could (i) downsize (ii) do equity release and invest into a DGT (discounted gift trust) for immediate IHT out of the estate, or a loan trust (iii) release capital and make gifts (even into trust for themselves) – to reduce the property value to below the nil rate band.

The laws of intestacy

If you do not have a will, then your assets devolve according to the laws of intestacy. These laws are slightly different in Scotland and Northern Ireland as opposed to England and Wales. If you do not have a will, then you could find yourself not inheriting at all, or sharing the late dearly-departed's assets with family relatives, such as brothers, sisters, uncles, aunts, grandparents and the like. In the final analysis, even the Duchy of Cornwall can inherit from you, if you leave no relatives.

The **rules of intestacy (England and Wales)** changed for deaths after 1st October 2014. The new Inheritance and Trustees Powers Act 2014 (ITPSA 2014) made a number of reforms. The single biggest change is to rules affecting married couples and civil partnerships where there are no children. In the past, they received the first £450,000 from the estate with the rest split between the deceased's blood relatives. Under the new law, the surviving spouse will receive everything with wider family members not receiving anything from the estate. Another important change affects couples who have children. Under the old rules, the spouse of the deceased received the first £250,000 and a 'life interest' in half of the remainder with the children splitting the other half. Under the new rules, the life interest concept is to be abolished with the surviving married partner receiving the first £250,000 and also half of any remainder. The children will receive half of anything above £250,000 and will have to wait until they are 18 to access any funds

After the payment of funeral expenses, tax and other debts owed by the deceased, the rest of the estate will devolve as follows: *(note that children includes children born in or out of wedlock and legally adopted children, but not step-children)*

- If the deceased leaves a spouse or civil partner, and no children or parents or brothers or sisters of the whole blood – then everything goes to the spouse or civil partner.

- If the deceased leaves a spouse or civil partner and children:
  1. For net estates of up to £250,000 – everything goes to the spouse or civil partner.
  2. For net estates of over £250,000 – the first £250,000 'statutory legacy' (index linked) plus personal chattels (possessions) goes to the spouse or civil partner; the balance of the estate is divided equally between the spouse or civil partner (50%) and the children at age 18 (50% shared equally).

- If the deceased leaves a spouse/civil partner and no children, and either parents, or brothers and sisters of the whole blood, the spouse receives the whole estate.

- If the deceased leaves children, but no spouse or civil partner, everything goes to the children in equal shares.

- If the deceased leaves no spouse or issue, the estate will pass to the deceased's parents. If neither parent is alive, the deceased's nearest relatives will inherit. The order of priority is as follows:
  1. Brothers and sisters, of the whole blood and the issue of any who have predeceased
  2. Half-brothers and half-sisters and the issue of any who have predeceased
  3. Grandparents
  4. Aunts and uncles (being brothers and sisters of the whole blood of a parent of the intestate) and the issue of any who have predeceased
  5. Half-brothers and half-sisters of the deceased's parents and the issue of any deceased half-uncle or half-aunt.

- If no living beneficiary, the deceased's estate will pass to the Crown, the Duchy of Lancaster or the Duchy of Cornwall.

The following article appeared in *Tax Insider* in November 2014 and shows the changes made:

Tony Granger examines the new intestacy rules which became effective on 1st October 2014, and what changes have been made following the Inheritance and Trustees Powers Act 2014 (ITPSA 2014).

Over 70% of eligible UK residents do not have a will. In addition, some existing wills may be invalid or out of date due to marriage, divorce, death of a spouse. If you do not have a valid will then on your death your assets will devolve according to the rules of intestacy. Under the reforms a larger portion of the estate will pass to the surviving spouse outright and matters are further simplified without a complicated trust structure, which is to be welcomed.
Note the term 'spouse' includes 'civil partner'.

The Changes

The new intestacy rules mean changes for spouses and children where the assets of people who die without wills are shared out. The previous position was that a surviving spouse with no surviving children shared the estate with the deceased's relatives (parents, brothers and sisters and others) where the estate value was greater than £450,000. Under the revised rules, the spouse could inherit the whole deceased estate without sharing it.

Previously, where the deceased left a spouse and children, the estate was shared with him or her and the children. For estates larger than £250,000 the survivor received £250,000 as a statutory legacy and a life interest in 50% of the residue – children being entitled to the remaining 50% on attaining the age of 18. From 1 October 2014 the surviving spouse receives 50% of the residue outright, not only the income. If no spouse, children or relatives, everything goes to the Crown, the Duchy of Lancaster (the Queen) or the Duchy of Cornwall (Prince Charles).

Table showing previous and current intestacy rules

Deceased dies leaving	Previous – before 1 October 2014	After 1 October 2014
A spouse and children	Spouse receives: • Statutory legacy of £250,000 • Personal chattels • Life interest in 50% of the residue • Children entitled to remaining 50% of residue at age 18	Spouse receives: • Statutory legacy of £250,000 (which is index linked) • Personal chattels • 50% of the estate outright • Children entitled to remaining 50% of the residue at age 18

A spouse, no children, with surviving parents and/or siblings	Spouse receives: • Statutory legacy of £450,000 • Personal chattels • 50% of the residue Parents receive 50% of residue equally, then siblings if no parents	Spouse receives the whole estate Parents, siblings (brothers and sisters) receive nothing
No spouse, but children	All to children in equal shares	All to children in equal shares
No spouse, children or relatives	Everything goes to the Crown	Everything goes to the Crown

Unmarried Partners

The revised intestacy rules do nothing for unmarried partners, who receive nothing on intestacy. You may, however, have a claim under the Inheritance (Provision for Family and Dependents) Act 1975. The act specifies four categories of claimants:

The surviving spouse; cohabitee who lived with the deceased for at least two years; Children; legitimate, illegitimate or adopted; and any other child, such as a stepchild, supported by the deceased and treated as her or his own; Others supported by the deceased such as an elderly relative, or anyone receiving regular maintenance from the deceased.

The time limits to bring a claim are very strict, with the Act providing that a claim must be brought within 6 months of the grant of probate being issued.

Inheritance Tax (IHT)

IHT is payable on intestate estates at 40% of the net estate after deduction of applicable nil rate band – currently £325,000 plus the unused portion of a deceased's spouse nil rate band.

Tax Tip

Consider making or reviewing your will. This will give you direction and certainty and ensure that intended beneficiaries benefit from you. IHT savings could be made, and if no relatives remain then a charity could benefit instead of Prince Charles or the Queen.'

The Changes

*   Where a couple is married, the whole estate passes on intestacy to the surviving spouse in all cases where there are no children or descendants.

*   Where there are children, both spouse and children inherit outright. There is no longer interest payable to the spouse on the children's half. If under age 18 their share is held in statutory trusts, and interest accrues from the date of death at the Bank of England base rate.

*   The new Inheritance and Trustees Powers Act 2014 (ITPA 2014) will protect children from the risk of losing an inheritance from a parent in the event that they are adopted after the death of that parent; amend the rules that currently disadvantage unmarried fathers when a child dies intestate; reform trustees' statutory powers to use income and capital for the benefit of beneficiaries (subject to any express provisions in the trust document).

*   There is a new modernised statutory definition of personal chattels under s55(1)(x) of the AEA 1925 which covers all tangible movable property other than any such property which consists of money or securities for money, or property used at the death of the intestate solely or mainly for business purposes, or was held at the death of the intestate solely as an investment.

*   Under the Inheritance (Provision for Family and Dependants) Act 1975, A person who was maintained by the deceased immediately before the death will be eligible to claim under the IPFDA 1975 whether or not, beyond the fact of providing maintenance, the deceased had formally assumed responsibility for that person's maintenance. A person claiming as a dependant under the IPFDA 1975 need no longer show that the deceased contributed more to the relationship than the applicant did.

*   In a judgment handed down by the Court of Appeal in July 2015 (Illott v Mitson [2015] EWCA, the Court awarded £163,000 to Heather Ilott, the daughter of Melita Jackson who left her £486,000 net estate to three charities. Despite a letter written by the deceased explaining the decision on beneficiaries, the court overruled the will. The legislation cited in the case – the Inheritance (Provision for Family and Dependent)s Act 1975 – only applies to the estate of a deceased and not to a trust. The courts have always had the power to overrule or ignore a will if they deem it unreasonable. It is stipulated in the Inheritance Family and Dependants Act 1975. If for example you have multiple children and leave an inheritance to only two and not the third, the courts can overrule this.

*   One of the proposed changes did not happen. It was expected that co-habiting persons would receive automatic rights on death to intestate

assets if they had children or had been together for 2- 5 years. To ensure a co-habitee inherits, the only two ways are marriage or making a will.

Converting Intestacy income to a lump sum

This was possible where there was a life interest arising under an intestacy for a surviving spouse. The future stream of interest income could be capitalized for a lump sum (S47A of AEA 1925) which had to be elected within 12 months of the grant date of Letters of Administration. Under the new rules, the surviving spouse inherits outright and no longer receives income/interest from the child's portion of capital, so the income capitalization to a lump sum has become irrelevant.

Common law wives

They obtain no benefit under the intestacy rules although anyone financially dependant on the deceased can make a claim for financial provision out of the estate under the *Inheritance (Provision for Family Dependants) Act 1975.*

Post-death deeds of variation or deed of family arrangement

These can be made within 2 years of the date of death, whether there was a will, or on intestacy. The will is effectively re-written to make use of IHT exemptions not utilised before. All beneficiaries must be aged over 18 and must agree. Following the 2015 Budget, the Government reviewed IHT avoidance through deeds of variation. It feels that using deeds of variation may be a form of avoiding IHT, and decided not to change the tax treatment but continue to monitor their use. A beneficiary who gives up their entitlement makes a lifetime disposition which may be a gift or for consideration. However, if made within two years and there is no consideration, it is treated as if made by the deceased for inheritance tax and capital gains tax purposes. (S142 Inheritance Tax Act 1984 and s 62(6) – (10) TCGA 1992).

Estate planning

Estate Planning is the planning procedure whereby accumulated assets are used for income in retirement and long-term care; where assets are protected from the ravages of inflation and death and other taxes; where beneficiaries are protected and provided for; where on death, assets and future income streams devolve where you want them to go. Estate planning covers all age groups and social classes, and can begin at any time. Wealth preservation and asset protection for future generations is important to most people, as is providing for the maintenance and welfare of your loved ones and possibly even children and grandchildren yet to be born. Estate planning includes your personal as well as your business assets. Reducing liabilities and mitigating taxes is part of the estate planning process, meaning that you keep more of what you have.

Having enough cash

One of the most important aspects of successful estate planning is to have sufficient liquidity – usually cash, but it can be easily realisable investments – available in your estate to provide for inheritances, to fund trusts that you may set up, to pay estate liabilities, such as mortgage loans, inheritance taxes, contractual and other financial commitments. You will have assets that are not liquid – such as the family home or holiday cottage, shares in the business that are difficult to realise, or assets such as well-performing investments that you would not dispose of under normal circumstances. For example, you would not want the family home to be sold in order to pay inheritance taxes. Nor would you want a top-performing investment portfolio to be encashed, when future income is required from it. Cash can be provided through life assurance in most instances, when more liquid investments are not available. You would use a joint-life second death policy, underwritten in trust. The proceeds of the policy would be payable outside of your taxable estate and would escape probate, being immediately available to meet your liabilities and commitments.

Does your plan work?

Proper planning is essential. In the past thirty-five years I have come across plenty of estate planning clients who have perfect wills in theory, which in practice just do not work. Many wills are drawn up without regard to estate planning, and in particular liquidity planning, and completed without a realistic outcome.

Example

Mr Bobbitt, who is aged 37 now and a successful business owner, wishes to leave £100,000 to each of his three children on his death, £500,000 into trust to provide an income for his beloved Mrs Bobbitt, and a further trust amount of £300,000 for his elderly parents to help them with their long-term care as they cannot survive on the State Pension alone. He also has an inheritance tax liability of £250,000. How much cash or investment assets does he require on his death? A total of £1,350,000. He has private company shares worth £1 million, a house worth £450,000 and ISA investments of £150,000. Cash at bank is £30,000.

On his untimely demise from a heart attack on the 14th tee on his favourite golf course, his accountant cannot find anyone to purchase his private company shares (he was the brains behind the business and had the business contacts, so there was really no business without him) and the shares drop in value for a fire sale value at £300,000 – but still there are no takers. The family still need to live in the house, although they could downsize to release some cash. His total liquid assets are thus ISAs of £150,000 and cash of £30,000, making some £180,000 in total. Barely enough to pay his inheritance tax liability, let alone fund the two trusts or make legacy payments to the children. Result: dreams shattered – not uncommon. However, with simple liquidity planning, at his age, he could have had £1 million worth of life cover to provide cash in the estate, as follows:

Maximum cover whole-of-life: Premium cost is £57 per month for £1 million whole-of-life cover (premiums are reviewable after ten years).

Balanced cover whole-of-life: Premium cost is £272 to £449 per month for £1 million whole-of-life cover (premiums are reviewable after ten years, but the policy reserve is better than maximum cover and any premium increases may be lower).

Guaranteed whole-of-life cover: Premium cost is £492 per month for £1 million guaranteed cover with no reviews.

Level Term assurance cover to the age of 65: Premium cost is £67.51 per month for guaranteed premiums and cover.

Premium costs vary greatly depending on the type of life cover selected. I have included term cover to the age of 65, to provide for family protection over the period up to retirement, as alternative IHT reduction strategies could be in place after that period, and he may require lower-costed but guaranteed outcomes over the planning period.

Note that all life policies should be written in to trust to avoid IHT on the policy proceeds.

Alternatively, he could have planned to reduce liabilities such as the inheritance tax payable; he could have made provision now for his parents for when they get older; he could have funded a pension plan for his spouse's income with tax-deductible contributions (depending on her tax rate), and taken advantage of a number of other cash and income-producing possibilities thus reducing his reliance on life assurance as the only answer. The result: his will would work – and he would die happy.

2

Planning Your Estate

The need for estate planning. Knowing the whole picture before proper advice can be given or taken. Liquidity needs analysis. Life assurance needs analysis. The will is at the end of the estate planning process, not the beginning. Client needs, requirements and financial and lifestyle objectives.

You may feel that you have a single need, such as the saving of inheritance taxes, or multiple needs, such as protecting wealth for future generations, ensuring the family home remains available to your family after you have died, providing for income in retirement, planning for long-term care, succession planning for your business, or whatever.

It is important to establish at the outset what your financial planning needs are now, and to combine these with your future needs, lifetime objectives and goals. It is also important to decide how far into the future you wish to plan. For example, to plan for yourself, your children and your grandchildren will require three generations of planning. To decide on a strategy in isolation, without covering all the bases or contingencies that may arise in the future, could be folly. You and your financial planner(s) must have all the facts available about your present circumstances, and what your idea of the future looks like. This is your opportunity not to leave anything to chance.

It is also important to know that some actions taken may be flexible and open to change in the future (for example, you can change your will at any time before your death), whereas other structures may be inflexible and limit your future planning should your circumstances change. For example, the gifting of your house to your children (unless they gift it back to you), or taking income from a discounted gift trust, once done, cannot be reversed.

Some decisions are based on facts dictating circumstances. Others are emotional. A factual situation may lead you to sell a certain type of asset, for example shares in your favourite energy company, and invest the proceeds into an investment that gives you IHT protection; however, emotion may sway you the other way, as you inherited the shares from a favourite aunt, and they remind you of her, so you will wish to keep the shares. Decisions based on emotion usually cost you or your estate money.

You may also have issues that conflict with your estate planning needs. You may not wish for a certain person to inherit from you, such as a child or parent; you may not have enough liquidity (cash) to make your wishes come true; or there may be other reasons why you feel planning is not important. Many people cannot be bothered with effective planning. They are either rich enough to pass assets to their heirs and pay inheritance taxes, without wishing to be bothered with complex plans – or poor enough not to be concerned. Some have no dependants and the choice is then either to pay the Chancellor his dues or perhaps to benefit a charity – however, there may be that nagging feeling that you could have done more, but didn't.

Estate planning phases

There are three distinct phases or life cycles involved in estate planning. You do not need to wait until retirement to begin your planning. Start right now. The bottom line is that you accumulate assets over your lifetime; consolidate them at retirement and have them distributed at your death. Those receiving assets from you continue the process, thus building wealth and conserving it through successive generations.

1. **Accumulation** *...to retirement.* Includes property, investments, inheritances, life assurance, funding pensions and savings; protection of assets; gifting excess assets and income. Hand in hand with large expenditures such as mortgage payments, school fees. Building an asset base and platform for a financially secure future.

2. **Consolidation** *...at retirement.* Pensions, investments, property consolidated for capital and income requirements; long-term care requirements; IHT mitigation and reduction; debt reduction. Securing asset base and protecting it.

3. **Distribution** *...at death.* Assets devolve to heirs after liabilities deducted. Taxes paid, if any, and post-death protection planning begins. Further asset, pension and investment consolidation for dependants' income and capital requirements. Others take over the decision-making process.

Issues to be considered

The following are some of the main issues that have to be considered. There is a big fear of the unknown, and death is one of these fears. Irrational though it may seem to many, there are a considerable number of people who believe that if they plan for it, it will hasten the process, usually to their detriment. The making of a will falls into this category. If you make your will, you will definitely die – almost immediately in fact, so better not to make one. Not making a will is not only the preserve of the elderly. Dealing with personal mortality also affects the younger generation where death is usually something that happens to someone else. Only 30% of those who should have wills in fact have them. In a recent seminar given to solicitors, I canvassed the group and around 50% of those present did not have a will – I was not unduly surprised, having done this survey 11 years ago, and found that the percentages have not changed. In a most recent case, a young wife with two minor children asked me to persuade her husband to have a will, and take out life assurance to protect the family. His response was to allow other family members to shoulder his financial burdens and commitments after he had died. Denying your own mortality can be troublesome for those who come after you. What financial planning can do for you is to help you deal with these fears – if you have them.

The issues in estate planning are broadly the following:

- Protecting and preserving wealth for yourself, your dependants and future generations.
- Dealing with inheritance and other taxes on your death and the death of a spouse or civil partner, or cohabiting partner.
- Not having to pay inheritance tax up front, if it can be avoided.
- General tax mitigation and reduction, and provision for tax to be paid.
- Protection of beneficiaries who are young, profligate, immature, or financially unable to deal with money, or disabled.
- Providing sufficient income and capital for yourself and your dependants when no longer working or retired, or going into long-term care.
- Providing for medical and other expenditures and costs.
- Emigrating abroad – before and at retirement.
- Whether to set up trusts whilst alive or on death, the costs of doing so and whether they are indeed necessary or not.
- Asset allocation and investments, taking into account attitude to risk and what the investments are for.
- Changing existing investments to 'wrap' them for IHT protection, and what is involved in the process.
- What to do with the family home: staying in it or passing it on to the children; losing it if going into long-term care; equity release issues to provide for usable capital and increasing income and the implications of doing so.
- How best to deal with business assets and succession planning.
- If farming, how to deal with a small farm and many dependants to be viable.
- Who should inherit from you? Do you leave inheritances to your parents? Your children? Your grandchildren? How much to leave and whether to be equitable or not. One or more children may have had support during your lifetime, others not.

- Leaving money to charity or political parties.
- What to put into your will and what to leave out.
- The whole issue of executors and administrators and trustees, how they get paid and how competent are they in dealing with your affairs. Who will advise on bereavement issues?
- Who will advise your heirs after you have gone? Will they be competent? What happens after you die, and what are the processes involved? How up-to-date must your current personal book-keeping be?
- Once a course of action has been chosen, can it be changed?
- Costs involved in estate planning and who does it?
- What more can you do to ensure a successful outcome?
- What if the laws change and I am too old to deal with new issues?

The above are very real concerns and have to be dealt with at some time – otherwise they remain largely unanswered questions. They affect those with substantial assets, as well as those with next to nothing.

The discerning financial planner should guide you through the above check-list in helping you with your estate and general financial planning. It's not just about saving taxes; it is about preparing yourself throughout life to make the best decisions and choices. The more you know, the better prepared you can be.

Threats in the estate planning process

Be aware of the following when doing your planning:

- The value of investments and savings can rise and fall, depending how and where you have invested. Your risk profile for investments is crucial, as is the amount available for investment. Can you afford to lose capital through taking on particular investment strategies? What is the purpose of your investment? If to grow for the next twenty years and then to provide an income, try to avoid an investment that can be eroded by inflation. Whilst the CPI 12-month rate to July 2019 was 1.9%, real inflation (RPI) is currently in the range of 2.9% per annum, and to make a 'real return' you need to be in inflation-beating investments. How well diversified are you? If one particular class of investment falls, will another type compensate by rising? Asset allocation amongst investment classes is key to diversified performance expectation.

- Beware of not having enough cash (liquidity) in your estate to provide for your wishes. Those without a strong investment base will consider alternatives such as life assurance to provide cash on death. You may wish to fund trusts and to provide for paying taxes without having to sell assets to do so.

- Having incompetent advisers can be a major threat. They may not have the whole picture, or may sell you unsuitable investments. They may not ensure that the correct protections are in place. As much as 70% of new clients seen by me do not have existing life policies in trust, which is a prime example. A simple trust form means that life assurance escapes both probate and inheritance tax. Policies can be written into trust after being taken out, generating substantial IHT savings. Even today, only 30% of policies that should be in trust are written into trust.

- Unsuitable products and trusts either in existence or affected by new legislation can put your financial planning at risk.

- Changes in financial circumstances can make prior planning obsolete. For example, say your son is a successful businessman with a substantial estate. Assets you leave him on death will make his estate taxable, and he may not have planned for this – his existing planning does not take into account what you may do. In these circumstances, family estate planning is important.

- Changes in legislation may require you to rethink your existing planning. Some legislation is retrospective, although there may be a transition period to get things right. For example, the Chancellor (in 2006) changed the basis of taxation for interest-in-possession and accumulation-and-maintenance trusts. Largely used in will trusts to give a spouse an income from trust assets (interest in possession), that interest was previously not taxable on the spouse's death, but has been after 2008; for accumulation-and-maintenance trusts, a child could receive income to the age of 25 and then capital – now the age limit has dropped to the age of 18 – above that age there are tax consequences. You may not wish a child to inherit at the age of 18, and may need another course of action or changes to be made to a trust to reduce the incidence of trust taxation. The introduction of transferable nil rate bands may mean an examination of current wills and trusts.

- You should also plan for *future* changes in legislation which could affect existing planning. For example, the Government may make potentially exempt transfers taxable (at present you can make a gift to anyone and the value of the gift and the growth on it would be out of your estate after 7 years); business property relief is given up to 100% on qualifying business assets such as private company shares; up to 50% on certain farm assets from your estate – there is no certainty that these exemptions from inheritance tax will always be there.

- Changes in the tax treatment of financial products that have current legislated-for tax advantages, may result in the removal of these advantages in the future. There again, a new Chancellor may be more generous, but this is considered unlikely, as the Treasury can expect around £5.3 bn+ from inheritance taxes in 2019/20. Only 4.5% of estates pay inheritance tax in the UK.

• Not having a financial plan that deals with your issues will be a major threat to your financial well-being, as well as for the well-being of those who succeed you.

The current economic and political environment is not conducive to the reduction of inheritance taxes, nor the preservation of your carefully built-up assets over your lifetime, nor the safeguarding of your families in the long term – nor the preservation of your pension assets for the use of future generations and your dependants. There is no protection of the family home and future financial stability for your dependants. The only things you can be fairly certain of in the future are an increase in life expectancy, possible falling pension provision from the State and employers, increased council taxes, income taxes and trust taxes and increasing costs of medical care, to mention a few.

Successful Estate Planning is where you take control, plan as best you can under current circumstances, and make sure that you use the best available financial planning mechanisms to level the playing field.

The Government tax-take will continue to increase, supported by general public inertia, as the majority of people continue to do nothing about it, and just accept the present position. Believe it or not, but there remain very advantageous procedures that can be undertaken to reduce your estate liabilities, including inheritance taxes, and they are all quite legal. In the same way that your car needs an MOT every year, or you would have a medical check-up from time to time, you also need to engage in a financial plan or have your present planning checked. The benefits are there to be claimed by you.

Starting the process

The following are the steps in the financial planning and estate planning process:

1. Complete a statement of your goals and objectives for yourself at the present time; then project forward how you see the position at retirement, after retirement and on death. What do you see as the result of your planning? You need to do this because if you don't know where you are going or intend to go, it is almost impossible to measure your journey milestones. You can be as general or as specific as you wish – it's your plan.

2. Decide how far ahead you wish to plan for. Will you planning be for yourself, your spouse or partner, your children, your grandchildren, and even more future generations?

3. Consider your need requirements now, at retirement, and after your death (for your dependants).

4. Prioritise your objectives and need requirements in order of importance to you. I find it useful to use a scale of '1-4', where '1' is most important and '4' is least important. For example, an important need requirement may be private medical insurance, but because your company provides this and you already have it, it will be a '4' on the scale. Inheritance tax reduction may be a '1', as an issue that must be resolved, on which nothing has yet been done.

5. Taking your circumstances into account (provided, usually, through a 'fact-find'), produce a report leading to recommendations and an action plan.

Example

For example, Huw and Mary Hefner are married and have two minor children. Huw is aged 35 and Mary is aged 30. Huw is a sales director who has recently sold his shares in his design company. Mary is a trained teacher but currently looking after the children and not working.

Life objectives and goals

Huw's and Mary's core objectives are given as follows. These can be added to and changed as their personal circumstances change.

Financial objectives (on a scale of 1-4 where 1 is most important):

1. Family Protection '1'
2. Income protection '2' Huw '1' Mary
3. Critical illness cover '1'
4. Private medical insurance '1'
5. Long-term care '4'
6. Mortgage/loan arrangements '4'
7. Regular savings '2'
8. Planning for retirement '1'
9. Inheritance tax planning '1'
10. Lump sum investment for growth '1'
11. School and university fees planning '1'
12. Reduce income tax '1' for Huw – and improve tax efficiency
13. Use of ISA allowances for 2019/20 '1'
14. Financial Track to run on '1' with investment ideas
15. To have a financial plan '1'

Lifestyle planning objectives

1. Provide for school fees
2. Best for the family and family security and protection
3. A decent retirement – early, if possible
4. Mary to return to work at some stage
5. Financial security
6. To be healthy and active
7. Using money most efficiently – including the investment of future lump sums received or generated

In particular, they wish the financial planning process to include the following:

1. To keep track of investments and investment management
2. Keep £30,000 in a high interest account for access
3. Advice on capital gains tax – Huw sold chargeable assets in the 2019/20 tax year and estimates £100,000 to be paid in capital gains taxes
4. General capital gains tax savings and saving income tax
5. Children's savings to achieve £50,000 at the age of 23 for each
6. School and education fees planning
7. Planning around wills and inheritance taxes
8. Reduce the risk of IHT for their life policies, through trusts
9. They can invest up to £1,000 per month for savings
10. They have £100,000 for capital gains tax payments, in Mary's account
11. For investments, they are interested in IHT and CGT wrappers.

Future planning

They wish to plan for at least three generations. This would include Huw and Mary, their children and their grandchildren. They will also inherit a substantial sum from their parents, and need to take this planning into account. Mary is an only child and will inherit from her parents, who are elderly and in poor health.

Their present position is that they have sold a business interest and have paid off their mortgage and are debt free. They are accumulating assets through investments, properties and pension funds and wish to have a retirement income jointly of £50,000 in today's terms at retirement at the age of 60. At first death in retirement they expect the best financial security for their family and a liveable income of at least £40,000 in today's terms, with all debts and liabilities paid.

They wish to plan effectively so as to mitigate and reduce taxes, and are particularly concerned about inheritance taxes eroding your estate. They do have wills, but they need a review.

They are concerned that you need to make the right choices now and in the future to meet your objectives.

Results of recommendations and action plan

(abbreviated to deal with one specific issue only)

Huw and Mary have a combined estate of £3,500,000 on death, of which £1 million was in life assurance not underwritten in trust. Total inheritance tax payable is over £800,000 (after liabilities are deducted). By introducing a bypass trust into their wills and moving their existing life policies into trust, inheritance tax savings is over £500,000. The remaining £300,000 inheritance tax payable is covered through a joint-life second-death policy in trust for £300,000 at a cost of £15 per month. (This is a minimum premium which actually provides, at their ages, cover of over £900,000). Further planning around investments includes removing them from the taxable estate, whilst ensuring they remain fit for purpose. Also, a family conference promoted the idea of planning *up* a generation to deal with their parents' likely inheritances to them and inheritance tax mitigation in their estates.

It is important from a financial planning point of view to ensure that all the objectives were covered and the correct recommendations made.

This includes the undertaking of a life assurance analysis as well as a liquidity analysis.

Life assurance analysis

Huw and Mary had a number of existing policies that were not written in trust. As a result, on death, the proceeds of the policies fall into the estate and may be subject to inheritance taxes. There are other problems too, as the bulk of the policies were taken out to cover previously-held mortgages and were underwritten on a joint-life first-death event. Some also had critical illness cover, also on a first-death basis. Being for mortgage protection, the term of cover was decreasing term. As the mortgage reduces, so does the amount of the cover.

The result is that on death or critical illness of either Huw or Mary, each policy would only *pay out once*, leaving the survivor with no cover. The level of cover is also decreasing annually, thus effectively reducing available cover. If either suffered a critical illness first, that would pay out but the life cover for both would be lost. In short, their existing life and critical illness cover is now inappropriate for their current needs objectives. Huw and Mary do not now have a mortgage liability, but they do have a large potential inheritance tax liability, and require cash in their estates at death. The original purpose of the life cover is now obsolete. A further recommendation would have been for each to have their own life cover and critical illness cover for family protection (another objective) for a longer term – to retirement at least, with the life cover written into trust.

As your circumstances change, then so do your objectives and the products that may have been appropriate at one stage (covering the mortgage), may have become unsuitable for their present and future circumstances (reducing and paying inheritance tax, providing for family protection and personal protection issues.)

Liquidity needs analysis

Huw and Mary need to work out how much cash is required in the event of death of either one of them, or both together. Then they must ascertain where the required cash is going to come from. Some investments may be encashable, yet other assets, such as the family home, may not be. Cash can be provided through life assurance, and joint-life second-death policies are usually the likely route.

Cash is required to pay liabilities, such as a mortgage, inheritance and other taxes, to fund trusts and leave legacies. If not available, then executors can sell assets and even take loans. No one can inherit from the estate until inheritance tax has been paid.

The will

Once the financial and estate planning exercise has been completed, it is time for the wills of the parties to be reviewed, and if necessary, for changes to be made.

Usually, couples leave their assets each to the other, and if they have both died, to their heirs, most often their children. If they are married or in a civil partnership, then the spouse exemption will apply. This means that any assets left to a spouse or civil partner will not be subject to inheritance tax. However, when that spouse or civil partner dies (as long as they have not remarried), then after the nil rate band (£325,000 in 2019/20) and other exemptions and liabilities have been deducted, the estate could be subject to inheritance tax at 40% on the last death.

If the parties are not married, or if assets are left to anyone else who is not a spouse or civil partner, then after the nil rate band and exemptions and liabilities are deducted, the excess is subject to inheritance tax.

One of the main estate planning devices to reduce inheritance tax where the spouse exemption has applied is to set up a bypass trust in the will to bequeath the value of the nil rate band to the children, so as not to lose one of the nil rate bands due to the 100% spouse exemption. This means that assets left in trust for say the children, up to the value of the nil rate band, can bypass inheritance tax on the amount of that nil rate band in the second estate. In other words, you still can use the second nil rate band to save £130,000 in 2019/20. This strategy may still be applied even though the NRB is now transferable between spouses and civil partners. The first-death spouse's unused NRB can be uplifted and used in the second-death's deceased estate, at the current value, no matter when the first spouse or civil partner died.

The will is important and should be reviewed at the end of the estate planning process. Changes can be made to mitigate inheritance tax, and also to direct where assets should go, to set up will trusts and provide for guardians, deal with the business and its assets, and to give general direction to the testator's wishes. This is all the more important now, as deeds of variation as an estate planning tool may fall under the microscope as a tax avoidance methodology.

Estate planning is a process that needs constant updating as your circumstances and objectives change. Inheritance tax provision or mitigation is a part of the estate planning process. This process also includes many different forms of analysis to be completed, ranging from cash flowing to future income projections; tax planning, life assurance and dealing with all of your objectives.

$$3$$

Inheritance Tax

The mechanics of inheritance tax. What taxes are payable during your lifetime and on death, and why. Why inheritance taxes are probably here to stay. Exemptions from inheritance tax.

Legislation governing inheritance tax is found in the *IHTA 1984*, and annual Finance Acts, as changes are made. For example, the nil rate band for 2009/10 was set in the *Finance Act 2006* at £325,000 and is now frozen at that level until the 2020/21 tax year as announced in the Emergency Budget of 2015.

The concept of a death duty or a death tax on assets has been with us since the last century, and is deeply imbedded in our national psyche as well as in our tax legislation. The Exchequer gains many billions from such a tax, and it is highly unlikely that it would be removed or significantly watered down in the future. It is a fact that exemptions have not kept pace with inflation (mainly house inflation, at an average real rate for the UK of 3.1% p.a. over the last ten years) and more and more of your assets will become inheritance-taxable in the future – that is, unless you plan properly to mitigate and reduce inheritance taxes payable. It is a common precept in our law that anyone can arrange their affairs in such a way as to legally avoid taxes payable. This has to be distinguished from tax evasion, which is a different matter, and a criminal offence. Often there is a fine line drawn between what is legitimate tax planning and tax evasion; between what is perfectly acceptable as a tax planning strategy today, but with a stroke of the Chancellor's pen, becomes unacceptable and taxable tomorrow.

The main areas that have come under attack by the HMRC in recent years are the protection of the value of your house from future inheritance taxes, and the protection of assets for future generations who may inherit from you. There has been some respite for home owners though with the introduction of a new family home allowance effective from April 2017 (an additional nil rate band starting at £100,000 and rising to £175,000 by 2021). Attacks have come from income tax legislation as well as from inheritance tax, pensions and trust legislation. They all add up to the same thing. You have attempted to deplete your estate of otherwise taxable assets. Do what you can, but the Government may find a way to tax you – even retrospectively. Yes, that fine principle that what you have done in the past should stand because it fairly reflects the laws pertaining at the time has sadly been eroded, so that uncertainty, and confusion often reigns. A prime example is where you gifted your house to your children and continued to live there, rent-free. The Pre-Owned Assets Tax (POAT) was introduced in the 2005/06 tax year and ensures that if you are not paying a commercial rent if you continue to live in the house that has been gifted, then one will be determined for you. In addition, your gift to the children will be seen to be one that reserves a benefit to you (the use of the asset), and will therefore fall back into your estate for inheritance tax purposes. The *Finance Act 2007* has increased the time within which you can make an election to have your house fall back into your estate for IHT, rather than to pay the POAT.

Similar attacks were mounted against pension scheme assets, with up to 82% in tax charges being levied when passing on pension funds from an alternatively secured pension (ASP). Pension funds on death are now not subject to IHT (Finance Act 2011).

The overall effect of deliberate capital reduction and erosion through State action will be to impoverish future generations; to impair the accumulation of wealth; to reduce the certainty for families building assets to provide financial security for old age and dependants; for people to lose their homes; and I guess, ultimately for the State to shoulder the burden of what they have created.

These are very sensitive issues. The Government response has been that it only affects a few thousand very wealthy people. However, most know that they are wrong, and statistics forecast that a considerable number of people in London (where property prices are higher) will pay inheritance tax in 2019/20, and considerable numbers outside of London will also be affected. Inheritance tax will continue to be a political 'hot potato' as it encourages disincentives to save, own your own home, financially protect and provide for your families – and reduces the overall feeling of well-being of people generally. The very wealthy seldom pay much in inheritance taxes – they are far too clever for that.

Statistically, more and more people would previously fall into the IHT net because of rising house prices. It is estimated that four in ten families face paying IHT and one in three detached property owners will pay IHT. The new transferable NRB for married couples and civil partners will reduce IHT payable for many families, as will the introduction of the new additional residential nil rate band for home owners who leave their home to direct descendants (children and grandchildren).

Having said that, there remain fairly generous inheritance tax mitigation and reduction plans and procedures. Many are not without risk, and older people are reluctant to commit hard-earned assets to tax planning, unsure of their futures. A sensitive and light touch is required for estate planning as so many other issues always lie under the surface. For example, if you gift your house to your children, and you remain there for life, what if a son divorces his wife and has to share his assets with her – including your gifted house – where do you stand, then?

Having a Plan is better than having no plan. It is important to know what inheritance tax is and when it applies, and how it may affect you, if at all. It is equally important to know what exemptions there are and how you may make use of them.

Chargeable lifetime transfers (CLTs)

Inheritance tax applies to certain gifts or transfers made within the lifetime of the donor ('lifetime transfers') as well as to gifts or transfers made on death. Certain types of lifetime transfer are immediately chargeable (see Chapter 5 for further details); these are known as 'chargeable lifetime transfers' (CLTs). The charge to tax is on the value of this loss to the donor's estate, as opposed to the value of the benefit received by the donee (person receiving the gift). If making a chargeable lifetime transfer, unless exemptions apply, inheritance tax is payable at 20% (half the death rate of 40%).

The death rate for inheritance tax is 40% on a taxable estate. If lifetime IHT was payable at 20% then the balance of 20% owing is collected at death.

The nature of the asset transferred need not be tangible. It can be a value placed on failing to exercise a right to income, for example.

On death, the value subject to inheritance tax is the aggregate market value of all assets, after deducting liabilities, certain expenses, allowances and exemptions. Note that loans are not deductible unless charged against the asset against which the loan applied.

If you are domiciled in the UK then all of your worldwide assets are liable to inheritance taxes in the UK. These assets may also be subject to taxes in other tax jurisdictions, and double taxation agreements may apply so that taxes are not paid twice on the same asset.

Any gifts made within the previous seven years also form part of your estate if you die within the seven-year period, but are reduced or tapered depending on when you died.

Potentially exempt transfers (PET)

Many lifetime transfers can be exempt from inheritance tax if made more than 7 years prior to the death of the donor (see Chapter 5 for further details). These transfers are known as 'potentially exempt transfers' (PET). For example, you may wish to gift an asset to your children, grandchildren or a third party. You may do so at any time, and providing you survive the making of the gift by seven years, it will be out of your estate. If you die within the seven-year period, then a proportion of the value of the gift made will fall back into your estate and may become subject to inheritance tax. All lifetime transfers not covered by exemptions and made within seven years of death will be added back into the estate to calculate the overall inheritance tax payable.

Transfers made between spouses and civil partners have the spouse exemption and will be 100% exempt. Additionally, transferable NRBs may reduce the values of PETs that become chargeable.

Less is taxable the longer you live – the seven-year rule

The amount that could be subject to inheritance tax is reduced by the following percentages, for years survived within the seven-year period:

Years before death	0-3	3-4	4-5	5-6	6-7	7+
Tax reduced by	0%	20%	40%	60%	80%	100%

If you survive for the full seven years after making the gift, the asset becomes fully exempt.

The years must be full years. Note that transfers falling within the full nil rate band do not benefit from taper relief.

The nil rate band (NRB)

Every person has an exempt amount in his or her estate that is known as the 'nil rate band' (NRB). After allowing for the nil rate band, tax is paid at a flat rate of 40%. Lifetime chargeable transfers (CLT's) are charged at 50% of the flat rate, currently 20%. On death, the full rate applies, but is tapered for transfers made more than 3 years before death (see the above table).

The NRB is a most important exemption. Every person has it, and no inheritance tax is payable on gifts made, whether as a CLT (chargeable lifetime transfer) or as a PET (potentially exempt transfer), where the value is below the level of the nil rate band. The previous years' and future nil rate band rates of exemption are as follows:

Tax Year	Nil Rate Band
2006/07	£285,000
2007/08	£300,000
2008/09	£312,000
2009/10-2020/21	£325,000

The spouse exemption

- There is an additional exemption known as the 'spouse exemption' whereby any assets left to the spouse or civil partner are 100% exempt from inheritance taxes. This makes planning for proper exploitation of the nil rate band particularly important for married couples or civil partners, as the nil rate band should not be utilised in making transfers to spouses which are already exempt under the spouse exemption. To utilise the nil rate band exemption as well as the spouse exemption, you leave in your will 'so much of the nil rate band as it may be at the time plus any transferable NRB from a deceased spouse or civil partner' in trust for your children or others, as the case may be (known as a 'bypass trust' or 'nil rate band trust'). This effectively allows the value of the first-dying's nil rate band to escape inheritance tax in the second-dying's estate – allowing the couple to utilise two NRBs rather than just the NRB of the second-dying, when the assets pass to their children and heirs. In the tax year 2019/20, this would amount to an IHT saving of £130,000 (40% x £325,000). However, there could be greater savings under the new transferable NRB regime, than if using a NRB discretionary trust in a will. Ensure that you leave both the unused NRB of a deceased spouse or civil partner, plus your NRB, in your will.

- Previously, if a spouse was non UK domiciled the spouse exemption was £55,000. FA 2013 radically changed the IHT treatment where one spouse is UK domiciled and the other (recipient) is not. Up to 5 April 2013, such transfers were subject to a lifetime allowance of £55,000. After 6 April 2013 the IHT exempt amount that can be transferred from a UK domiciled spouse/civil partner to a non UK domiciled spouse/civil partner is increased to the NRB amount, currently £325,000. A non UK domiciled spouse/civil partner can elect to be treated as UK domiciled for IHT. This means assets can pass between spouses without an IHT tax charge. There are rules governing the election. The election ceases to be valid if the individual making the election lives outside the UK for more than 4 successive tax years. So you can be UK resident and live in the UK and retain the non UK domicile, and the election would be valid.

New family home allowance (residential nil rate band - RNRB)
From 6 April 2017 the government introduced a 'family home allowance' that will raise the Inheritance Tax threshold to £500,000 for an individual and £1 million for couples.

- The additional nil rate band (increases gradually: £100,000 in 2017/18; £125,000 in 2018/19; £150,000 in 2019/20; and £175,000 in 2020/21. If the estate is worth more than £2 million the RNRB reduces.

- Any unused RNRB on the first death of a married couple or civil partners is transferable – even if the first death occurred before 6 April 2017.

- The RNRB can only be used by those who held a 'qualifying residential interest' at some time during their lifetime. If you do not own your own home, the RNRB cannot be used. However, it can be used if you downsized or sold a property to move into care after 8.7.2015.

- The RNRB cannot be used to offset against other properties owned by the deceased – such as buy to let or investment properties.

- It is the net value of the home that is used for the RNRB (after any mortgage or equity release loan is deducted).

- The property must pass to direct descendants and be 'closely inherited'. These include children, grandchildren, remoter descendants, spouse, civil partner and their widows, widowers and survivors who have not remarried. It includes a step, adopted or fostered child and a child where the deceased was appointed as a guardian, or special guardian when the child was under age 18.

- Nephews, nieces, siblings and other relatives are excluded under the direct descendant category.

- A qualifying residential interest placed into a bare trust or interest in possession will trust will qualify for the RNRB provided the beneficiaries are direct descendants. However, it will not qualify if placed into a discretionary trust, unless the trustees appoint out to direct descendants within two years.

- The RNRB is transferable between spouses and civil partners when the survivor dies regardless of when the first death occurred and whether or not the deceased had a qualifying residential interest. Claim this within two years from the end of the month of the second dying.

- For large estates. Where the value is more than £2 million, the RNRB is reduced by £1 for every £2 that the value exceeds the threshold. Ignore reliefs and exemptions to determine the threshold. The £2 million threshold does not include lifetime gifts made by the deceased – even if included in the IHT calculation. After 5.4.2021 the £2 million threshold will increase with the CPI.

- The deceased's RNRB will be set off against the residence before the standard NRB is set off against the balance of the estate, including any value of the residence in excess of the RNRB.

• If the first death occurred before 6 |April 2017, the only check required is the £2 million taper threshold.

Quick succession relief (IHTA 1984 s 141)

If the same asset was taxed twice due to death of the first-dying and then the second-dying, within a five year period, then the IHT payable on the second transfer is reduced by a percentage of the tax charged on the first transfer. This is not to be confused with taper relief applying to CLTs and PETs falling into your estate within a seven-year period. The amount is reduced as follows:

Years between transfers	Percentage
0-1 year	100%
Over 1 but less than 2	80%
Over 2 but less than 3	60%
Over 3 but less than 4	40%
Over 4 but less than 5	20%

Making gifts

Whilst making a gift may be exempt (as a PET) or chargeable (as a CLT over the nil rate band), there are also other tax considerations to make. If a gift is a chargeable asset, it may be liable to capital gains tax (CGT), as a disposal. If the donee (the person receiving the gift) pays the CGT, the value of the transfer is reduced for IHT purposes (*IHTA 1984 s 165*).

For certain gifts, the capital gains tax payable can be 'held over' (not paid now). Hold-over relief includes gifts to and from trusts, gifts of business assets, gift of shares in an unquoted trading company (or personal trading company, even if the shares are quoted or on the AIM). The donee must be a UK resident, and where there is a settlor, he or she must have no interest in the settlement made. The held-over gain reduces the donee's acquisition cost. Stamp duty is not chargeable on lifetime gifts, except where, for example, there is a mortgage on land and the mortgage charge is assumed by the donee.

Inheritance tax exemptions

Certain gifts made by donors enable estates to be reduced by the amount of the gift, or to build up assets outside an estate, where they will not be subject to inheritance tax. These exemptions are available to husband and wife as well as civil partners. If you do not use some of these exemptions each year they are lost.

Outright exemptions

The following are outright exemptions, and do not fall back into your estate for inheritance tax purposes once made.

Annual exemption – IHTA 1984 s.19

Anyone can make a gift of up to £3,000 each year, free of inheritance tax. Any unused balance from the previous year may be carried forward, giving you £6,000 in that tax year – but you must use the current exemption first. Gifts can be made to any person or trust, including a discretionary trust and would be free of inheritance tax. The gift also qualifies for hold-over relief for inheritance tax. Note that from 1 March 2011 any gifts over the exemption could be potentially chargeable if not out of normal expenditure, and made up to 7 years before death. This could add considerable value back to an estate.

Small gifts exemption – IHTA 1984 s.20

You may make gifts of up to £250 to any person in a tax year and such gifts would be exempt. Any number of gifts may be made to different people in this way. This is in addition to the annual exemption.

Gifts in consideration of marriage or civil partnership – IHTA 1984 s.22

The limits for any one marriage are as follows:

- £5,000 given by a parent of a party to a marriage (£20,000 in total)
- £2,500 by a grandparent or ancestor or by a party to the marriage (potentially £10,000 or more in total)
- £1,000 if given by anyone else.

The happy newly-weds could hopefully expect at least £30,000 to see them on their way into married life – these gifts reducing the estates of the donors.

Gifts between spouses and civil partners – IHTA 1984 s.18

Previously, as long as the recipient spouse or civil partner was domiciled in the UK then lifetime and after-death transfers of property were exempt from inheritance tax. Where the recipient spouse or civil partner was not UK domiciled, the exemption was limited to £55,000. However, FA 2013 has changed this with the non domiciled spouse allowed up to the value of the nil rate band, currently £325,000 from 6 April 2013. A UK domiciled spouse or civil partner can make a transfer to another UK domiciled spouse of any amount who can then make a gift to make use of the IHT exemptions. This is useful where one spouse has funds or assets and the other does not. The first gift must not be conditional on the spouse (or civil partner) making the second gift, otherwise the 'associated operations' rules may apply

Gifts for maintenance
Qualifying gifts for the maintenance of a spouse, civil partner, child, or a dependant relative made by the donor can be exempt.

Gifts to a charity – IHTA 1984 s.23
These must become the property of the charity or held in trust for charitable purposes.

Payments made from normal expenditure out of income – IHTA 1984 s.21
If you have excess income, not required for normal living expenditures, then this income may be gifted to third parties, for example, a grandparent making regular payments to a grandchild for his mortgage loan. The payment must be from earned income and cannot be made from capital, to qualify. It is important to maintain records of the source of the income and the dates when payment was made. The transfer must be made out of post-tax income taking one year with another, i.e. continuously, and the person making the transfer must have sufficient income left to maintain their usual standard of living.

Other exemptions

* Gifts to qualifying political parties
* Waivers of remuneration or dividends – conditions apply
* Transfers of national heritage property – conditions apply
* A reversionary interest under a trust – conditions apply
* Trust property which is outside the UK and where the trust settlor was not UK domiciled
* If not domiciled in the UK at death, nor resident or ordinarily resident, certain foreign currency accounts
* Charitable covenants and Gift Aid payments, which are tax deductible
* Transfers conferring pension benefit
* Holdings in an authorised unit trust or share in an open-ended investment company (OEIC) if the holder is domiciled outside the UK
* Interest free loans payable on demand
* Shares to an employee trust by individuals are exempt if the trustees hold over 50% of the ordinary shares in trust and have voting control; beneficiaries must include most of the employees

Nil rate band – personal IHT allowance

Although not an exemption, the first £325,000 of chargeable transfers is charged at a nil rate. If you make a gift to anyone or a trust, then after seven years the value of the gift and the growth on it is out of your estate for inheritance tax purposes. After seven years, there is the benefit of another nil rate band.

Proposed legislation to limit the number of nil rate bands on multiple trusts was not proceeded with.

Exemptions on death

These include business property relief (BPR) and agricultural property relief (APR), which are covered elsewhere. Also, life assurance proceeds underwritten in trust should be exempt from inheritance taxes.

Transferable Nil Rate Band

From 9th October 2007 the inheritance tax nil rate band became transferable. between spouses and civil partners. If a person dies with an unused NRB allowance, the unused part may be claimed by their surviving spouse or civil partner.

If, for example, the NRB is not used because the entire estate passes to their surviving spouse or civil partner, the NRB available on the second spouse or partner death is effectively doubled. In the 2019/20 tax year, the NRB is £325,000 each, so £650,000 is available, plus the additional RNRB amount if leaving your house to a direct descendant of up to £175,000.

The NRB is transferable, regardless of the date when the spouse or first partner died. It is effective from 9 October 2007 and is totally retrospective – to even before the introduction of IHT in 1986.

Amount of the NRB and RNRB available to transfer

- A proportion of unused NRB at the time of the death of a spouse or civil partner, using the NRB rate applicable at the death of the second spouse.
- If you die having survived more than one spouse, the NRB can be accumulated for each spouse.
- If A died on 10th October 2007 and left all assets to spouse B, there is 100% spouse exemption and the NRB of £300,000 is unused. When B dies in October 2014, his or her NRB at the time, now £325,000, is doubled to £650,000.
- Where chargeable transfers had been made then the uplift is limited to the balance of the NRB available at that time. For example, in the 2011/12 tax year a £100,000 chargeable transfer was made, leaving £225,000 of the £325,000 nil rate band available on the first spouse death. On the death of the surviving spouse in October 2014, the available nil rate band is £225,000 plus the current year's nil rate band of £325,000 = £550,000.
- Any unused portion of the new additional RNRB of up to £175,000 can be transferred to the surviving spouse. From April 2017, this is £100,000, rising to £175,000 at 2020/2021.

Inheritance Tax Planning

The new transferable NRBs do not apply to single people, divorced or unmarried couples. NRB trust planning is still required for those individuals.

If you have a nil rate band trust in your will, there is probably no need to change it other than a clause to include the transferable NRB. Previous planning using NRB will trusts did so precisely to use both nil rate bands.

There is no need for all assets of the first-dying to pass to the surviving spouse or civil partner absolutely. You can still use a life interest trust for the surviving spouse and on his or her death the remainder of the estate passes to children or third parties (100% exemption whether the spouse is UK domiciled or not). FA 2013 radically changes the IHT treatment where one spouse is UK domiciled and the other (recipient) is not. Up to 5 April 2013, such transfers were subject to a lifetime allowance of £55,000. After 6 April 2013 the IHT exempt amount that can be transferred from a UK domiciled spouse/civil partner to a non-UK domiciled spouse/civil partner is increased to the NRB amount, currently £325,000. A non-UK domiciled spouse/civil partner can elect to be treated as UK domiciled for IHT. This means assets can pass between spouses without an IHT tax charge. There are rules governing the election. The election ceases to be valid if the individual making the election lives outside the UK for more than 4 successive tax years. So you can be UK resident and live in the UK and retain the non UK domicile, and the election would be valid.

Where a NRB discretionary trust is used on the first death and then appointed to the surviving spouse after three months and within 2 years, this would be as if left to the spouse outright and the unused NRB is transferable.

Planning will be easier for many families as the NRB would not be wasted because of the spouse exemption at 100%. It will be easier to deal with private residences and estates below £650,000 in 2019/20 and 2020/2021 as the individual NRB is frozen at £325,000. It is then proposed to be £329,000 in 2021/2022.

If the NRB was used on the first death there is no increase on the second death. Estates above the nil rate band are still taxed at 40%. You could have been a basic rate taxpayer all your life, paying tax at say 20% on earnings, but on death you are taxed at 40% on your accumulated wealth after exemptions.

There may be good reasons for still having a will trust and leaving your wills as they are (as opposed to changing your wills because of the transferable nil rate band). Reasons may include protecting assets for spouses and children, divorce issues, disabled people trusts and a host of other reasons to not give up the will discretionary trust. Assets left in trust grow outside of your estate and may mean that other inheritable estates end up paying less IHT. For combined estates worth more than £650,000 in 2019/20, lifetime gifting and loan planning using trusts will enable assets to grow outside of the estate and bear in mind that the NRB again becomes available every seven years, and should be used. The NRB applies to people as well as to trusts, and each trust has its own NRB.

For planning purposes, much thought will go into the need for severing tenancies where homes are owned as joint tenants so that each owner can deal separately with their portion of the home, using discretionary will trusts and even deeds of variation – especially where the nil rate band of a deceased spouse that was not used at the time can now be used by the second-dying to increase their own NRB and thus save IHT wherever possible.

Where you leave 10% or more of your estate to charity – after deductions of IHT exemptions, reliefs and the NRB- a reduced rate of IHT will apply. The 40% rate is reduced to 36%, and applies from 6 April 2012.

Trust Charge Calculation Rules

The relevant property regime applies to trusts such as discretionary trusts and lifetime interest in possession trusts.

At outset, if the gift (together with any other chargeable lifetime transfers in the last seven years) exceeds the available nil rate band then there is a 20% lifetime inheritance tax charge on the excess. If within the available nil rate band, the gift is taxable at 0%.

During the life of the trust, there will be calculations needed on every ten-year anniversary and when any assets are distributed by the trustees to the beneficiaries.

Periodic charges

The trustees calculate, report and pay any periodic charge for the trust. On every ten-year anniversary, the trustees will need to compare the value of the trust fund with the level of nil rate band in force at that time.

If the value of the trust fund plus any distributions of capital to the beneficiaries in the previous ten years is greater than the available nil rate band on the ten-year anniversary a periodic charge will apply. The available nil rate band used is the nil rate band on the ten-year anniversary, reduced by any other chargeable lifetime transfers made by the settlor in the seven years before commencement of the trust.

If this total exceeds the available nil rate band, the excess is taxed at 6%.

Where there have been no distributions of capital to the beneficiaries and no previous chargeable lifetime transfers by the settlor, the calculation is as follows:

Periodic charge = (value of trust – nil rate band) x 6%

Exit charges

When money is distributed to beneficiaries, an inheritance tax exit charge could apply. These may differ during and after the first 10 years.

Exit charges in the first ten years:

Any exit charge due in the first ten years of a trust is based on the value of the assets settled into the trust when they were gifted.

If lifetime inheritance tax was payable at outset, exit charges will apply in the first ten years. If there was no lifetime inheritance tax payable at outset, there will be no inheritance tax exit charges on any distributions of capital to the beneficiaries in the first ten years. (The position can change on death if a failed PET causes a subsequent chargeable lifetime transfer to exceed the available nil rate band).

Where a discretionary trust has been set up on death through a will then exit charges can apply, even if there is no entry inheritance tax charge. A trust with a single settlor is only entitled to a single nil rate band when considering exit and periodic charges.

Exit charges after the first ten years

Once the trust has passed its first ten-year anniversary, inheritance tax exit charges are always based on the effective rate of tax used for the previous ten-year anniversary charge. If this was zero, there will be no inheritance tax exit charges on any distributions of capital to the beneficiaries in the following ten years.

For the calculation, you must establish the effective rate of tax applying to the trust at outset or at the ten-year anniversary.

This tax rate is then applied to the amount of the capital distribution. However, there is a proportionate reduction based on the number of complete calendar quarters since the last ten-year anniversary, or since outset if within the first ten years.

The calculation is therefore:

Exit charge = amount of capital distribution x (tax suffered by trust / value of the trust at inception or the 10th anniversary) x X/40

The 'X factor' represents the number of complete calendar quarters, with 40 representing the number of quarters in a ten-year period.

4

IHT and Trusts

The in's and out's of the charging structures for entry to a chargeable trust, periodic charges and exit charges.

The current settled property regime is known from 22nd March 2006 as the 'relevant property' regime applying to lifetime trusts. The chargeable gifts history of the settlor to a trust, in the seven years before the date of the settlement, must be taken into account to determine the tax charge on the settlement (the gift made to the trust). The trust itself can be taxed at every tenth anniversary from the date the trust was set up (the 'periodic charge), and whenever capital is paid from the trust to a beneficiary (the 'exit' charge). The charges apply to all discretionary trusts, including now accumulation-and-maintenance trusts, interest-in-possession trusts and flexible trusts.

There are three ways in which trust tax charges apply.

Immediate charge on lifetime transfers that are not exempt

Where a chargeable lifetime transfer is made to a trust, and where the value of the gift to the trust after the annual exemption of £3,000 (you may use two year's exemptions in the current tax year, if one was not used in the previous tax year), and any BPR or APR exemptions that may apply, and where the value of the gift exceeds the settlor's available nil rate band (£325,000 in 2019/20), will be taxed at 20%, which is the current lifetime rate. The available nil rate band is reduced by any CLT (chargeable lifetime transfer) made in the previous seven years, as well as any PET (potentially exempt transfer) that becomes chargeable within the seven-year period.

If the tax is paid by the trustees, then the rate is 20%. If the person making the chargeable gift pays the tax then the rate is 25%.

Example

Molly wishes to gift £400,000 into a discretionary trust. She has a full nil rate band available and has not used her annual allowances. The tax could be paid by either Molly or the trustees, and this requires different calculations.

Where the trustees pay the tax, the calculation is as follows:

Chargeable transfer	£400,000
Less two annual allowances	£6,000
Less the nil rate band	£325,000
Taxable	£69,000
Tax at 20%	£13,800
Net value after tax	£386,200
Value that has left the estate	£400,000

If Molly paid the tax, then 25% x £69,000 is £17,250. Her estate is further reduced by the extra tax of £3,450. However, the net value in the trust is increased by the trustees not having to pay the tax, and will be £400,000.

Taper relief is available to reduce the amount of tax payable, should Molly have died within the seven-year period. Every seven years, Molly can make use of the nil rate band again, at its value at that time. If Molly was to die within seven years, the tax is recalculated at 40% using the nil rate band applicable at death. In the example below, it is assumed that the nil rate band is £325,000. Tax that has already been paid will reduce the tax now payable (it is credited to Molly's tax account). Taper relief applies to the balance payable after three years.

Assume Molly made a chargeable settlement into a discretionary trust of £400,000, when the nil rate band was £325,000, and she had no other exemptions. Tax payable is £400,000 – £325,000 x 20% = £15,000 to be paid by the trustees. If Molly had paid the tax, it would have been £400,000 – £325,000 x 25% = £18,750. Total tax payable is recalculated at 40%.

Years survived	% reduction for taper	Total tax payable	Tax already paid by trustees	Balance of tax to pay
0-3	0%	£30,000	£15,000	£15,000
3-4	20%	£24,000	£15,000	£9,000
4-5	40%	£18,000	£15,000	£3,000
5-6	60%	£12,000	£15,000	£0
6-7	80%	£6,000	£15,000	£0

No tax refund is available, even though more tax would have been paid by the trustees in years 5 to 7.

Periodic anniversary charge

Where there is a relevant property trust in existence, HMRC seeks to tax the trust every ten years for inheritance tax as if the property was a lifetime gift made every ten years. The periodic charge is collected every ten years, at a maximum rate of 6%. The 6% figure is arrived at through the following formula: 20% every 33 1/3 years, rounded down to make 6%. More conventionally, this is 20% (the lifetime rate) x 30% to give you 6%. 6% is the maximum rate applying, but this can be less, when the nil rate band is applied, giving the 'effective rate'.

The chargeable amount will be based on the value of all 'relevant property' in the settlement immediately before the ten-year anniversary. The chargeable amount is reduced by BPR (business property reliefs) and APR (agricultural property reliefs).

The rate of tax applying is 30% of the effective rate which will give the actual rate of tax payable.

The ten-yearly periodic charge at a maximum of 6% is levied on the excess of the trust funds over the nil rate band at the time of the calculation. In other words, the nil rate band at the time of the ten-year anniversary is used.

At present these principles can be applied across multiple trusts each with its own £325,000 nil rate band. The 2013 Autumn Statement announced a consultation to end this practice by splitting nil rate bands across multiple trusts, and some proposed changes were announced. However, these proposed changes were reversed by the 2014 Autumn Statement and multiple nil rate bands will still be with us for the foreseeable future. Notwithstanding this, the Government will further consult on multiple trust avoidance and legislation is expected to follow.

Exit charge

An exit charge is calculated every time capital is appointed to a beneficiary or leaves the trust. On leaving the trust, capital ceases to be relevant property, and an exit charge may be payable. The rate of tax on the exit charge is the amount distributed x 30% of the effective rate. This is then multiplied by the number of complete quarters since the settlement date or the 10-year anniversary (whichever of these is the most recent). This is then divided by 40.

Example

If the distribution made is £20,000 and the effective rate is 2.5%, and the number of quarters since the settlement date is 30, then the exit charge is £20,000 x 30% x 2.5% x 20 divided by 40 = £75.

Note that the transferable NRB from 9th October 2007 on second deaths for married couples and civil partners could provide a further IHT allowance thus reducing the overall chargeable event IHT payable.

5

Chargeable Transfers

Potentially exempt transfers (PETs) and chargeable lifetime transfers (CLTs), both before and after the 2006 budget and Finance Act 2006. The interaction with entry, periodic and exit charges.

Whilst certain transfers are fully exempt, others are potentially exempt (PET) or chargeable lifetime transfers (CLTs).

Potentially exempt transfers (PET)

You may make a gift to any individual and certain trusts, and as long as you survive for seven years, the value of the gift and the growth on it will be out of your estate for inheritance tax purposes. No IHT is due at the time the PET was made, and while the donor is still alive PETs are ignored for the purpose of the calculation of the cumulative lifetime total of gifts made.

It is important to note the order in which gifts should be made. Some gifts are potentially exempt, others are chargeable lifetime transfers (CLTs). Always make chargeable gifts first before gifts that may qualify as being potentially exempt. This is because any gift made uses up any available exemptions. This is particularly the case with the annual exemption of £3,000 per year (and using the previous year's exemption if not used, to make it £6,000 in the first year). The annual exemption is allocated by HMRC in chronological order of transfer and set off against the gift whether a PET or a CLT, in that order. If, in the same tax year, a PET gift is made first and a CLT second, then the annual exemption is reduced by the PET first before any allocation to the CLT (and will be wasted unless the donor dies within seven years). It is always better to make the chargeable lifetime transfer (CLT) first, and then the potentially exempt transfer (PET).

Potentially exempt transfers are:

* Transfers by individuals to other individuals
* Transfers by individuals to certain trusts for the disabled

nsfers by an individual into an interest-in-possession trust where, on or after 22nd March 2006, the beneficiary has a disabled person's interest
- Certain transfers on the termination or disposal of an individual's beneficial interest in settled property (restricted following FA 2006)
- Transfers on or after 22nd March 2006 by an individual to a bereaved minor's trust on the coming to an end of an immediate post-death interest
- Transfers before 22nd March 2006 by an individual to an accumulation-and-maintenance trust.

Surviving seven years

If you make a gift as a potentially exempt transfer and survive for seven years, then the value of the gift and all growth on it will be out of your estate. If you die within the seven-year period, then the gift made becomes a chargeable lifetime transfer – and the date of calculation is from when the gift was made. In order to work out the IHT liability, all chargeable lifetime transfers in the seven years preceding each gift is accumulated. Exempt transfers and potentially exempt transfers where the donor has survived for seven years are not included in the cumulative total. The rate of IHT is applied to the cumulative total at the date of death. Taper relief is given depending on the number of full years the donor has survived within the seven-year period.

It is important to keep accurate records of all transfers or gifts made to others as well as to trusts. It could be that the period taken into account is longer than seven years as the calculation is made from the date the gift is made.

The recipient of the gift, the donee, is responsible for reporting that a previous PET has now become chargeable and is also liable for the payment of the inheritance tax. If the donee is unable to pay the IHT, then the personal representatives of the deceased must pay.

Inheritance tax may not be the only tax payable. Capital gains tax may be payable as the making of the gift will be treated as a disposal for capital gains tax purposes. The capital gains tax is payable by the donor. The recipient donee can only add the cost of the IHT payable by him to the gift when making a subsequent disposal of the gift if the original gift was subject to 'hold-over' relief. This is important as it 'revalues' the gift made for the CGT that he may have to pay.

The benefits of making a potentially exempt transfer is that cash, shares and other assets may be gifted without limit to any person and to trusts for the disabled and bare trusts, and will be out of your estate for IHT purposes, so long as you survive for seven years. Business assets qualifying for BPR and those with CGT holdover reliefs may also be gifted in this way – the reliefs continue to apply for the recipients in most cases. Obviously you must have good health to survive for seven years, but even if you don't make it within the time period, taper reliefs will apply to lessen the impact of IHT payable. You may wish to insure yourself with a seven year decreasing term policy to cover the PET period of seven years, especially for large gifts where you intend your estate to pay the IHT, or where the donee would be liable for the IHT payable, for the donee to insure you.

Example

Tom Chumley is 65 next birthday and is a non-smoker. A decreasing term policy for 7 years for £100,000 starting cover reducing to nil over 7 years, would cost him £28.07 per month, with guaranteed premiums and cover.

His wife Bunty, at the same age and for the same cover, would pay a guaranteed premium of £28.07 per month. The premiums can be paid by the donee who would receive the proceeds to pay the IHT liability when it occurs.

Chargeable lifetime transfers (CLT)

Lifetime transfers made to discretionary trusts, including (since *FA 2006*) interest-in-possession trusts and accumulation-and-maintenance trusts (but not trusts for the disabled or bare trusts), and lifetime transfers made that are in excess of the nil rate band, will be chargeable lifetime transfers, or CLTs.

The donor is responsible for paying inheritance tax in advance on CLTs at 50% of the current inheritance tax rate of 40% (20% is the lifetime rate of tax payable). On death the balance of IHT payable becomes due.

Initial charges

Unless otherwise exempt, transfers into trusts are chargeable lifetime transfers (CLTs). The tax payable is at half of the death rate (20%). The tax can be paid by either the settlor or the trustees. If the settlor pays the tax then the transfer is grossed up to reflect the loss to the estate. Essentially trustees pay the tax at 20% and the settlor at 25%.

Initial charges are only payable if the chargeable amount is over the nil rate band at that time. Other exemptions, such as BPR and APR will also apply, in the same way as the nil rate band. The lifetime tax charge is therefore only payable on entry to the trust if the cumulative amount of exemptions has been exhausted.

Example

Sally Phillips created a discretionary trust in 2015/16 of £375,000 on 1st June 2015 and has no other exemptions than the nil rate band available. The trustees would pay tax of of £375,000–£325,000 (nil rate band) x 20% = £10,000. If Sally paid the tax then the amount payable is £375,000–£325,000 = £50,000 divided by 80% = £62,500 x 20% = £12,500. £12,500 divided by £50,000 is 25%.

If Sally died within the seven-year period then taper relief applies to the balance of the tax payable after three years. Tax paid may be greater than the total tax due in later years, and no tax refund is available. This is shown in the following table:

Years Survived	Total IHT payable at 40%	Tax already paid at 20%	Balance of Tax payable on death
0-3	£20,000	£10,000	£10,000
3-4	£16,000	£10,000	£6,000
4-5	£12,000	£10,000	£2,000
5-6	£8,000	£10,000	0
6-7	£4,000	£10,000	0

After seven years, Sally will again have the use of her nil rate band. The nil rate band is therefore not available only once, but can be regenerated every seven years.

Had Sally made a gift to the trust of £250,000 as a CLT, there would be no initial charge as the nil rate band of £325,000 in 2019/20 is greater than the CLT.

Exit and periodic charges

The general rule is that a capital distribution made from the trust could be subject to an exit charge. Every ten years, a trust could also face a periodic charge on relevant property within it. However, depending on the size of the trust assets at the relevant periods, there may or may not be charges payable.

When capital leaves a discretionary trust, it ceases to be relevant property, and there may be an exit charge payable. If the property settled is below the nil rate band and no chargeable transfers were made in the seven years preceding the settlement, there would probably be no exit charge tax payable on property ceasing to be relevant before the first ten-year anniversary. If you make a capital distribution within the first ten years and no tax is payable, the value of the trust fund at the tenth anniversary could be kept below the nil rate band *available at that time*.

Rate of tax on the exit charge
Distribution amount x 30% of effective rate* x number of complete quarters since settlement date or 10-year anniversary (the most recent of these) divided by 40.

*Effective rate = [CLT Tax] / [Current value if Trust Fund]

Example

If the CLT tax is £10,000, and the current value of the trust fund is £500,000, then the effective rate is £10,000 divided by £500,000 = 2%.
   If the distribution amount is £15,000 and the number of quarters (4 quarters in a year) is 16 (for 4 years), then the calculation for the exit charge is:

£15,000 x 30% x 2% x 16 divided by 40 = £36

Rate of tax on the periodic charge
10-year anniversary charge = current value of trust fund x 30% of effective rate*

*Effective rate = [CLT Tax] / [Current value if Trust Fund]

Example

If the CLT tax is £50,000, and the current value of the trust fund is £700,000, then:

Effective rate = £50,000 / £700,000 = 7.14%
Rate to be used is 30% of this: 7.14% x 30% = 2.14%
Periodic Charge: 2.14% x £700,000 = £14,980

Where chargeable lifetime transfers are within the nil rate band

On 1st June 2013 Jane Morgan made a trust settlement into a discretionary trust of £256,000 – £6,000 is covered by 2 x annual gift allowance, therefore chargeable lifetime transfer is £250,000. She has made no previous gifts. The trustees distribute £15,000 to daughters Katy in 2015 and £20,000 to Phoebe in 2016. No exit charges arise as neither distribution cumulatively exceeds the nil rate band in the year in which it is made.

10-year periodic charge

Example

At the tenth anniversary of the trust on the 1st June 2019, the trust fund has grown to £700,000, and the nil rate band is then worth say £450,000.

Value of the trust fund	£700,000
Add any distributions where there are exit charges	£0
Less nil rate band	£450,000
Taxable amount	£250,000
Tax at 20%	£50,000

Effective rate £50,000 / £700,000 = 7.14%
Rate to be used is 30% of this: £50,000 / £700,000 x 30% = 2.14%
Periodic Charge: 2.14% x £700,000 = £14,980

Had the trustees distributed £260,000 just before the 10th anniversary, there would be no exit charge and no periodic charge.

Value of the trust fund	£440,000
Add distributions subject to exit charge	£0
Less nil rate band in year 10	£450,000
Taxable amount	£0

Periodic charges and exit charges for the next ten years will be nil.

The rate of inheritance tax chargeable between ten-year anniversaries will be the appropriate fraction of the rate at which it was charged at the last ten-year anniversary. The effective rate is recalculated every ten years using the trust value at the anniversary, and adding on any withdrawals on which an exit IHT charge is paid. That effective rate is then used to calculate the periodic and exit charges in the next ten years.

Where chargeable lifetime transfers exceed the nil rate band

Example
Ken Collin gifts £456,000 into a discretionary trust on 20th June 2012. £6,000 is covered by 2 x annual gift allowance, therefore chargeable lifetime transfer is £450,000 He has made no previous gifts, other than using his annual exemptions.

Entry charge

Chargeable Lifetime Transfer (CLT)	£450,000
Less available nil rate band	£325,000
Taxable amount	£125,000
Immediate tax paid by trustees at 20%	£25,000

Exit charge

The trustees distribute £60,000 to Miss Nollie Collin and pay the tax from that amount, on 20th June 2017.

Previous lifetime transfers	£0
Initial value of the trust fund	£450,000
Less the trust's NRB at date of distribution (2017/18)	£325,000
Taxable amount	£125,000
Tax at 20%	£25,000

Effective rate = CLT Tax (£25,000) divided by Current Value of Trust Fund (£450,000) = 5.55%

of which 30% is 1.66%

The exit charge is calculated as follows:

Distribution amount (£60,000) x 30% of effective rate (1.66%) x number of complete quarters since settlement date or 10-year anniversary (the most recent of these) (16 quarters). Divide this by 40.

£60,000 x 1.66% x 16/40 = £398.40 exit charge to pay

10-year periodic charge

At the 10th Anniversary the Ken Collin discretionary trust has grown to a fund of £820,000.

Previous chargeable transfers in seven years before creation of this trust	£0
Distributions on which exit charge paid in first 10 years	£60,000
Value of trust fund at 10-year anniversary	£820,000
Total	£880,000
Less NRB at 10th anniversary on 20 June 2022	£325,000
Taxable amount	£555,000
CLT tax at 20%	£111,000

Effective rate = CLT Tax (£111,000) divided by Current Value of Trust Fund (£820,000) = 13.539%

of which 30% = 4.05%

The 10-year anniversary charge is calculated as follows:

Current value of trust fund x 30% of effective rate

= £820,000 x 4.05%

= £33,210

Previous lifetime transfers

Where previous lifetime transfers have been made within the seven years prior to settling an amount into a new discretionary trust, the scenario is as follows.

Example

On 2nd January 2006 Francis Prior made a chargeable lifetime transfer of £291,000 into a discretionary trust – £6,000 is covered by 2 x annual gift allowance, therefore chargeable lifetime transfer is £285,000 (being equivalent to the NRB applying at the time). He creates another discretionary trust in January 2008 for £146,000 – £6,000 is covered by 2 x annual gift allowance, therefore chargeable lifetime transfer is £140,000.

   As the first transfer used up Francis's nil rate band, the second transfer into trust is immediately chargeable as a CLT at 20%.

Previous CLT	£285,000
Current settlement to new trust	£140,000
Total	£425,000
Less available current nil rate band in 2008	£300,000
Taxable amount	£125,000
Assume trustees pay tax at 20%	£25,000

(if Francis paid the tax it would be £31,250)

Exit Charge

The trustees of the second discretionary trust distribute £25,000 to Michelle, Francis's daughter in June 2012.

   The distribution is in the first ten years since the trust was established in January 2008, so the settlor's chargeable transfers in the past seven years before the new trust was set up in January 2008, plus the initial value of the trust fund, are taken into account.

Previous chargeable lifetime transfer	£285,000
Initial value of the trust fund	£140,000
Total	£425,000
Less the trust's nil rate band at the date of distribution (2012/13)	£325,000
Taxable amount	£100,000
Tax at 20%	£20,000

Effective rate = CLT Tax (£20,000) divided by Current Value of Trust Fund (£140,000) = 14.28%

of which 30% = 4.28%

The exit charge is calculated as follows:

£25,000 (distribution amount) x 30% of the effective rate x complete quarters since settlement date or ten-year anniversary (16), divided by 40:

= £25,000 x 4.28% x 16/40

= £428 tax to pay on exit

Had the distribution occurred say two years earlier, then the exit charge would have been £25,000 x 4.28% x 8/40 = £214.

Periodic charge at 10-year anniversary

On the 10th anniversary the second trust fund has grown to £155,000.

Previous chargeable transfers of settlor	£285,000
Distribution in 1st ten years	£25,000
Value of trust fund at 10-year anniversary	£155,000
Total	£465,000
Less nil rate band at 10th Anniversary in January 2018	£325,000
Taxable amount	£140,000
CLT tax at 20%	£28,000

Effective rate = CLT Tax (£28,000) divided by Current Value of Trust Fund (£155,000) = 18.06%

of which 30% = 5.41%

The 10-year anniversary charge is calculated as follows:

Current value of trust fund x 30% of effective rate

= £155,000 x 5.41%

= £8,385.50

The freezing of the nil rate band has caused a much larger 10 year anniversary charge, than had the NRB increased with inflation. If the NRB had risen to say £460,000 in 2018 (instead of being frozen at £325,000), then the charge would have been a mere £294.

Updated position 2019

The Office for Tax Simplification (OTS) and HMRC proposals in the Inheritance Tax Review second report of July 2019 is recommending on simplifying the periodic and exit charges by taking out the need for previous settlements and initial values to be calculated, and applying a flat rate of 6% instead of having a complicated charging structure.

Multiple trusts and the Rysaffe principle

The 'Rysaffe Principle' (*Rysaffe Trustee Co (CI) v IRC (2003)*) relates to a series of trusts created on consecutive days. Each individual trust has its own nil rate band and by using a series of smaller trusts instead of one large one, the impact of the 10-yearly periodic charge and the exit charges can be minimised. However, the creation of the trusts must not be on the same day. Section 62 of the *IHTA 1984* considers 'related settlements', and for a trust to be a related settlement the settlor must be the same in each case, and the trusts must commence on the same day. By creating a series of smaller trusts on different days, inheritance tax can be saved.

Because of the cumulative effect of adding back previous chargeable settlements made within seven years of the current settlement, it may mean that one or more trusts do suffer periodic and exit charges – particularly if growth in the trusts' investments outpaces the growth in the nil rate band. For both PETs and CLTs you can give away your nil rate band every seven years, and have a new nil rate band at the value at that time.

Under the Rysaffe multiple trusts arrangement, the calculation applies a nil rate band to each trust separately, so settlements made under that nil rate band in each case may or may not have exit and periodic charges to pay (depending on the level of the amounts settled into trust). The nil rate band is, however, cumulative as far as entry charges are concerned and each settlement made uses up a portion of the nil rate band.

The 2013 Autumn Statement announced a consultation to end this practice by splitting nil rate bands across multiple trusts, and some proposed changes were announced. However, these proposed changes were reversed by the 2014 Autumn Statement and the Rysaffe principle remains with us for the time being.

Should the proposed changes be re-introduced in the future, the following could be the effect on increasing tax charges.

Some trusts set up under such multiple arrangements could be liable for a tax charges for the first time. A person benefiting from four such trusts could be liable for a tax charge exceeding £50,000. The tax charges are likely to be retrospective, applying to both old and new trusts.

Setting up trusts on different days, each below the £325,000 IHT limit has proved a popular wealth planning strategy for people over the years. The new proposals could introduce a single nil rate band, i.e. the amount you can inherit without being liable for an IHT charge, across all such trusts. This proposed change in legislation means these trusts may now face a tax charge at what is known as the 10-year periodic charge point and if these trusts already exceed the IHT limit, their tax liability could be even greater.

For example, if a client has created four trusts, all below the IHT threshold, then under current legislation, depending on when the trust was set up, the trust would not be liable to a 10-year tax charge. Under any future proposed legislation, the nil rate band would be split between the four trusts, and a maximum 6% tax charge will be applied on the excess over the nil rate band on each trust.

		Current legislation		Proposed legislation	
Trusts	Value	Nil rate band – each trust has its own nil rate band	10-year tax charge	Nil rate band split 4 ways	10-year tax charge*
1	£320,000	£325,000	£0	£81,250	£14,325
2	£320,000	£325,000	£0	£81,250	£14,325
3	£320,000	£325,000	£0	£81,250	£14,325
4	£320,000	£325,000	£0	£81,250	£14,325
Total	£1,280,000		£0		£57,300
* Uses a maximum 6% tax charge as proposed in the consultation paper					

Using the example above, the proposed change could result in the trustee being liable to a £57,300 tax charge at the 10 year periodic charge point (as opposed to a nil charge under the current legislation).

Planning

Estate and IHT planning with gifting to individuals and trusts can be a simple or complex procedure. Settlements made into trust must be carefully considered, both as to amount as well as to the type of trust to be used. You can make a chargeable lifetime transfer, but it will only be taxable if not exempt. Exemptions include your annual allowances, the value of the nil rate band (£325,000 in 2019/20), and business and agricultural property reliefs attaching to assets, usually at 100%. In the tax year 2019/20, you could gift up to £325,000 into trust without paying the up-front 20% tax charge (provided your nil rate band is available).

Once the asset is in the trust, any growth on it will normally be captured in the trust and not in the estate on death, unless the GWR (gift with reservation) rules apply. Trust assets can be distributed to beneficiaries and the taxation aspects on distributions are covered elsewhere.

Both potentially exempt transfers (PET) and chargeable lifetime transfers (CLTs) can make use of the nil rate band exemption – for example a PET may become chargeable if you die within a seven-year period of making it. If it does, you may be covered by the exemption in the nil rate band. It is important to remember that only previously chargeable lifetime transfers come into the reckoning when calculating the periodic and exit charges, and not PETs made as exempt gifts. The PET only becomes chargeable should you not survive the seven -year period after making the gift – and then taper reliefs may apply to reduce the incidence of taxation. Planning will include the order of the gifts made, the type of gift made and whether you reserve a benefit after making it, the use of the nil rate band, equalisation of assets between spouses or civil partners and the respective taxation consequences.

Note that the transferable NRB from 9th October 2007 on second death for married couples and civil partners could provide a further IHT allowance thus reducing the overall chargeable event IHT payable on joint estates, as could the RNRB for homes directly left to descendants.

6

The Inheritance Tax Regime

What is taxable and what is not taxable in your estate.
Reporting requirements on gifts made, making payments
out of income. Keeping the HMRC happy.

It is important to have a 'bird's eye' view of the inheritance tax regime for your estate. Some assets and gifts made may fall into your estate for inheritance tax purposes, and others may be exempt or deductible in your estate when calculating inheritance tax.

Exempt and allowable assets

These include:

*   All estates which, after allowable deductions, fall within the nil rate band, currently £325,000 in 2019/20.
*   Qualifying lifetime gifts, including: any gifts falling within the annual exemptions (presently £3,000 per annum); small gifts of £250 to any person; gifts made in the contemplation of marriage, excess income over normal expenditure that is gifted; gifts to charities and political parties; gifts of heritage property; gifts and transfers subject to business property and agricultural reliefs; lifetime gifts for spouse, civil partner and child maintenance and others mentioned previously.
*   Gifts between spouses and civil partners (but limited to £325,000 if the recipient spouse is domiciled outside the UK).
*   Life assurance proceeds in trust (also bypasses probate).
*   Pension funds passing to a spouse or a civil partner.
*   Pension annuities ceasing on death.
*   Gifts to interest-in-possession and accumulation-and-maintenance trusts made before March 22nd 2006; these are treated as PETs where the settlor has survived 7 years.
*   Assets passing on death to a spouse or civil partner (spouse exemption).
*   Assets gifted on death to a bypass trust for the amount of the nil rate band (for example assets left to children or grandchildren in trust rather than to

the spouse, where the spouse exemption has already been used); these will bypass IHT in the second spouse dying.
- Non-UK assets if domiciled outside the UK – note that there are specific IHT rules affecting domicile.
- UK authorised unit trusts or shares in open-ended investment companies (OEICs) if domiciled outside the UK ("non-dom"); otherwise all UK assets held by a non UK domiciled individual are subject to IHT.
- Certain foreign currency accounts of those dying not domiciled, resident or ordinarily resident in the UK.
- Shares in qualifying Enterprise Investment Scheme (EIS) companies, if held for more than two years (these shares fall out of your estate after two years).
- Woodlands – the ownership of woodlands is treated as a business for IHT purposes and can therefore attract 100% business property relief (BPR). It may also attract agricultural property relief (APR) connected to farming. Income is not taxed and losses are not allowable against income tax. Growing timber and underwood passing on death has a special IHT relief, where the charge may be deferred until actually sold.
- The discounted portion of a discounted gift trust investment.
- Capital gains tax dies with you. If you were deferring a capital gain then this tax is not payable on your death.

Taxable assets

The general rule is that all of your assets, wherever situated are subject to UK inheritance tax if you are domiciled in the UK. You may live abroad, but if you have not severed all ties and even if you have no intention to return to the UK, you may still be deemed to be domiciled in the UK and assets could be subject to inheritance tax.
Taxable assets include:

- Your house, holiday property and other properties, such as buy-to-let investments.
- Foreign property owned by you, such as holiday homes.
- Household contents, cars, and personal effects.
- Gifts that you made 'with reservation' – where you gifted the asset but still enjoyed the use of it; these will fall back into your estate and will be taxable.
- All non-exempt investments. These include ISA's (except for qualifying EIS shares held in an ISA), VCTs, share portfolios, investment bonds, national savings and most other investments
- Life assurance not underwritten in trust.
- Gifts made as a potentially exempt transfer where you die within 7 years; these will fall back into your estate for the portion that is not relieved.

- Gifts made as chargeable lifetime transfers (CLTs) that are in excess of the nil rate band; these will be chargeable, less inheritance tax already paid. CLTs will include gifts made to discretionary trusts by a settlor.
- Certain interests in possession flowing from a trust will be chargeable after 22nd March 2006 unless in the transition period to 22nd March 2008 in which case certain transitional arrangements apply.
- Business assets and shares unless relieved through business property relief. This would include a close company, for example which is used to manage investments, where there is no definable trade, or where there are large cash holdings instead of assets; such companies may not get business property relief. Likewise, certain agricultural assets not used in farming may not qualify for agricultural property relief.
- Agricultural assets unless relieved through agricultural property relief.
- Loans that you have made to other people that are repayable on demand.
- The non-discounted portion of a discounted gift trust, if you die within seven years. This is a PET that will become chargeable, subject to taper relief for the years you have survived.
- The capital value of an immediate or voluntary annuity, available at death
- Certain pension funds passing to a non spouse or civil partner – this could be a pension fund passing to your children or others on your death. Pension funds passing to a spouse or civil partner are not subject to inheritance tax but there are other tax charges that will apply.
- A director's loan account in a company.

The above are broadly the assets that may fall into your estate as taxable assets.

All assets must be brought into account in your estate on death. This only applies to your assets, not those of your spouse or civil partner. If you jointly own an asset, then your share of the asset falls into your estate. From your gross estate assets are then deducted the various liabilities you may have, such as debts, and funeral and hospital expenses, then exemptions and allowances that further reduce your estate. Your nil rate band is then applied to further reduce your estate (or so much of it as is left after accounting for PET's and CLT's), and the balance is subject to inheritance tax at 40%.

Deductions allowable

- Your share of the mortgage loan outstanding at death.
- Creditors owing.
- Loans outstanding.
- Credit cards and store card liabilities.
- Income tax payable.
- Last expenses, such as funeral and hospital costs.

- Certain professional fees.
- Other liabilities. These may include claims for redundancy from employees if you were a sole trader, or contractual maintenance payments where a lump sum is set aside, for example to satisfy a divorce court order.

Restrictions on the deduction of liabilities

One of the changes brought about by *Finance Act 2013*, contains provisions that restrict the extent to which liabilities may be deducted to compute IHT. Section 162A (applies irrespective of when the liability was incurred) disallows a liability where the money has been used to acquire, enhance or maintain excluded property, although this basic approach is relieved if the excluded property, or the consideration from its sale, turns out to be subject to IHT. Section 175A (applies irrespective of when the liability was incurred) disallows a liability on death where the liability is not actually repaid out of the estate (which includes excluded property owned by the deceased, with the proviso that where there is a real commercial reason for not repaying the loan and the non-repayment does not give rise to a tax advantage, the liability may still be deducted. Where the liability can be deducted and was used to acquire, enhance or maintain property that qualifies for agricultural (APR), business (BPR), or woodlands relief, Section 162B stipulates that the liability must first be taken as a deduction against that relievable property, so that relief is only applied to the net value, notwithstanding that the liability may be charged against other property. The new rules apply to deaths and other chargeable events after 17 July 2013. For example, from 6 April 2013 a mortgage taken out on the family home and invested into 100% IHT-exempt assets (farmland, EIS, AIM, etc.), where the loan reduces the value of the home subject to IHT, and the assets acquired do not attract IHT, after 6 April 2013, the amount of the loan must first be deducted from the value of the assets it was used to acquire, not the property it is secured on. The loan and the IHT-exempt assets cancel each other out in the IHT calculation and no tax is saved. HMRC expects liabilities to be repaid. So in completing Form IHT400, include all the deceased's liabilities at death, unless a particular liability will not be repaid and should not be deducted.

In summary:

- A deduction for IHT purposes will only be available to the extent that a loan is actually repaid.
- A deduction for IHT purposes will not be allowed to the extent that a loan has been used directly or indirectly to acquire property excluded from the charge to IHT. This is unless the property has been disposed of or the loan is greater than the value of the excluded property.
- Where a loan has been taken to acquire assets which qualify for BPR, APR or WR, the loan will reduce the value of the assets that can qualify for the relief. The deduction for the loan will be matched against

the assets acquired and relief will be restricted to the net value of the assets. Any excess liability will be allowable as a deduction, subject to it being repaid in full in money or monies worth.

It is important to note that the reliefs themselves remain untouched and are very valuable. It is the legislation concerning the deductibility of the loans which is being changed.

The process

Gross Assets (including chargeable lifetime transfers)
less liabilities, and allowable deductions
 = Net Estate

Less exemptions (such as spouse or civil partner exemption)
Less nil rate band
= Taxable Estate

Tax is paid at a 40% flat rate.

When must the tax be paid by?

An account must be delivered before the later of (a) 12 months from the end of the month in which death occurs and (b) 3 months from the date on which the personal representatives first act or the person liable to inheritance tax first has reason to believe he is required to deliver an account. Inheritance tax is payable 6 months after the end of the month in which death occurs or on delivery of the account by the personal representatives of the deceased, if earlier. Interest is chargeable from the due date of payment to the actual date of payment. The rate of interest at October 2019 is 3.25% per annum.

If the tax is due between the 6th April and 30th September then it must be paid by the 30th April in the following year; if between 1st October and 5th April then tax must be paid six months after the end of the month of the CLT transfer (see **www.hmrc.gov.uk/rates/iht-interest-rates.htm**).

If you cannot afford it at the time, it is possible for IHT to be paid in instalments over a 10 year period and interest is charged at 3% per annum.

Accounting for CLTs

The HMRC reporting thresholds for chargeable lifetime transfers (CLTs) made by individuals are as follows. These new rules apply to gifts made on or after 6 April 2007. There are now two tests, summarised below. The accumulation period for reporting has been aligned to the inheritance tax system and has been reduced from ten years to seven years.

Where an individual makes a CLT, the regulations introduce two new tests to determine when a report at the time the CLT is made to HMRC is NOT required and these can be summarised as follows:

Excepted transfers (Test 1)

1. The asset transferred is cash or quoted shares or securities, AND

2. The value transferred by the chargeable transfer, together with the values transferred by any previous chargeable transfers made by the transferor during the seven years preceding the transfer, does not exceed the IHT threshold. ('IHT threshold' means the available nil-rate band taking into account previous transfers.)

This means that CLTs of cash, quoted shares or securities will not be required to be reported where all CLTs made by the client in the previous seven years (including the CLT now being made) do not exceed the value of the individual's available nil-rate band. In principle this means that reports in these circumstances will only be required where IHT is due.

Excepted transfers (Test 2)

1. The value transferred by the chargeable transfer, together with the values transferred by any previous chargeable transfers made by the transferor during the seven years preceding the transfer, does not exceed 80% of the IHT threshold, AND

2. The value transferred by the transfer of value giving rise to the chargeable transfer does not exceed the net IHT threshold.

The net IHT threshold means the IHT threshold (currently £325,000 for 2019/20) less the summed values of all previous chargeable transfers made during the seven years preceding the current chargeable transfer (not including the CLT now being made). For the purposes of Test 2(2) above, business property relief and agricultural property relief will not apply in determining the value of the chargeable transfer. The 80% limit in Test 2(1) means the reporting level in 2019/20 is £260,000.

For example, for a CLT not to be reportable it must pass two tests; firstly that the cumulative total (for example, current CLT £100,000 plus previous CLTs £125,000 = £225,000) does not exceed 80% of the current NRB (£325,000 x 80% = £260,000), and secondly that the current CLT (say £100,000) does not exceed the net IHT threshold (NRB £325,000 less previous CLTs £125,000 = £200,000).

So in this case, both tests have been met so reporting is not required.

Forms IHT100 and IHT100a must be used for reporting.

You will need to complete form IHT100 Inheritance Tax Account if Inheritance Tax is due on assets passed into or out of a trust, or on the trust's ten-year anniversary if it's above the Inheritance Tax threshold.

This form is required if the following chargeable lifetime events are made:

* assets are transferred into a trust
* someone who transferred assets into a trust dies within seven years of making the transfer
* an 'interest in possession' - where a beneficiary can use or enjoy a trust asset as if it is theirs - comes to an end
* trustees dispose of or transfer assets out of the trust
* the trust reaches a ten-year anniversary and is liable for a ten-year anniversary charge
* a special trust, for example a charitable trust, ceases to be entitled to special tax treatment

Some trusts may fall within what are known as 'excepted estates' and will not need to send in an IHT100 Inheritance Tax Account. These are usually trusts with a low value. The following forms are used for different chargeable events:

* IHT100a - Gifts and other transfers of value
* IHT100b - Ending an interest in possession in settled property
* IHT100c - Assets in a relevant property trust ceasing to be relevant property
* IHT100d - Discretionary trust ten-year anniversary
* IHT100e - Assets ceasing to be held on special trusts
* IHT100f - Cessation of conditional exemption and disposal of trees and underwood
* IHT100g - Alternatively secured pension chargeable event

You may also need to fill in supplementary pages for certain types of asset held in the trust, or if the person making a transfer into trust lives overseas.

You can obtain these forms by ordering them through the Probate and Inheritance Tax helpline on Tel 0845 302 0900.

(Note the above information is supplied by the HMRC website).

7

Avoiding Double Taxation

The double whammy of IHT on tax-paid assets. The extent of IHT payable.

Assets can be taxed more than once

Accumulation of assets will be from many different sources. Some of these may be tax efficient; however, in most instances you will have paid tax on your assets during your lifetime or used tax-paid income to acquire assets.

In the 2019/20 tax year the rates for *individuals* are: 0%; 20% basic rate up to £37,500 and 40% higher rate on £37,501 to £150,000; 45% additional rate for those with income over £150,000. That's not all – from £100,000 earnings you begin to lose your personal allowances on a £1 for £1 basis, thus increasing your income tax rate to 60% effectively at this level (to £125,000). If you earn dividends from investments, then these are the rates:

- Basic rate tax-payers 7.5%
- Higher rate tax-payers 32.5%
- Additional rate tax-payers 38.1%.

The personal allowance (an exemption from taxable earnings) is £12,500 in 2019/20. Capital gains are taxed at 10% and 20% but 18% and 28% on residential property sales. Trusts are taxed at a 20% flat rate. The CGT personal allowance is £12,000 and the allowance for trusts is £6,000.

From your earned income, investments and savings may be made, and on your death, these could be subject to inheritance tax at 40%. If assets are inherited from you, they could form part of the person's estate inheriting from you, and again be subject to inheritance tax at 40%.

You may feel that no matter how hard you save, and invest into the best performing investments over your lifetime, that 0% to 45% of your hard-earned wealth could go to the taxman. This could be more in fact, because on the way to accumulating your nest egg, you may have paid income taxes or capital gains taxes on the money before you invested it, and then again during the term of the investment.

Some investments are not subject to income and capital gains taxes, but may nevertheless be subject to inheritance tax. Into this category fall ISAs, where many sizeable holdings have been built up over the years – some couples have in excess of £250,000 in ISA holdings that will fall into their estates and be subject to inheritance tax (unless relieved by investing into qualifying EIS shares from 6 April 2013).

From 3 December 2014 on death, husband or wife or civil partner can inherit their ISA and keep it income tax or CGT tax free – 40% of Britons save or invest in ISAs.

From 6 April 2015 a surviving spouse can invest as much into their own ISA as their spouse used to have on top of their usual allowance. Also the surviving spouse will then be given an additional one-off allowance equal to the amount the deceased had in their Isa, which would become available from April 6th 2015.

Some investments are protected from inheritance tax

Some investments not only give you tax relief when you make the investment, but will also escape inheritance taxes and capital gains taxes. For example, an Enterprise Investment Scheme (EIS) investment is deductible for income tax purposes at 30% of the investment made up to £1 million for normal EIS or 50% for a Seed EIS (SEIS) at up to £100,000 in 2019/20 (if the latter is backdated to the previous tax year for 2018/19 when in 2019/20 now). There is no capital gains tax on any gains made, and if held for at least two years, the investment will not be subject to inheritance tax. However, dividends from EIS shares are subject to dividend taxation. General EIS and SEIS tax relief can be backdated to the previous tax year at 100% of the amount available. A SEIS investment made in 2019/20 will qualify for capital gains tax relief and in 2019/20 gains of up to 50% with a maximum of £50,000 may be tax relieved.

Pensions contributions are deductible for income tax purposes if a higher rate taxpayer at 20% (and 25% for additional rate taxpayers) subject to contribution restrictions of up to £40,000 p.a., although in all cases for non-defined benefit schemes, the HMRC adds 20% to your pension fund; the growth in the pension fund is tax free; a tax free lump sum may be taken (usually at 25%); and on the first death, the remaining pension fund may pass to your dependant(s) free of inheritance tax. The pension income is subject to income tax. From 6 April 2015 the whole of a defined contribution pension fund, if uncrystallised, can be taken as cash from age 55. 25% of this is tax free, the balance taxed at marginal rates

Certain investment bond investments can be made with an immediate discount from inheritance tax payable, the balance of the bond value falling out of your estate over a seven-year period. These are known as discounted gift trusts (DGT's).

To avoid the double whammy of having tax-paid investments again being taxable on your or your spouse's or civil partner's death, there are investments that can be made that both reduce tax and save on future inheritance taxes. Not all of them may be appropriate for your particular risk profile, but substantial savings can be made through proper planning. It is always wise to find out if inheritance tax mitigation 'wrappers' can be made around your investment, or if a suitable trust could be created to 'freeze' the value of your investments so that the growth is not subject to inheritance tax in your estate.

Lifetime inheritance tax

Is inheritance tax a death tax only? The answer is no. As referred to earlier in this book, certain 'chargeable lifetime transfers' (CLT) will render you liable for the payment of inheritance tax in advance, during your lifetime, as well as on death. The rate for such lifetime charges is 50% of the full inheritance tax rate at the time (currently 40%), making the lifetime IHT rate 20% at present. For example, if you gift an asset into a discretionary trust in the current tax year 2019/20, and the value of the gift is over the value of the nil rate band of £325,000 in 2019/20, then the portion over the nil rate band is taxed at 20%. On your death, the balance of the IHT owed is collected from your estate. This could be alleviated through transferable NRB's if a second death, and the first-dying's NRB was not fully utilised on his or her death. There is now a new additional nil rate band for home owners leaving the family home to direct descendants under the RNRB, starting at £100,000 in 2017 and rising to £175,000 in 2020/21. In 2019/20 the RNRB is £150,000.

Notwithstanding the various exemptions available, it could be that those inheriting from you, and succeeding generations inheriting from them, will find the same assets subject to inheritance taxes. Much of this erosion of estate capital can be protected with proper planning.

Estates can be further reduced where at least 10% is left to charity. The effective tax rate is then 36%.

8

How Trusts Work

*The various parties to a trust – settlor, beneficiary, trustee –
and their roles. Onshore and offshore trusts.*

Trusts have been with us for many hundreds of years, and they have been set up for both monetary and non-monetary reasons. Monetary reasons include tax advantages and the ability to direct cash flow to different beneficiaries; non-monetary reasons could be as diverse as protecting the interests of minors and non-financially-minded spouses or civil partners, protecting assets from dissipation and passing on assets to others. Under English law, trusts have a lifetime of up to 125 years (*Perpetuities and Accumulations Act 2009*). In other tax jurisdictions, trusts can endure for much longer.

The settlor

The person setting up the trust is known as the settlor. The settlor will make a contribution to the trust, called a settlement. This can be in money or property, and is a gift or donation made to the trust. The settlor or others can also make loans to the trust.

Trustees

Trustees are appointed to manage the trust assets and to invest the trust assets in terms of their investment powers. The trust deed or trust instrument is the source of trustee powers, and the trustee can now own the assets, not merely manage or safeguard them. It is usual to have at least two trustees, preferably three. It is not uncommon to have a professional trustee, usually a solicitor or accountant, or a trust company, to guide the lay trustees and to carry out the functions of the trust. Trustees act jointly and the actions of one trustee will impact on all the trustees. Trustees can be personally liable for acts and omissions. Usually the trust instrument will have exemptions to protect the trustees.

Beneficiaries

The beneficiaries of the trust may receive or have a right to receive income or capital, or both, as the trust instrument dictates. Some beneficiaries may only be entitled to income and others to capital. The former are known as 'life tenants' and the latter as 'remaindermen'. The trustees hold or administer the asset for the benefit of the beneficiaries. Terminology is different in Scotland.

The trust itself and the gift made

The trust itself is seen as a separate persona in law. A gift of property to the trust is called a settlement which is described as a transfer of value by the settlor for inheritance tax purposes. This is calculated as a loss of the value of the asset to the settlor's estate. The transfer of value made and whether it is subject to inheritance tax now or in the future, will depend on the type of trust to which it is made. Once the gift or donation has been made, its ownership passes from the donor or settlor to the trustees of the trust, and the donor's estate is reduced for inheritance tax purposes. The trust is subject to trust income taxation, as well as capital gains tax and inheritance tax, VAT and stamp duties, where applicable.

Starting a trust

The trust begins with the trust instrument or trust deed. The donor or settlor makes a gift to the trust or trustees, which can be as low as say £10. Other gifts can be added at a later date, or loans made to the trust. A settlor grandparent can set up a trust and his adult child could make a loan to it, for example.

A lifetime gift to the trust will either be chargeable or potentially exempt, depending on the type of trust concerned. A lifetime gift to a discretionary trust will be a chargeable lifetime transfer (CLT). The same applies after 22nd March 2006 to a life-interest trust (also known as an interest-in-possession trust). A disabled person's trust where there is a life interest will not be an immediate chargeable transfer and is exempt.

The chargeable lifetime transfer is valued after deducting the annual lifetime exemption of £3,000 (£6,000 in the first year, if not used in the previous tax year); then the cumulative lifetime chargeable transfers made over the past seven years by the same settlor are added together and if below the nil rate band there is no inheritance tax to pay. The chargeable lifetime transfers are further reduced through other exemptions, such as business or agricultural property relief that may apply to the gift made by the same settlor.

The nil rate band for 2019/20 is £325,000. If the chargeable lifetime transfer is in excess of available exemptions then it is taxed at the lifetime rate of 20%. If the settlor dies within seven years of making the gift, a further 20%

is payable. However, this is subject to taper relief depending on the number of years the settlor survived within the last seven years.

IHT can be paid by the settlor or the trustees. If the trustees pay the IHT, the rate is 20%. If the settlor pays the IHT then the tax is grossed up to 25%.

A gift made to an interest-in-possession (IIP) or accumulation-and-maintenance trust (A&M) before 22nd March 2006, was known as a potentially exempt transfer (PET), and as long as the settlor survived the making of the gift by seven years, would fall out of his estate for inheritance tax purposes. If the settlor died within the seven years, then the transfer made becomes a chargeable lifetime transfer. After the 22nd March 2006, all transfers or settlements to an IIP or A&M trust (except for a disabled person's trust), are CLTs. PETs are now only available to bare trusts, and to individuals. HM Revenue and Customs (HMRC) have confirmed after the March 2007 budget that gifts to bare trusts will remain as PETs and will not be chargeable as CLTs.

The chargeable gifts made by the settlor in the preceding seven years is always taken into account in establishing what the tax charge is on the settlement made into a discretionary trust.

manuring or adjust (PS?)

The mechanics of the trust

The trustees will receive the trust property, and will manage and administer it. If investments are to be made, these are either done by the trustees or the nominated adviser, who has received the trustees' delegated investment powers. The objectives of the trust will be to manage the investments and trust property (which they can do as absolute owners), providing for income or capital as required for the beneficiaries. The trustees will deal with the reporting aspects of the trust and its taxation as well as dealing with beneficiaries. Trustees have a difficult and often onerous task in that different types of trusts deal with tax issues differently; particular rules apply where a settlor and his or her spouse or civil partner receive benefits from the trust, or where the income of minors is concerned (this is dealt with as if it was the settlor's income and taxed accordingly). There are also capital gains tax and CGT deferral processes that have to be dealt with, and record-keeping is a vital part of trust administration. The trustees are jointly and severally liable for acts and omissions and may be sued by the beneficiaries if they get things wrong. Professional trustees are entitled to fees and expenses, payable by the trust.

The Trustee Act 2000

This important piece of legislation has changed the landscape for all trusts. The Act came into force in February 2001 in England and Wales (other legislation affects Northern Ireland and Scotland – see below). The Act lays down criteria for the investment of assets, which is broader and more flexible than previous legislation (the *Trustee Investment Act 1961*), which had a much narrower scope. The *Trustee Act 2000* affects all trusts, whether created in the past, or new trusts. It governs both trusts *inter vivos* (those set up whilst you are alive) and trusts *post mortem* (those trusts that only come into effect once you have died). Note that the Act only applies to trusts set up in England and Wales; in Scotland the statutory investment powers are described in the *Trusts (Scotland) Act 1921*, the *Trustee Investment Act 1961* and the *Charities and Trustee Investment (Scotland) Act 1925*. In Northern Ireland the *Trustee Act (Northern Ireland) 2001* came into operation on the 9th July 2002. All UK tax jurisdictions follow the general more flexible approach towards wider investment powers and trust flexibility.

Duty of care

The *Trustee Act 2000* introduces a new *statutory* duty of care under **sections 1 and 2** of *TA 2000*. This is a 'must comply' position, as opposed to the common law duty of care, which is less onerous.

The new duty brings consistency and certainty to the standard of competence and behaviour expected of trustees. It is a safeguard for beneficiaries and balances the wider powers given to trustees elsewhere in the Act.

The duty is a default provision. It may be excluded or modified by the terms of the trust. This new duty will apply to the manner of exercise by trustees of a discretionary power. It will not apply to a decision by the trustees as to whether to exercise that discretionary power in the first place.

In relation to investments by trust funds, the new duty of care allows for the particular skills and experience of the trustee and is a subjective test. To comply with the statutory duty of care a trustee must show such skill and care as is reasonable in the circumstances of the case making allowance for his or her special knowledge, experience or professional status (**sections1(1) (a) and (b)**). Higher standards are expected of experienced trustees, and in determining what constitutes reasonable care consideration should also be given to the nature, composition and purposes of the trust being administered.

Section 2 (and **Schedule 1**) of the Act defines when the duty will apply. In general terms it applies to any exercise by a trustee of a power to invest trust property or to acquire land; to appoint agents, nominees and custodians; or to insure trust property.

Note that although the trust instrument may provide exemptions, including an exemption from the statutory duty of care, the *Law Commission Consultation Provisions 2003* relating to trustee exemption clauses suggested a need for legislation for professional trustees to take responsibility for their actions, especially when being paid for their services, in the future.

The Act lays down functions and procedures that form part of the usual compliance and investment compliance framework.

General power of investment

Section 3 creates the general power of investment. Trustees will have the same power to invest trust assets as if they owned the assets outright rather than holding them on trust. Trustees can hold investments jointly or in common with other persons not necessarily related to the trust. The general power of investment permits trustees to invest assets in a way that is expected to produce an income or capital return.

Section 4 (1) provides that where exercising a power of investment, a trustee must have regard to the suitability to the trust of the investment, and where appropriate, to the need for diversification of the trust's investments. **Section 4(3)** defines this as standard investment criteria. 'Suitability' includes the type of investment proposed, and to consider its size, the risk of the investment, and the need to produce an appropriate balance between income and capital growth to meet the needs of the trust; as well as ethical considerations. The standard investment criteria is core. Other considerations may also have to be made with regard to diversification, the need for tax planning, asset allocation and other factors.

Section 4(2) requires the trustees to keep investments of the trust under review and to consider whether, in the light of standard investment criteria, they should be varied. This provision codifies the common law position, under which 'a trustee with a power of investment must undertake periodic reviews of the investments held by the trust': *Nestle v National Westminster Bank plc (no 2) [1993] 1 WLR 1260, 1282G, per Leggatt L.J.*

Section 5 provides a safeguard for beneficiaries in relation to powers of investment. The trustee, when considering the exercise of a power of investment or carrying out a review of the investments of the trust, must obtain and consider proper advice about how, in view of the standard investment criteria, the power to invest should be exercised or the investments of the trust be varied (**sections 5(1) and 5(2)**). However, the trustee does not have to obtain advice if he or she considers it is unnecessary or inappropriate to do so: **section 5(3)**. The investment proposed may be too small or the trustee may possess the skills to make this judgment without advice. The obligation of the trustee to take advice (if any) is dependent on the application of the rule that trustees must act with reasonable prudence in exercising powers of investment. 'Proper advice' is defined in **section 5(4)** where other expert skills may also be relevant.

Section 5(1) states that the taking of advice need not be in writing, 'but to do so will no doubt be regarded as best practice in many circumstances, and may be necessary for trustees to show compliance with the general duty of care in **section 1**' *(Explanatory Notes to Trustee Act 2000 part 28)*

Delegation of powers

Investment powers may be delegated to nominated advisers, such as IFAs and fund managers, who must be given the *Policy Statement* and *Guidelines* prescribed by the Act by the Trustees stating what the nominated adviser must do, how he or she must do it and what the review processes are for the investments undertaken as well as the review of the adviser – including the power of revocation of the appointment as nominated adviser and how that will be applied.

The powers of delegation and appointment are subject to the duty of care (**section 1**), and are a default provision for most trusts. The duty of care is limited to trustees and does not apply to the agent in the performance of an agency. However, agents will owe a separate duty of care to trustees under the general law of agency. The obligation to comply with specific duties and restrictions attached to the trustee function delegated under **section 11** (power to employ agents) will most commonly apply in cases where the trustees delegate their investment function. In these cases the agent will be obliged to have regard to the standard investment criteria in accordance with **section 4**. The agent may also be required to obtain and consider proper advice in accordance with **section 5**. The duty to consult beneficiaries is not delegable and only trustees can consult and give effect to the wishes of beneficiaries. (**section 13 (4)**).

Section 15 relates to the delegation of asset management functions by trustees. That includes the investment of trust assets and the acquisition, disposal and management of trust property (**section 15(5)**).

The terms of an agreement authorising the agent to exercise asset management functions on behalf of the trustees must be in writing or evidenced in writing (**section 15(1)**) and must require the agent to secure compliance with the trustees' guidance as to how the functions are to be exercised for the time being (**section 15(2)**).

This guidance must be in writing or evidenced in writing (**section 15(4)**) and must be framed with a view to ensuring the functions will be exercised in the best interests of the trust (**section 15 (3)**).

The document containing the guidance is referred to in the Act as a 'policy statement' (**section 15(2)(a)**). The policy statement must be prepared before the agent is authorised to act, but can be revised or replaced (**section 15(2) (a) and (b)(ii)**). The duty of care under section 1 applies to the preparation of the policy statement (**sch 1 para 3(2)(c)**). The policy statement constitutes a record of the trustees' policy on how the functions in question should be exercised.

Personal liability

Trustees can be personally liable for the acts and omissions of current and previous trustees. For this reason professional trustees often provide services and administration to their trusts that are not fully recovered in order to protect their vulnerable position from adverse criticism or claims of breach of duty. Trustees should take out Trustee Liability insurance to protect themselves from trust claims.

Onshore and offshore trusts

If UK resident and domiciled, you can form a trust both in the United Kingdom (onshore), and in any non-UK trust and tax jurisdictions (offshore). Offshore trusts are governed by the laws of that offshore jurisdiction. For example, a trust set up in Jersey or Guernsey is governed by the trust and tax laws of that tax and legal jurisdiction. Offshore trusts are usually more expensive to establish and manage as costs will generally be higher. However, there may be tax advantages in doing so, and so long as the trustees of the trust are based offshore, the trust itself will be deemed to be offshore, even if the settlor and beneficiaries live in the UK. Most local offshore jurisdictions, such as the Isle of Man have adopted the England and Wales version of the Trustee Act 2000, and follow it closely.

Trusts *inter vivos*

These are trusts set up whilst you are alive, and continue to operate on your death, for the benefit of your beneficiaries.

Trusts *post mortem*

These are trusts that are provided for in your will, or on intestacy, and only come into effect on your death.

9

Trusts and the Finance Act 2006

Finance Act 2006 affecting trusts. Types of trusts and trust taxation. Bare and absolute trusts, interest-in-possession trusts, accumulation-and-maintenance trusts, discretionary trusts, offshore trusts and private charitable trusts

The *Finance Act 2006* introduced a new regime for inheritance tax after March 22nd 2006. This came without warning and as a surprise to most tax planners. This new regime sought to impose a single 'relevant property' IHT regime on all trusts created on or after 22nd March 2006, with a transitional period for those trusts in existence at that date. There have also been changes made subsequently, following representations made by the financial services industry, in particular relating to accumulation-and-maintenance trusts (see below). Over the past few years, modernisation of trusts has been in progress, with widening investment powers and generally increased income taxes and new rules for capital gains tax purposes for UK resident trusts.

Trusts can be categorised as non-discretionary or discretionary. The *FA 2006*, which passed into law on 19th July 2006, introduced a new tax regime for trusts, essentially making interest-in-possession and accumulation-and-maintenance trusts subject to the rules of discretionary trusts. Gifts to such trusts cannot now be PETS, subject to the seven-year rule, but CLTs, whereby the gift or donation is chargeable if above the nil rate band in value. The Potentially Exempt Transfer regime has therefore ended for Interest in Possession (IIP) trusts as well as Accumulation and Maintenance Trusts (A&M) created during the lifetime of the settlor.

Update on trust consultation and proposed legislation at 2014

There have been a number of consultations with regard to trusts, with an emphasis on removing complexity, and tackling tax avoidance through trusts. This included an attack on multiple trusts with their own nil rate bands, whereby it was proposed that a settler should only have one nil rate band over multiple trusts, thus increasing the tax take to the fiscus. There is also an emphasis on simplifying trust tax charges and inheritance tax on trusts. The following tracks

the various consultations.
There have been five major consultations:

1. *'Inheritance Tax: Simplifying charges on Trusts'* in July 2012
2. *'Inheritance Tax: Simplification of Trust charges – the next stage'* in May 2013
3. *'Inheritance Tax: A Fairer way of calculating trust charges'* in June 2014
4. *'OTS Inheritance Tax Review'* first report 2018 on administration
5. *'OTS Inheritance Tax Review'* second report July 2019 – simplifying the design of Inheritance Tax with recommendations

The above related to a proposed new regime on for calculating inheritance tax charges on relevant property trusts, affecting the treatment of relevant property trusts established on or after 7 June 2014. Some resulting legislation has already been enacted, and further legislation is expected in 2015 in respect of the proposals.

The **first consultation** outlined the current burdensome calculation methods (including the number of chargeable transfers previously made within seven years before the date of the trust; value of trust property before the trust started and the value after the last 10 year charge, the value at the date of the charge; the length of time the property was in the trust (or each part of it); rates of IHT at the date of the charge; the amount of any reliefs available such as APR or BPR. The first consultation noted areas for reform, including the treatment of accumulated income.

The **second consultation** dealt with proposals to simplify periodic and exit charges on relevant property trusts, the treatment of accumulated income and payment and filing dates for periodic and exit charges. Legislation is in FA 2014 on these aspects.

Simplification was to be achieved by ignoring the cumulative lifetime transfers of the settler; ignore non-relevant property; apply a 6% rate to the periodic charge (on any excess above the NRB); splitting one nil rate band equally across all relevant property trusts in existence at any time during the 10 years before the time of the tax charge in question – regardless whether there was any value in the trust – such as a pilot trust set up with say £10 to receive death benefits on a life policy.

Various concerns were raised by the financial adviser community and finance industry including the loss of the regeneration of a nil rate band after 7 years; the retrospective manner of one NRB over multiple trusts (and the proposal itself for one NRB over the lifetime of the settler, and the increased administration this would bring.

The **third consultation** showed how the periodic and exit charges would be simplified. The 7-year cumulative total of lifetime chargeable transfers would be ignored; as would be the non-relevant property and property in related settlements to calculate periodic and exit charges; and a rate of 6% would be applied to the deemed chargeable transfer exceeding the NRB for the periodic and exit charges.

Under the proposed change the calculation of the periodic charge would be:

> The current value of the property in the trust (£x)
> *Less* the nil rate band/settlement NRB (£y)
> Multiplied by 6%, to give the tax due at the 10-year anniversary

The new rules apply to IHT charges on or after 6 April 2015 and apply to:

- new trusts made after 6 June 2014
- trusts created prior to 6 June 2014 where additional funds or property is added to trusts after 6 June 2014
- trusts changed after 6 June 2014 where relevant property comes into being.

It was further proposed that a Settlement Nil Rate Band (SNRB) be created from 6 April 2015 to allocate to settlements created after 6 June 2014. This is an additional NRB where the Settlor can elect to allocate to all the relevant property trusts created after 6 June 2014 or earlier trusts that have been added to after 6 June 2014. The Settlor must elect the percentage amount of the SNRB for each trust. This can be amended when new property is added to the trust. However, once the percentage allocated has been used in a calculation of a 10-year periodic charge or an exit charge, it is believed it will not be possible to reduce it.

In addition the third consultation sought to close the multiple trusts loophole whereby an individual could set up multiple trusts each with its own nil rate band (see Multiple Trusts page 76). However this element of the proposed changes was cancelled in the Autumn Budget 2014.

Autumn Budget 2014 changes

On 3 December 2014 the Government announced a 'U' turn on plans to introduce a single settlement nil rate band on trusts. However, the door seems to have been left open to further attack against tax avoidance using trusts.

The Office of Fair Trading (OTS) Reports 2018 and 2019

These make recommendations across a number of key and relevant areas (see introduction in this book).

Summary

Trusts set up before 6 June 2014 will continue to function under the old rules. Existing trusts with added property to the trust will be subject to the new rules. Do not add property to existing trusts until the rules become clearer. It is still possible to set up new trusts on different days to take advantage of multiple nil rate bands under the Rysaffe principle at £325,000 NRB each.

Draft legislation issued subsequently as part of the draft Finance Bill 2015 appears to still provide opportunities for further multiple settlements to be established, each benefiting from a nil rate band, provided the additional property is added on different days.

The proposals do, however, introduce new measures when property is added to multiple settlements on the same day, to ensure the value of all the settlements are be taken into account for both periodic and exit charge calculations.

Different types of trust

The main trusts in use today are as follows:

1. Bare trusts
2. Interest-in-possession or life-interest trusts
3. Accumulation-and-maintenance trusts
4. Discretionary trusts
5. Offshore trusts – can be a combination of the above trusts and excluded property trusts
6. Pilot trusts
7. Charitable trusts – private sector

1. Bare trusts (absolute trusts)

These are trusts which have no discretionary element, and the gift made is considered to be absolute. Parents or grandparents can create a bare trust for the benefit of a child. Assets are transferred to the trustees, who then hold the assets for the benefit of the child. When the child attains the age of 18, the child will have a right to the property held in trust for him or her.

Inheritance tax

The gift made to the bare trust is a potentially exempt transfer (PET). If the settlor survives for seven years, the value of the gift made and any growth on it will be out of his estate for inheritance tax purposes.

Bare trusts had largely fallen out of use until the *Finance Act 2006*, when the Chancellor increased trust taxation on other trusts, but did not attack bare or absolute trusts in the same way. Some product providers recommend the use of a bare trust for discounted gift trust schemes, but these are largely seen to be inflexible, compared to a discretionary trust.

Income tax

Income in excess of £100 is assessed on the parent if the parent was the settlor, until the child reaches the age of 18 (16 in Scotland for legal capacity), whether the income is retained or paid out to the child or for the child's benefit. From the age of 18, the income may be reduced by the child's personal allowance for income tax, and the child will be taxed on the income. If a grandparent was the settlor, then income will be taxed on the child at any age and using his personal allowances. The child could also make a stakeholder pension payment, further reducing his tax liability. In 2019/20 the basic personal allowance is £12,500, which could be used by a child.

Capital gains tax

The trust property is treated as owned by the child, and if the trust has any capital gains, the child's personal allowances can be used to reduce this. The capital gains tax allowance for an individual is £12,000 in the 2019/20 tax year. The CGT allowance for trusts is £6,000 (but can be apportioned up to five trusts). Capital gains tax is charged at a flat rate of 20% with no indexation or taper reliefs for individuals and trusts. Individuals are taxed at 10% and 20% for CGT.

HMRC on Bare Trusts

It had been reported that HMRC (ABI circular TDG 1/07) had received legal advice that gifts to a bare trust with a minor as a beneficiary might now be considered as a CLT (chargeable lifetime transfer) as opposed to the present position as a PET (potentially exempt transfer). It has now been confirmed that gifts to a bare trust will not be treated as a settlement for IHT purposes. (Citywire 24 March 2007).

2. Interest-in-possession trusts (IIP)

This type of trust is managed and controlled by trustees to provide an income benefit for one or more named beneficiaries. The donor or settlor wishes the beneficiary to have an income only, but no control over the capital. The capital will pass to other beneficiaries. In this way, personal wealth can be passed to others, with flexibility over who receives the capital. The trustees retain control of the capital.

The trust deed will define the interests of the beneficiaries to the income of the trust, as well as the beneficiaries of the capital in due course. For example, the income could be for a surviving spouse or civil partner or the adult children of the settlor, and the capital beneficiaries could be the grandchildren of the settlor. The trustees would have wide flexible powers and could also make capital distributions to an income beneficiary, or even change the flow of income away from one income beneficiary to another. The settlor can be a trustee and could retain the power to appoint and remove trustees.

Inheritance tax

The settlor could use a life-interest trust or IIP trust to reduce his estate for inheritance tax purposes. This would be the case where adult beneficiaries are involved, such as family members, and where control of the capital does not pass to those income beneficiaries. Interest-in-possession trusts can be set up whilst the settlor is alive, or after death via the will ('will trusts'), where a life interest to income can be provided to a beneficiary.

The IHT position on IPP trusts changed significantly for trusts established after 22nd March 2006. A gift into trust is a transfer of value by the settlor for inheritance tax purposes. Prior to 22nd March 2006, such a transfer was a potentially exempt transfer (PET), and if the settlor survived for seven years after making the gift, it would be out of his estate for inheritance tax purposes. After 22nd March 2006, the transfer is a chargeable lifetime transfer – a CLT – and tax at the lifetime rate of 20% is payable on transfers made over the nil rate band. The gift remains a PET if made to a trust for the benefit of a disabled person.

Ownership of trust property

Prior to 22nd March 2006, the beneficiaries entitled to a share of the income from the trust are treated as owners of the proportionate share of the trust property for IHT purposes. An income beneficiary receiving a third of the trust income, will have a third of the trust capital deemed to be in his own estate for IHT purposes. If capital distributions are made to that beneficiary thus reducing income, the IHT position remains the same, as the capital is deemed part of his or her estate. The trustees will pay the total IHT owing from the beneficiary's deemed share of the trust capital.

After 22nd March 2006, the beneficiaries are not treated as being owners of the trust assets for inheritance tax purposes. Instead, the tax liability falls on the trust as it does for discretionary trusts. Here, the trust funds will be subject to periodic and exit charges if applicable. Gifts made to a trust after 22nd March 2006 will be chargeable lifetime transfers (CLTs), and tax will be charged at the lifetime rate applicable to trusts, currently 20%, if the gift is over the nil rate band (or accumulatively over the nil rate band, if combined with other gifts made within the past seven years). The nil rate band at present is £325,000 in 2019/20.

Capital gains tax

A gift to trust of a chargeable asset may create a disposal for capital gains tax purposes. If the trustees are UK resident, the gains may be held over until realised by the trustees, who will then be liable for capital gains tax (subject to an annual CGT exemption, currently £6,000 in 2019/20). Tax is payable at 28% by the trustees. However, if the settlor, the spouse of the settlor or minor child of the settlor is a beneficiary, then capital gains tax will be charged to the settlor at 20% (and offset by his personal allowances for CGT – £12,000 in 2019/20). The settlor has a statutory right to reclaim tax paid by him from the trustees. (*TCGA 1992 Sch 1 para 1*). There is a flat rate of 20% for capital gains tax.

Note that if the trust is for mentally disabled persons, persons in receipt of a disability allowance (with criteria), or an attendance allowance, then the trust can use the full individual's CGT personal allowance of £12,000 in 2019/20 and not the trust's reduced CGT allowance of half that rate at £6,000. This is a valuable benefit, especially if there is more than one trust, and the trust's CGT annual allowance is spread amongst them.

Income tax

The changes made to trust income tax rates for discretionary and A&M trusts (on 6th April 2004) do not apply to life-interest trusts. Income tax is payable at the basic rate of 20% by the trustees, including savings and investments (tax credit from dividends).

Beneficiaries are taxed at their marginal rates of income tax, where entitled to income, with a credit for the tax paid by the trustees. A beneficiary can reclaim part or all of the tax paid by the trustees, but cannot reclaim the dividend tax credit from UK dividends. If the beneficiary is the spouse or civil partner of the settlor, then the settlor is liable to any higher rate tax payable.

3. Accumulation-and-maintenance trusts (A&M)

A&M trusts are used to benefit younger beneficiaries. Assets are gifted or transferred to the trust to be used for the benefit of younger beneficiaries, usually children or grandchildren of the settlor. This type of trust offers certain protections and provision for income for a period and then at a certain age, a capital entitlement. Beneficiaries can include those yet to be born, and need not be named individually. There must be at least one living beneficiary of that class when the trust is set up. There are inheritance tax advantages in making gifts to the trust, as the settlor's estate can be reduced for IHT purposes.

The settlor selects the payment age for the income from the outset, but it may be income tax effective to begin income payments earlier. Otherwise income can accumulate to be paid at a later date. The trustees can control both the income and capital. This type of trust has been popular to provide for the general welfare, maintenance and education of minor beneficiaries through to adulthood. Usually income is payable to the age of 25 and capital distributions made after that age.

On attaining the age set by the settlor, the beneficiaries must receive the current income. The beneficiaries do not have a right to capital, and capital may pass to them or to other beneficiaries. For example, children could receive the income, and grandchildren the capital. Any undistributed income is accumulated in the trust.

Whilst a settlor can be a trustee and retain the power to remove and appoint trustees, care should be taken so that the settlor is not seen to reserve a benefit to himself, as the gift could again be taxable in his estate.

Inheritance tax

Prior to 22nd March 2006, gifts made to the trust were potentially exempt transfers (PET); after that date, gifts are chargeable lifetime transfers (CLTs), and may be chargeable to inheritance tax at the lifetime rate of 20%, if over the nil rate band and not subject to agricultural or business property and other reliefs.

Accumulation-and-maintenance trusts have now been brought into the same tax regime of discretionary trusts, and are subject to periodic and capital exit charges. This applies to all new A&M trusts created after 22nd March 2006.

Accumulation-and-maintenance trusts: at various ages

(i) Up to the age of 18

Following financial services industry representation to HMRC no periodic charges will be payable for trusts in existence at 21st March 2006 and where beneficiaries become absolutely entitled to the trust funds before age 18, or if the terms of the trust were amended before 6th April 2008 to ensure that the entitlement is before age 18. After that date, for trusts coming into effect on the death of a parent by will or on intestacy for the benefit of a child, there will be limited exemption from periodic trust charges.

(ii) Up to the age of 25

Where a child becomes absolutely entitled to the trust funds at age 18, there is no further IHT charge; between age 18 and age 25, where the child becomes absolutely entitled, there will be an IHT charge, not exceeding 4.2% of the trust funds. There is no ten-year periodic charge – even if the trust goes on for more than ten years.

(iii) Age 25 and beyond

If entitlement is after the age of 25 then the periodic and capital distribution exit IHT charges will apply.

(iv) Any age
Where a grandparent creates a will trust which is an A&M trust, then the periodic and exit IHT charges will apply, irrespective of age. This does not apply to where a parent creates the will trust.

Income tax
Trust income is taxed at a basic rate of 20% on the first £1,000 and 45% on income over £1,000 in 2019/20, and 38.1% for dividends in 2019/20.

Beneficiaries who are classed as 'vulnerable' will have all trust income subject to income taxed on them at their personal rates. If the child is aged under 18, then all income (except the first £100) will be taxed in the hands of the settlor, if a parent; if the settlor is a grandparent, then income is taxed in the hands of the beneficiary, irrespective of age, which could be more tax efficient. Beneficiaries may be able to recover tax paid by the trustees, if their tax rates are lower than the trust tax rate. The settlor should ensure that no income or capital can be paid to him to avoid the 'revert to settlor 'rules.

Capital gains tax
The CGT rate applicable to trusts is 20%. The settlor may make a chargeable gain on disposal of assets or a gift to the trust. However, hold-over relief should apply for capital gains tax, until the trustees dispose of the asset, when the tax will become payable by them. Alternatively, the hold-over election can be made when the trustees distribute the asset to the beneficiaries, who then become liable for the capital gains tax. There is an annual exemption applying to trusts at half the rate for individuals, but this is spread over the trusts with the same settlor. The rate is currently £6,000 in 2019/20.

4. Discretionary trusts

The trustees have the discretion to distribute capital and income to the beneficiaries. The rules applying allow far greater flexibility with regard to providing for beneficiaries and potential beneficiaries, according to their needs. The range of beneficiaries can be wide and include the spouse or civil partner of the deceased settlor. Previously the trust could accumulate income for a beneficiary's lifetime plus up to 21 years. Now, we have the *Perpetuities and Accumulations Act 2009* which has abolished the rule against excessive accumulations of income for non charitable trusts. Because this type of trust is discretionary and flexible, it also attracts the greatest levels of taxation. Other previously less-taxed trusts, such as interest-in-possession and accumulation-and-maintenance trusts now fall within the regime for discretionary trusts, following the *Finance Act 2006*.

Trusts are set up for a maximum period of 125 years (it was 80 years until 2009) and can have a wide range of beneficiaries, who do not need to be named. This gives wide flexibility on who will benefit and when. The trustees have discretion as to the type of investments made and how they deal with the trust assets. There need be no income or capital distribution stipulations, and they will deal with the wishes of the settlor, as long as these do not conflict with their duties as trustees. The settlor would give the trustees a letter of wishes to guide the trustees with regard to trust matters, payment of income and capital and other areas, and this can be updated as circumstances change.

Inheritance tax

The transfer to the trust will be a chargeable lifetime transfer (CLT). If, after exemptions, including the nil rate band, there is an excess, this will be subject to IHT at the lifetime rate of 20%. The nil rate band is currently £325,000 in 2019/20, and value below this level will not be charged to lifetime inheritance tax. After seven years, the value of any cumulative transfers will fall out of the reckoning for inheritance tax purposes. It is important that the settlor is not included as a beneficiary, nor does he benefit from the discretionary trust in any way to avoid the value of the asset falling back into his estate for IHT, after gifting it away.

There are also periodic and exit charges applying to the trust. The periodic charges are every ten years. If capital is transferred to another trust (such as a sub-trust) or appointed to a beneficiary then the charge could apply. It may not apply in all circumstances, as its calculation often depends on whether there was a tax charge to assets entering the trust in the first place. The periodic charge is 30% of the lifetime rate, and the maximum charge at the ten-year anniversary will be 30% x 20% = 6%. *FA 2014* introduced a new rule to treat income arising in trusts that remain undistributed for 5 years or more as part of the trust capital when calculating the 10 year anniversary charge will increase the exit charges.

To avoid the incidence of inheritance tax, an individual gifting chargeable assets to the trust can make use of available exemptions. These include the value of the nil rate band as well as other available exemptions – for example, business property relief (BPR) applying to qualifying private company shares being gifted, or agricultural property relief (APR). Each spouse can set up their own trust, and have the same exemptions. Inter-spouse or civil partner transfers between each other are not subject to any taxes, and may provide capital to a spouse or civil partner with no assets to gift to the trust. If setting up multiple trusts, be sure to make them on different days, as each trust can have its own nil rate band exemptions that can be effective. As the assets held within the trust grow, they could in future years fall into the IHT net. However, a discretionary trust, if planned properly, can shelter assets from inheritance taxes for many years into the future. There is also an order in which to make gifts to make use of all available exemptions, without losing the exemptions.

Order of making gifts is important

First, fully exempt gifts should be made, then loans to trusts, then chargeable lifetime transfers (CLTs), and finally potentially exempt transfers (PETs). It is important that CLTs are made to discretionary trusts before PETs, as the ten-year periodic charge on the discretionary trust will depend on what other CLTs were made in the seven years before the discretionary trust was established. Had the client made a PET within the seven-year period and died within the seven years, the now failed PET becomes a CLT and will be included in the calculation at the ten-year anniversary for the discretionary trust. If the PET was made after the CLT then, on failing within the seven-year period, it cannot be included in the calculation, thus reducing the tax bill.

Getting the order wrong could result in higher IHT bills. Getting it right could save a massive amount in IHT. If a gift of £325,000 was made in the 2019/20 tax year to a discretionary trust, and treated as a CLT, and the same amount to a bare trust (treated as a PET), then the estate could be reduced by £650,000 without any IHT consequences.

Income tax

The trustees pay income tax at the trust rate of 45%, and 38.1% on UK dividend income. Beneficiaries will receive income net of income tax at the above rates and may reclaim part or all of the tax paid from the trustees.

Note that special rated trusts (such as discretionary trusts) have a £1,000 standard allowance where income is taxed at 20%. This allowance is divided by the number of trusts that settlor has in existence in the tax year, but to a figure no less than £200.

If children are minors, under the age of 18 and unmarried, and receive income or capital from the trust, this will be assessed as the settlor's income and taxed accordingly in his hands. If the settlor and his spouse or civil partner derive any benefit from the discretionary trust they will be taxed. This does not apply to his widow or a widower.

The 2010 March budget introduced an income tax adjustment measure for settlor-interested trusts (from 6 April 2010). Where the settler receives repayments of tax on trust income where liable to income tax at a lower rate than the trustees, they will be required to repay any such repayments received by them to the trustees. These repayments to trustees will be disregarded for inheritance tax purposes.

Special treatment applies for 'vulnerable' beneficiaries under *Finance Act 2005 ss 23-33*. Here the trustees pay tax at the rate of the beneficiary, not the trust, and a joint election must be made to this effect. The beneficiary in this case may have a tax rate of, say, 0% or 20% (on savings and 7.5% on dividends) after personal allowances, which would represent a saving in cash flow as the trust income tax rate is 45% and dividends are taxed at 38.1%. *Finance Act 2013 (Section 216 and Schedule 44)* make provision for trusts with vulnerable beneficiaries. A main test to qualify for favourable tax treatment as a disabled person's trust is that the person concerned is in receipt of the Disability Living Allowance (DLA). This is now replaced by the Personal Independent Payment (PIP), and the 1984 IHT Act is amended to reflect this.

Capital gains tax

If the trustees are UK resident when the asset is transferred and the beneficiary is UK resident when receiving it, then hold-over relief applies to the asset transferred to the trust. If the beneficiary becomes UK non-resident within six years of the distribution being made, then CGT could become payable immediately. Trustees pay capital gains tax at 20%, after the trust annual exemption (currently £6,000 in 2019/20) has been deducted (or as much of it as remains after being apportioned between up to five trusts) – unless there has been hold-over relief or other capital gains tax deferral relief. If the settlor or his or her spouse or civil partner is a beneficiary, then CGT is charged at his marginal rate. He can then claim the tax that he paid from the trustees.

5. Pilot trusts (also known as feeder trusts or family bypass trusts)

Whilst not a separate category of trust ,as it is usually drafted as a discretionary trust, the Pilot trust is mentioned here as it is becoming more popular to increase the number of nil rate bands you may have to save IHT. It is set up in your lifetime with a small amount of money (usually £10) which can be added to, usually in your lifetime or on your death, in your will. Pilot trusts are not 'related' trusts, (related trusts are those set up on the same day) and are set up before your will leaving money to the trust is signed. At the date of death you may leave assets to the trusts on the same day, but so long as the trusts were set up on different days they will not be 'related' trusts. Each pilot trust can use one nil rate band, currently £325,000. Assets can be placed in trust at any time during your lifetime or by will. These assets can be used for a surviving spouse and for children and grandchildren. You can include a NRB discretionary trust in your will and also leave further monies to your pilot trust. This would give you the advantage of 2 or more nil rate bands. Money or assets in trust would not be part of a surviving spouse's estate but available for their lifetime use.

If a cohabitee, then there is no transferable NRB available to a surviving cohabite, however assets up to the nil rate band can be added to the pilot trust through the will and the residue left to the cohabite for life. These two trusts will not be 'related' trusts. If under the nil rate bands, monies in trust will not be subject to IHT, at least for the first 10 years. Pilot trusts can be set up for children and grandchildren, They can provide protection for assets against divorce, bankruptcy, nursing home fees. Pilot trusts are also useful to receive pension death benefits to fall outside your estate, a surviving spouse's estate or cohabitee's estate. This means trust value is readily available without the need for probate and generating considerable tax savings. The inheritance tax treatment of pilot trusts was confirmed in *Rysaffe Trustee Co (CI) v CIR [2003] STC 536*. The Government proposed to attack multiple trusts by stating that the settler should only have one nil rate band – but this proposal was not proceeded with following the Autumn statement 2014.

6. Offshore trusts

These are trusts where the trustees are resident outside the UK – mostly established by wealthy individuals to protect their family and business assets from taxes, including inheritance tax. The status of the trust depends on where the trustees are resident, regardless of whether the settlor and the beneficiaries are in the UK or not (as residents or domiciled in the UK). The trusts are usually discretionary, life-interest or accumulation-and-maintenance. The law in this area is complex and there are many anti-avoidance tax provisions applying. From the 6th April 2007, where there is a transfer between settlements, the domicile and residence status of the settlor will be tested at the time of the transfer as well as at the time the property was first settled.

Domicile and residence are the main aspects to be considered. If the settlor was non UK domiciled as well as the beneficiary, then there is no UK IHT or capital gains tax payable. If income arises in the trust and is not remitted to the UK then no income tax is payable. Where the settlor is non-UK domiciled and the beneficiary of the trust is UK domiciled, then no IHT is payable. Income tax is usually payable on income arising, but can be deferred. *FA 2013* amends the ordinary residence rules by removing the ordinary residence test. For example, the ordinary residence test as regards bank accounts is removed for deaths on or after 6 April 2013.

Inheritance tax
For trustees, their liability to IHT depends upon the tax status of the settlor when the trust was set up. If the settlor was not UK domiciled and the property is situated abroad, the assets are excluded property and exempt from IHT. In all other cases, the trust assets will remain liable to UK inheritance taxes. A non-UK domiciled settlor who sets up a trust abroad (and has an interest in possession or is a beneficiary of the trust) who subsequently becomes UK domiciled could find such a trust useful to protect his non-UK assets from IHT.

If the settlor is domiciled in the UK and transfers assets to a non-UK trust, this will be a CLT (chargeable lifetime transfer), above any exempt limits. Unless classed as excluded property (where the trustees of the trust are not UK resident), if the settlor retains an interest in the trust as a discretionary beneficiary, this will be seen as a reservation of benefit and subject to IHT.

Where the settlor is neither domiciled nor deemed domiciled in the UK, he can make a transfer of foreign assets to trustees offshore without any IHT liability.

A beneficiary of a discretionary offshore trust may be charged to UK IHT on that beneficiary's interest if the settlor was UK domiciled when the settlement was made – if he was not UK domiciled when the settlement was made, then usually no IHT liability arises on the beneficiary.

Income tax

If the trustees live abroad, then income tax is only payable by the trust if income arises in the UK. How the income is taxed, depends on what it is used for. If it merely arises to the trust then income tax is at the basic rate of 20% or the 45% trust rate on trust income from the UK; 7.5% and 38.1% on dividend income. If the trustees have the discretion to pay it to beneficiaries or can accumulate it, then the rate of tax is 45% (38.1% for UK dividend income).

If the settlor or his spouse or civil partner retain an interest in the property, then they pay tax at their marginal rates on income received – unless not resident or ordinarily resident in the UK when the income arises.

If the beneficiary is domiciled in the UK and resident or ordinarily resident in the UK, he or she will be taxable on income from the trust. If the trustees accumulate income for the beneficiary, the beneficiary will only be taxed on receipt of income from the trust, and not during the accumulation period. It may be more tax efficient for the beneficiary to receive income (or capital) on a regular basis and make full use of personal tax allowances and perhaps lower tax rates, than to wait for a larger accumulation of income to be paid to him. If the beneficiary is not resident or ordinarily resident at the time that the accumulated income is paid to him, then a liability to UK income tax may be avoided.

If the settlor has been taxed on the beneficiary's income (through falling foul of the anti-avoidance legislation), then the beneficiary can avoid paying income tax.

Capital gains tax

Capital gains tax depends on where the trustees are resident, and also on the domicile and residency status of the settlor at the time of the disposal leading to the capital gain arising.

There is no liability to foreign trustees to pay capital gains tax – unless the offshore trust carries on a trade. From 6th April 2007, if any of the trustees are resident in the UK, the trust is treated as resident in the UK –unless the settlor was not domiciled, resident or ordinarily resident in the UK at the time the settlement was created or transfers made between trusts (settlements).

The UK domiciled and resident settlor making a transfer of assets into the offshore trust will be liable to capital gains tax. There are exceptions to this rule – for example, beneficiaries of a trust created before 17th March 1998 who are grandchildren of the settlor. A settlor incurring personal capital losses may offset these losses against an offshore trust's gains.

A beneficiary who receives a capital payment or benefit from the trust is potentially chargeable to capital gains tax. The beneficiary must be both resident and domiciled in the UK for this to occur. The beneficiary could be liable to a CGT surcharge as well. A calculation is made according to the time it takes for the trustees to pay the gain to the beneficiary and a surcharge is payable at 10% per year for up to six years.

Tax treatment for overseas trusts depends on a number of factors, including: when the trust became non-UK resident; the domicile and residence status of the settlor when the trust was settled; the tax year in which the settlement occurred; the status of the beneficiary when payments are received from the trustees; the relationship of the settlor to the beneficiaries; additions to the trust assets; changes to the beneficiaries themselves.

Excluded Property Trusts (EPT)
The EPT is mentioned here, not specifically as a different type of trust, but as an example of how an offshore trust that has offered IHT mitigation, has now had tax avoidance legislation (from 6 April 2012) passed to counter its benefits. IHT is normally charged on the value of a person's estate at death after deducting reliefs and the nil-rate band. There is a separate relevant property regime that charges IHT on assets held in trusts, which are not included in a person's estate. If a UK-domiciled individual settles assets into an offshore trust, the transfer into trust will be charged to IHT and the value of the trust assets above the nil rate band will also be subject to IHT.

But if the settlor is not UK-domiciled, settled property situated outside the UK is excluded from the IHT charge and is referred to as excluded property. Anti-avoidance provisions ensure that where an 'interest in possession' (IIP) in such excluded property is purchased for value, the trust assets are subject to IHT as part of the purchaser's estate. However, if a UK domiciled individual acquires an interest in excluded property which is not an IIP, there may be no charge to IHT when the interest is acquired and the settled property may escape any subsequent charge to IHT either as part of the individual's estate or under the relevant property regime. In addition, the individual's estate may be reduced by any debt where the acquisition is financed by a loan. The amendments to the settled property provisions relating to excluded property will apply to avoidance schemes where arrangements exploit the excluded property rules by converting UK assets to ones that are excluded from the IHT charge and do not give rise to a transfer of value when that conversion occurs. In future, a transfer of value will arise and the assets will no longer be treated as excluded property and will fall within the relevant property regime.

There were tax avoidance schemes available whereby the UK domiciled individual used his UK estate assets to purchase a share in an EPT – in an offshore trust. In other words, he was buying in to a trust that excluded property and thus protected his assets 100% from IHT. This legislation is to counter these types of schemes

7. Private Charitable Trusts

An individual can set up a private charity, properly registered with the Charity Commission, and can be one of the trustees administering the trust. Donations made to this type of trust are exempt from inheritance tax as well as capital gains tax. The gift of capital is irrevocable and must be outright. Charities also have income tax exemption reliefs, and tax deducted at source and tax credits can be repaid to the charity by HMRC. However, the tax credits on dividends are not repayable.

New rules for non-UK domiciled individuals ("non-doms")

The Pre-Budget statement of 9th October 2007 introduced tax changes for UK-resident non-doms from 6th April 2008. The *Finance Act 2009* introduced minor amendments limited to clarification of amounts when applying for a low income (£2,000) exemption from reporting on an arising basis or electing to report on a remittance basis. These only apply to income tax and capital gains tax, but not inheritance tax. There is a £30,000 per annum flat fee payable which enables the non-UK domiciled person to claim the remittance basis of taxation, if you have been UK resident for 7 years out of the past 10 years. Those with foreign income or gains of less than £2,000 p.a. will be exempted. Income and gains actually remitted will attract additional taxation without the benefit of personal allowances – whether or not they have paid the £30,000 p.a. flat fee, or been resident in the UK for 7 years. A tax credit may not be available in other jurisdictions where the UK non-domiciled individual pays tax.

The 2011 Budget announced that from 6 April 2012 there will be an increase to £50,000 in the annual charge (from £30,000) for non-domiciled individuals who have been UK resident for 12 or more years and who wish to benefit from the remittance basis of taxation. It is possible to remove the tax charge when non- domiciled individuals remit foreign income or capital gains to the UK for the purpose of commercial investment in UK businesses. However, the personal allowance and married couples allowance are not available to non UK domicilliaries and not ordinary UK resident individuals who elect to pay tax on the remittance basis.

There is an opportunity to use insurance bonds and roll-up funds to remit capital and thus avoid the flat fee of £30,000-£90,000 p.a. in any one tax year.

If you have been resident for 17 out of the last 20 years a non-UK domiciled person is deemed domiciled for IHT purposes. Three full years of non-residence resets the 17-year clock (for CGT, 5 full years resets the CGT clock). Possibly re-starting the 7-year period by becoming non-resident may be a possibility, but the period of non-residence is unknown at this stage.

In addition, the review on domicile and residence has been completed, and changes will be introduced so that days of arrival and departure from the UK will count towards establishing residence.

The Autumn Statement 2014 announced the following provisions concerning non-domicilliaries who use the remittance basis and resident in the UK:

- 7 out of last 9 years charge unchanged at £30,000 per year
- 12 out of last 14 years to increase from £50,000 to £60,000 per year
- 17 out of last 20 years – a new charge of £90,000 to be introduced. (This became obsolete from April 2017 with the introduction of the '15-year rule' – see the following section.)

The Government also consulted on making the election apply for a minimum of three years (Finance Bill 2015).

Changes in IHT payable come into effect from 2017

The following announcements were made in the 2015 Budget with regard to non-domiciled individuals There are extensive changes to the non-domicile status, which will have a significant impact on long-term UK resident non-domiciled people:

1. From April 2017, anybody who has been resident in the UK for more than 15 of the past 20 tax years will be deemed UK-domiciled for tax purposes and be liable for full UK tax. The tax status remains the same. Non-UK domiciled individuals will be subject to new legislation.

2. It will also no longer be possible for people born in the country to UK domiciled parents to claim non-domicile status if they leave but then return. From April 2017, individuals who are born in the UK to parents who are domiciled there, will no longer be able to claim non-domicile status whilst they are resident in the UK.

3. Permanent non-domiciled status will be abolished and replaced with a 15-year rule. Individuals who have been UK resident for more than 15 of the past 20 years will be deemed domicile for all tax purposes in the UK. This means that they will become subject to UK tax on their worldwide income and gains on an arising basis and subject to UK Inheritance Tax on their worldwide assets. Excluded property trusts will continue to have the same Inheritance Tax treatment as at present, with the exception of UK residential property held within such a trust. On departure from the UK, the deemed domicile status will be retained for five years.

4. UK residential property that is held by a non-domiciled individual will be assessed for UK Inheritance Tax on death, regardless of how that property is held. This means that properties held within trusts, corporate entities or other opaque structures will be subject to UK Inheritance Tax.

What the Government wants to achieve

The Government wants to tighten the tax receipt for non-domiciled people. They are able to claim the remittance basis of taxation, which does not tax foreign income and gains as long as they are not brought to the UK. To access the remittance basis, longer term UK resident non-domiciled individuals need to pay an annual remittance basis charge of up to £90,000.

All UK-resident non-domiciliaries will be subject to all UK taxes (exactly as if they were UK-domiciled) after completing more than 15 years out of the last 20 years as UK residents. We refer to this as the "15-year rule".

It also wishes to bring more assets into the IHT tax net.

What the Non-Domiciled Person can do

*   Ensure that an offshore excluded property trust is established at the most appropriate time.
*   Take particular note of the timing aspect in relation to the 15-year deadline – it could in fact be as little as just over 13 years after the date of arrival in the UK.
*   Carefully consider the pros and cons of retaining assets within excluded property trusts and stripping out income and gains.
*   Consider the use of alternative tax deferral structures such as offshore insurance bond wrappers to hold personal investment wealth once the remittance basis regime is no longer available.
*   Consider leaving the UK altogether and establishing permanent residency elsewhere.
*   Consider the possibility of the family splitting their tax residency status, i.e. one spouse and children living in the UK and the other spouse living and working abroad.
*   Consider the possible establishment of tax residency in a jurisdiction which has a suitable double tax treaty with the UK. The Budget papers suggest that the consultation process will include consideration of the impact of the new proposals on the application of these treaties but it is not clear whether the treaty benefits will be removed.

These are some guidelines given by the PFS to its members. This part of planning can be complicated and specialist advice may be required.

10

Taxation of Trusts

Trust taxation and reliefs generally

Income tax

Trust taxation depends on the type of trust involved. This depends on income received as income, interest or dividends. In 2019/20 the rates are as follows:

- **Bare trust:** income and dividends are taxed as an individual at their tax rates.
- **Discretionary trust:** a standard rate band of £1,000 is applied within which income is taxed at 20% and dividends at 7.5%. Above the standard rate band income is taxed at 45% and dividends at 38.1%. (Note that the 10% tax credit for dividends would reduce the actual tax to 28.1%). Note that this standard rate is not per trust – if the settler is interested in more than one trust the rate is divided proportionately down to a minimum of £200.

Trustees pay tax under self-assessment, by the 31st January following the end of the tax year. When the trust is formed, trustees must send in Form 41G Trusts to HMRC. Subsequently trustees must complete the self-assessment form SA 900. Where income payments are made to a beneficiary, the trustees must complete tax voucher R 185 to show (i) gross income (ii) tax at 10%, lower or basic rate, or the rate applying to trusts (RAT) and (iii) the net sum to which the beneficiary is entitled. On receipt of this voucher, the beneficiary can then submit his own self-assessment forms.

Where the settlor or his spouse or civil partner benefits from the trust property or any property derived from it, he has an 'interest in the settlement'. The whole of the trust income is then treated as his income (*section 624, ITTOIA 2005*). Under *section 629*, where a settlement has been made for the benefit of the settlor's minor children, that income will be assessed on the settlor as a parent (less the first £100 per parent and per child per annum). Before 9th March 1999, the rule applied only to income paid out to beneficiaries – after that date it applies whether income is paid out or retained by the trustees.

However, the settlor can reclaim tax from the trustees where he has not received the income.

Beneficiaries in receipt of a life income (interest-in-possession trusts)

A beneficiary of an interest-in-possession trust who is entitled to receive a life income as it arises from a trust, has to pay income tax on the income in the year in which the trust receives the income (even if the beneficiary received it after the end of the tax year), and the tax rates applying to that tax year are used. The trustees pay lower or basic rate income tax and the beneficiary any higher rate or additional tax.

Income received by discretionary and A&M Trusts

The first £1,000 of income received is taxed at 20% (standard rate for trusts). The balance is taxed at 45% (38.1% for dividends).

Dividends from UK companies carry a non-repayable tax credit of 10%. The dividend trust tax rate is 38.1%, of which 10% is met by the tax credit, leaving the trustees to pay 28.1%.

Interest income can be received gross. The trustees must pay to make 45% as a total tax liability. Where income is received gross, the trustees pay 45%. An example is rental income received by the trustees.

If a payment is made to a discretionary beneficiary, tax at 45% (or 38.1% on dividends) will have been paid by the trustees. The beneficiary may recover all or part of the tax paid – apart from the 10% non-repayable credit on dividends.

If a trust is for a vulnerable person, such as a disabled person, or a minor where at least one parent has died, an election can be made to disapply the normal rate applicable to trusts and have the income and gains of the trust taxed as if they arose directly to the beneficiary. However the trustees must show that the income payment has had tax paid on it by the trustees at 45%.

Trust Management Expenses

Trust expenses are allowable from trust income if properly charged against income and actually paid out of income in the tax year. The deduction will not apply if the expenses are incurred for the benefit of the whole estate or attributable to capital. This is a complicated area. Some trust expenses are set against capital for example. The HMRC publishes a guide to SA 900 which details some of the more common expenses that are allowable. Go to **www.hmrc.gov.uk/forms/sa900**.

Capital Gains Tax

Capital Gains Tax (CGT) is payable on actual and deemed disposals. Actual disposals can include a gift as well as a sale of an asset. CGT could also be payable on a deemed disposal – for example, where a beneficiary becomes absolutely entitled to the property – but does not apply where a life tenant dies who is treated as owning the property for IHT purposes. The taxable gain is the difference between the sale proceeds of the assets and the cost of acquisition (or its 31st March 1982 value if it was originally acquired before this date), less any costs of acquisition and disposal.

The previous position is: a deduction for indexation (inflation) as at April 1998 may be made if the asset was owned prior to that date. In the case of a gift, or a sale by the trustees to a connected person such as the settlor or relative, the deemed disposal value is the market value at the date of the gift or sale.

Once the taxable gain has been calculated, it could be further offset by reliefs applying. The main relief is taper relief, which is calculated over a ten-year period for non-business assets and two years for business assets.

The new position is: from 6th April 2008, there was a flat rate of 18% CGT with no indexation and taper reliefs. This rate is now 20%.

Rate of capital gains tax

Trustees are assessed at 20%.

The annual exemption

Each trust has an annual exemption from capital gains tax payable. This is half the annual personal exemption rate. In 2019/20 the personal rate is £12,000, and the trust annual exemption is therefore £6,000. However, where the same settlor has paid into multiple trusts, this exemption is spread over up to five trusts, so the lowest trust annual exemption is £1,200. If only one of these same-settlor trusts makes a gain in a tax year, the other annual exemptions will be lost.

Reliefs from capital gains tax

The main reliefs applying to trusts and trustees are as follows:

• **Taper relief (<u>abolished from 6th April 2008, but shown for earlier tax calculations</u>)**
   This reduced the value for capital gains tax purposes, depending on the time the asset has been held. Taper relief can be non-business or business relief in relation to assets, and is more generous for business assets.

Complete years from 6 April 1988	1	2	3	4	5	6	7	8	9	10
Business assets % relief	50	75	75	75	75	75	75	75	75	75
Non-business assets % relief	0	0	5	10	15	20	25	30	35	40

For non-business assets, add one year if the asset was acquired before 17th March 1998. The business asset taper relief will be apportioned where the asset has not been a business asset throughout the entire period of ownership.

- **Roll-over relief**
  A claim may be made for deferral of a gain, where trustees trade, selling one qualifying business asset and reinvesting the proceeds in another, when they can carry forward or "roll over" the original acquisition cost for tax purposes.

- **Hold-over relief**
  Where the trustees sell or gift an asset to a UK resident beneficiary, they may claim hold-over relief to defer the gain. The gain is taxable when the beneficiary sells the asset.

- **EIS – Enterprise Investment Scheme relief and Seed EIS (SEIS)**
  The trustees can defer the capital gain realised from the sale or gift of any asset through investing into a qualifying EIS or SEIS company. The investment is usually higher risk, as it is made into AIM stocks or unquoted company shares.

- **Main residence relief**
  Where the trustees sell a home that has been used as the main or only residence of a beneficiary, it may qualify for full or partial relief, depending on the circumstances.

Settlor-interested trusts

Where the settlor, spouse or civil partner can benefit from the trust, and the settlor's minor unmarried children can benefit – but where the children are not in a civil partnership – the trust gains are treated as those of the settlor and not the trustees. This may benefit the settlor as his personal CGT allowances apply (in 2019/20 this is £12,000 per person), and tax may be payable at 10% (basic rate) or 20% above that. There is a surcharge for residential property gains of 8% (28%). The settlor may also be able to use allowable losses, whereas the trustees may not be allowed to offset losses on a disposal to a connected person. The trustees can only carry the loss forward to be offset against another disposal to the same connected person.

The 2010 March Budget introduced an income tax adjustment measure for settlor-interested trusts (from 6 April 2010). Where the settler receives repayments of tax on trust income where liable to income tax at a lower rate than the trustees, they will be required to repay any such repayments received by them to the trustees. These repayments to trustees will be disregarded for inheritance tax purposes.

11

Planning a Trust

The use of trusts in estate planning; the different types of trusts and their uses

Trusts can be used for many different purposes and are very much a part of modern estate planning. Trusts can be set up when you are alive or when you die. On death, a trust can be part of your will, and if you do not have a will, a trust can be formed on intestacy.

The reasons for creating a trust can be summarised as follows:

- to protect the interests of vulnerable or immature beneficiaries
- to protect the interests of the mentally infirm and disabled people
- to protect the interests of those unable to deal with financial matters or the handling of cash lump sums
- to ensure that an income stream is provided for a beneficiary
- to direct capital to beneficiaries at certain times
- to reduce your estate for inheritance taxes
- to 'freeze' your assets so that the growth on the assets is captured in the trust and not in your estate
- to provide a mechanism to deal with estate assets well into the future and for succeeding generations (UK trusts can endure for 125 years from 2009)
- to bypass generations so that inheritance tax is minimised
- to protect assets against insolvency or bankruptcy
- for charitable purposes
- in the case of business trusts, to provide an independent means for the creation and distribution of employee benefits
- in the case of shareholder and partner trusts, to give cash sums for distribution to surviving shareholders or partners
- in the case of life assurance trusts, to deliver policy proceeds outside your estate that are free of inheritance taxes, and directed to your beneficiaries
- to enable management and control of your financial affairs
- to pass on your personal wealth

- to enable a 'tax spread' amongst beneficiaries using their personal allowances and tax rates in certain instances
- to deal with assets in different tax jurisdictions – for example, company shares or foreign properties.

Whatever your motives and intentions, trust planning could be a valuable part of your overall estate planning. Trust law was re-landscaped in the *Finance Act 2006*, when interest-in-possession trusts and accumulation-and-maintenance trusts, which had formerly been outside the discretionary trust regime, were now brought into it, and made subject broadly to entry, periodic and exit charges. The *Trustee Act 2000* brought in sweeping changes on how trusts must be managed and trust investments made, with a new statutory duty of care for trustees. Trusts have essentially been modernised, and the *Trustee Act 2000* applies to older established trusts, as well as to new ones.

The basic rule governing trusts is: the more power the creator (settlor or donor) retains, the harsher is the tax treatment of the trust. A trust is viewed as a separate persona in law, with its own tax regime and rules governing who is taxed on income and capital gains, and who is responsible for inheritance taxes to be paid.

Trusts can be simple to execute, or more complex, depending on your objectives. Different types of trusts are possible for diverse reasons. Whilst trusts may have different names or take on different forms, they essentially fall into two broad regimes: non-chargeable and chargeable.

The non-chargeable regime includes bare trusts, also known as 'absolute' trusts and certain exempt trusts, such as trusts for the vulnerable or disabled. In these instances, gifts or donations made to such trusts fall under the potentially exempt transfer rules (PETs) and the settlor or donor must survive for at least seven years for the value of the gift to be out of his estate. If the settlor dies within the seven-year period, then a portion of the gift made will fall back into his estate for IHT purposes.

All other trusts fall into the chargeable events regime. These are broadly known as discretionary trusts and now include interest-in-possession and accumulation-and-maintenance trusts (both types formerly within the PET non-chargeable regime). This means that when the gift or settlement is made, there could be a chargeable event and entry tax at 20% could be payable, i.e. within your lifetime, with the balance of 20% payable on your death.

You may escape this charge if the donation or gift is under the nil rate band, currently £325,000 in 2019/20, or if other exemptions apply, such as business or agricultural property reliefs.

You can set up a trust, or one may be set up for you. The following are the main types of trust instruments available and the reasons for having one.

Bare or absolute trusts

Purpose: To make a fixed gift, normally to a child. The time and amount of the capital received by the beneficiary is fixed and cannot be varied.

The trust is set up and the trustees hold the asset for the child's benefit. At the age of 18 the child has absolute rights in the property. The child's personal allowances for income tax and capital gains tax can be used for income and gains. If the parent made the gift the parent (not the child) is taxed on any income over £100, until the child reaches the age of 18, when the child can be taxed. If someone other than the parent makes the gift, then the child can be taxed on the income.

The gift made is a PET and the donor must survive for seven years for its value to be out of his estate.

The beneficiary must be in existence when the trust is created, i.e. this trust cannot be for the unborn.

The amount held for each child must be fixed and cannot be varied.

Bereaved Minor Trusts

Where a Will sets up a trust for children of the deceased, who will inherit subject to the condition that they attain the age of 18, this will normally create a 'Bereaved Minor Trust'.

A Bereaved Minor Trust must be distinguished from a gift in a Will made without any age restriction, where the beneficiary happens to be a child, or a gift left absolutely to a child but directed to be payable when they are older. These will create a Bare Trust, in which the gifts given belong to the child from the start.

Due to a change in the law, Bereaved Minor Trusts can now only be created by parents for their own children or stepchildren. Any money left to grandchildren, nephews and nieces or other minor beneficiaries will create either a Bare Trust or a Relevant Property Trust.

Accumulation-and-Maintenance trusts (A&M)

Purpose: To provide a discretionary flexible income stream, at the discretion of trustees, most commonly for the maintenance and education of children. Settlements made can reduce your estate for IHT purposes. These trusts are more flexible than bare trusts and the time and amount of income and capital received by a child is at the discretion of the trustees.

The trust is discretionary and can be for children born and to be born; however there must be at least one beneficiary of a particular class. Beneficiaries do not have a right to capital, which can pass to another beneficiary. Income should be paid to the age of 25 (it may be later), however, the Government introduced new legislation in the *Finance Act 2006* reducing this age to 18 for there to be no penal tax consequences.

18-25 Trusts

Where a Will delays the age that a child of the deceased can inherit, to age 25, or earlier, this can create an '18-25' Trust. The tax treatment of these trusts for income tax and capital gains tax are the same as for Bereaved Minor Trusts.

An 18-25 Trust can only be created by parents for their own children or stepchildren.

Tax treatment

Capital Gains Tax

Disposals and acquisitions of assets within the trust will be assessed for capital gains tax purposes. The Trust would benefit from an annual allowance equal to half the current individual annual allowance. For the tax year 2019/20 2018-19 the current annual trust allowance is £6,000 £5,850. The Trust must pay capital gains tax on any excess exceeding that allowance. The rate of capital gains tax applicable to trusts is 28% for residential property and 20% for everything else. This may change with Government budgets.

There are opportunities to mitigate capital gains tax on the transfer of assets out of the trust, however, certain conditions apply. Capital gains tax can also be mitigated where the trust sells or transfers a property which is occupied by a beneficiary.

Income Tax

Income tax will be charged to the trust at the rate applicable to trusts which is currently 45% on gross non dividend income exceeding £1,000. The rate applicable to dividend income is currently 38.1%. If the gross income does not exceed £1,000 then the standard rate of tax will apply which is 20%.

Inheritance Tax

Bereaved Minor Trusts and 18 – 25 Trusts differ from other trusts in the way that they are treated for inheritance tax purposes. Even if the value of the trust exceeds the nil rate band there will be no assessment for inheritance tax on a distribution at age 18 or at ten yearly intervals during the trust period.

In an 18-25 Trust, when a child over 18 receives a payment from the trust there may be a charge to inheritance tax if the trust fund exceeds the nil rate band. The charge will be a fraction of 6%, with the amount depending on how long after the age of 18 the payment is made. For example, if the child inherits at age 21 the inheritance tax rate will be 1.8%. If the child inherits at age 25 the maximum inheritance tax rate will be 4.2%

There will be no ten yearly anniversary charges to inheritance tax during the trust period, but when the child attains the specified age, there may be a charge to inheritance tax if the trust fund exceeds the nil rate band.

If the Will sets up a trust whereby a child inherits a share of the estate at age 18, a further share at age 21 and a further share at age 25, these will be treated as one trust for tax purposes. There will be no charge to inheritance tax at age 18. Distributions to the child after that age will be subject to an inheritance tax charge, if the trust exceeds the nil rate band. The rate of tax will depend on the age of the child at the date of the distribution.

However, the rates of inheritance tax applicable are very low and should be balanced against the advantage of additional control over funds left to young adults who may not be capable of handling large sums of money sensibly. Protection over tax considerations is often important.

Please note that H.M Revenue and Customs will usually treat a Will as setting up one trust, even if the Will contains several gifts to different children who will receive their shares at different times. In this case, the nil rate band, capital gains tax annual allowance and the £1,000 income tax standard rate allowance are applied to the whole Will trust and not just to one child's share.

If capital is received between the age of 18 and the age of 25, there will be a tax charge of up to 4.2%. Income may be paid to beneficiaries at any time, although it is not required to be paid out until an age selected by the settlor. Trustees can decide who will benefit, and when. The settlor can be a trustee. The gift made is a chargeable transfer and lifetime IHT may be payable if over the nil rate band and no other exemptions such as BPR and APR apply. If the A&M trust was created after 21st March 2006, there is a periodic charge after ten years and an exit charge. If created before that date, there will be no periodic charges if the beneficiary becomes absolutely entitled by the age of 18. The terms of an existing trust may be amended by 6th April 2008 for this to happen.

If the trust comes into effect by will or on intestacy after 21st March 2006, and was set up by a deceased parent for his bereaved child's benefit, then if the child becomes absolutely entitled at the age of 18, there is no further IHT charge. At the age of 25 for absolute entitlement, there is a maximum charge of 4.2%. There is no ten-year periodic charge in either case, even after ten years. If the child becomes entitled after the age of 25, then there will be periodic and exit charges. If a grandparent creates a will trust, there will be periodic and exit charges whatever the age of the grandchild.

Interest-in-possession trusts (IIP) or life-interest trusts

Purpose: To provide an income benefit for named beneficiaries, whilst leaving the capital to a different beneficiary. This type of trust is more suitable for adults, or those over the age of 25, but can be for minor children. One or more beneficiaries is entitled to income arising from the trust funds. The capital will vest (pass) to another beneficiary. These trusts can be established by will or set up whilst alive. An example may be where the settlor wishes a spouse or partner to have an income, but not to control the capital.

Where family company shares or agricultural property is gifted into trust, income is provided to named beneficiaries.

If the beneficiary is aged over 18, then that income is taxed in their hands. Where a parent-settlor sets up the trust for a child, then the parent is taxed on income and capital gains until the child turns 18. The trustees can distribute capital to the income beneficiaries if they so wish. They may also change a beneficiary for income in favour of another beneficiary.

For trusts created before 21st March 2006, the gift to trust was a PET; beneficiaries were treated as being the owners of the trust property for IHT purposes, and a proportion of the trust property forms part of their estates. For trusts created after that date, the gift is a chargeable transfer, with 20% charged on any excess over available exemptions, such as the nil rate band. Beneficiaries will not be treated as owners of the trust assets for the purposes of IHT. The trust assets will be subject to periodic and exit charges on distributions from the trust.

For Interest in Possession Trusts a transitional period was allowed between 6th April 2006 and 6th April 2008 to make any changes in respect of a life tenant's interest to avoid existing IIP trusts falling into the new discretionary trust regime. In order to give trustees more time to review existing IIP arrangements, this review period was extended to 5th October 2008. The extension of the deadline gave trustees more time to make alternative arrangements. This extension does not apply to A & M trusts, which now falls under the 'relevant property' provisions if income and capital do not vest in the beneficiary absolutely not later than age 18.

Discretionary trusts

Purpose: This is the most flexible type of trust and can be used for income and capital distributions to beneficiaries. The trustees have the discretion as to who benefits. Income and capital is distributed to the beneficiaries (and potential beneficiaries – who can be from a wide class, such as children and remoter issue of the settlor) according to their needs. The beneficiaries can include the widow or widower of the settlor. Income may be accumulated (for up to 21 years for most older trusts, but see the changes brought by the *Perpetuities and Accumulations Act 2009* where the time limit for accumulations was abolished), and the trustees have wide investment and distribution powers, even to sub-trusts.

A transfer into a discretionary trust is a chargeable event, subject to exemptions, such as the nil rate band and BPR and APR reliefs. The trust may suffer periodic ten-yearly charges as well as exit charges. Non-exempted settlements made over the nil rate band will attract lifetime inheritance tax (at 20%), and assets transferred would usually attract CGT hold-over relief. As spouses and civil partners have their own nil rate bands, they could set up two trusts, or multiple trusts on different days, each with its own nil rate band. These are known as Pilot trusts. In this way, unless growth in the trust assets are substantial, IHT could be minimised for many years, as well as the periodic and exit charges. Neither the settlor nor his spouse or civil partner should be a beneficiary. If they are included this will be a reservation of benefit and the settlement value could fall back into the settlor's estate for IHT purposes, and income tax would ordinarily be charged on the settlor. The settlor can include a widow or widower though without the income tax and GWR rules applying.

Where the trust is set up for the 'vulnerable' (*FA 2005 ss 23-33*), from 6th April 2004, there are dispensations for income tax and the trustees pay tax at the same level as the beneficiary would have paid, and the tax allowances and tax rates apply for the beneficiary. A joint tax election must be made by the trustees and the vulnerable beneficiary.

Life assurance policy trusts

Purpose: To pass on the benefit of life assurance policies without exposure to IHT. Life assurance policies held in trust will not be subject to IHT on death and can escape the estate of the policy owner. Policy proceeds also avoid probate and should be payable independently of the probate process. If a qualifying policy it will also be income tax and capital gains tax free.

The trust most commonly used is a flexible trust, and this is provided free of charge by the life office providing the policy. However, any form of trust could be used, and with some trusts there could be tax charges on periodic events and exits. In the main though, policy proceeds may arise into trust, but are usually immediately distributed to beneficiaries or used to pay for estate liabilities and therefore no accumulation takes place in the long term that would be taxable or subject to charges. Trusts that definitely escape charges and IHT at present are bare trusts. Also exempt are policies in trust to repay a mortgage, policies paying life cover for families on death, most policies where the proceeds are paid out of the trust and are not accumulated, or policies where the value is under the nil rate band.

There is a difference between life policies for family protection and investment bonds underwritten as life policies. The latter are not exempt unless under the nil rate band or part of a DGT (discounted gift trust) arrangement that has immediate IHT reliefs, where the balance is a PET falling out of your estate after seven years.

Business life policies held in trust for surviving partners or shareholders to fund their purchase of the deceased's business share will be exempt if in trust and written in conjunction with a suitable double option agreement governing the sale and purchase of the business share. There is unlikely to be an accumulation in the trust (which might qualify the trust as discretionary and therefore IHT-taxable) as the proceeds of the policy are usually paid out to surviving partners or shareholders immediately on the death of the deceased in order to fund the survivors' purchase of the deceased's business share. If there is no double option agreement then the proceeds of the sale of the business share could be taxable in the estate of the deceased; the proceeds will also fall into the estate for IHT if the agreement was a firm 'buy and sell' agreement (viewed by HMRC as a sale agreement pre-death) rather than a double option agreement.

Individual and business trusts are important trust instruments. They will receive the policy proceeds on death and distribute them in accordance with any agreements, or if no agreement is in place, to the named beneficiaries.

Private charitable trusts

Purpose: To provide funds to be used for charitable purposes. This is most appropriate where the individual wishes to support individual personal charities rather than make contributions to public charities. The charity need not be in the UK to qualify.

There must be compliance with the Charities Commission and tax exemptions are available if the criteria are met. The gift to the trust is exempt from IHT and capital gains tax. There is also an exemption from stamp duty. Trading profits may also be exempt from tax where the trade carries out the charity's primary purpose.

Offshore trusts

Purpose: To take advantage of beneficial offshore tax regimes, or to protect the gifting of overseas assets. To qualify, the trustees must be resident offshore (outside the UK). The type of trust will be discretionary, or life-interest (interest-in-possession) or an accumulation-and-maintenance trust. Settlors may favour this type of trust to deal with assets held abroad, and believe that offshore trustees can be more flexible.

Offshore trusts and their taxation largely depend on the residency status of the trustees, the settlor and the beneficiaries, and also the domicile of the settlor and beneficiaries. HMRC are seriously examining all of these aspects on a continuous basis, and especially where there is perceived loss to the Exchequer. Where the settlor and the beneficiary are both non-domiciled, then there is an exemption from IHT and CGT. If income arises and is kept offshore, there is no income tax payable. If the settlor is non-domiciled and the beneficiary is UK domiciled, there is an exemption from IHT. There are complex anti-avoidance measures for offshore trusts, and a settlor may be liable to UK tax even if he or she does not benefit from the trust.

If the settlor is UK domiciled and makes a gift into an offshore trust, there could be a lifetime IHT charge at 20% if the gift is in excess of available exemptions. Unless the property is excluded property, if the settlor is a discretionary beneficiary when the trust is created, the GWR rules will apply and the property will fall into his estate for IHT purposes. A settlor must not be domiciled or deemed domiciled in the UK to transfer assets held abroad to trustees to avoid IHT on making settlements to an offshore trust. Similarly, if a beneficiary has an interest in an offshore trust, this could be subject to IHT in his estate, depending on the interest held, and if the settlor was domiciled in the UK – if not, at the date the settlement was made, then usually there is no IHT payable in the beneficiary's estate. The rules are complex and professional guidance is required if contemplating an offshore trust.

Generally

There are many versions of different types of trusts available, depending on individual requirements. It is important to note that once a trust is set up and you make a settlement or gift to it, your actions are generally irreversible. If you, as settlor to the trust, reserve a benefit or benefit from a trust, then the value of the trust asset will be taxable in your estate, if you have used up available exemptions. Making a settlement usually implies a loss of control over the asset. However, for some trusts, the settlor may remain as a trustee, or will have the power to remove and appoint trustees, or leave a letter of wishes to trustees, and have some measure of control through the trustees. The Government has been tightening up on trust legislation, but have produced clarity in many respects on what is currently allowable or not. Trusts do give choices and options in financial planning, and different types of trusts suit different circumstances.

12

Your Home

IHT and the family home – how to save your home from the taxman, whilst staying in it. Passing on the value of the home to your heirs; using your home for long-term care costs and to draw down capital from it. Strategies to reduce your estate value, including equity release and taking loans. The importance of wills and trusts.

For many people, where the family home is the principal asset, the ability to pass it on intact on death, or to use its equity for long-term care and other capital requirements, is a most important aspect of their planning, if not *the* most important aspect. Most people purchase a principal residence to live in, and to provide accommodation for family members; the value of the home as an investment asset is usually secondary. Yet for many, the family home is also a store of value that can be used to supplement income in retirement, or to enable children to get themselves onto the housing ladder. For others, once the mortgage is paid off, the home itself will not be put at risk for any reason.

Over 10% of the present home-owning population will have their homes subject to inheritance taxes, and this could be higher in London and the South East than elsewhere. The nil rate band in 2019/20 is £325,000, and many homes are worth more than that, so becoming subject to inheritance tax, especially when investment and other assets are added. Losing your home because of inheritance taxes is therefore a very real possibility for some, and many tax and other strategies have been developed to protect the family home and families. The transferable NRB regime from 9th October 2007 will protect most homes from IHT by enabling married couples (and civil partnerships) to utilise both their NRBs. However, estates worth £650,000 or more will still be vulnerable to IHT (for married couples and civil partners) and for £325,000 or more for unmarried couples and single people. The Emergency Budget of 8 July 2015 has added an additional nil rate band known as the family allowance or residential nil rate band (RNRB), which began in April 2015 at £100,000 and rise to £175,000 per person if the home passes to direct descendants, which will ease the IHT burden occasioned by escalating house values.

Objectives

The main objectives in planning around the family home will be as follows:

- minimising inheritance tax for your heirs
- making sure the home does not have to be sold to pay inheritance taxes
- ensuring that children and dependants can inherit from you
- preserving the home as a 'store of value' to release equity to use for liveable needs, retirement income and long-term care, as well as debt reduction
- providing for spouse and dependants' accommodation on your death
- dealing with the home if you have to go in to long-term care.

Principal concerns in this planning process will be:

- deciding on the best planning strategies for your home now and in the future
- having simple structures to consider, rather than complex tax planning, if this can be avoided – for most people.

The present position

Ownership of your home may be as a single person, as joint tenants, as tenants in common, or through a structure such as a company or a trust. Your home may be in the UK or abroad. Your home may have a mortgage or be used as security for debt; or it may be unencumbered, with no liabilities attaching to it.

Most couples wish to continue living in the home until both parties have died. Most would wish the home or its value to be passed on to their children, dependants or relatives. You may have dependants living in the home, and these could range from children (who may be adults) to grandparents or remoter relatives, such as aunts or uncles. You would need to provide for them, should you die, and decisions need to be taken around the home.

The family home can be an emotive issue. You might wish to leave your home to your children for example, while they may actually be quite content to receive its cash value instead.

It is therefore important to ensure that family financial planning takes place and what you do is not done in isolation from family objectives. It could save you a lot of time and money with your planning.

Future planning

You can plan strategies for IHT mitigation which can be put into practice during your lifetime or after your death, the latter through your will and the use of trusts. It is pointed out at the outset that there are many different tax strategies available to you, and not all of them will be covered here. Over the years, the Government has come down heavily on the majority of tax planning strategies, in particular with regard to lease carve-outs and gifting the home but remaining in it, without paying any rent.

Planning for your own lifetime

Taking into account your objectives, you would have a home, which together with other assets could be subject to inheritance tax. Every individual, no matter what their age, has the nil rate band for inheritance tax purposes. Currently this is worth £325,000 in 2019/20 (and from 2017, if married and you own your own home and leave it to descendants, an additional NRB of £100,000 rising to £175,000 by 2020, is available per person – the residential nil rate band (RNRB) – but there are rules to be satisfied first). If the value of your total estate, including the family home, is below this figure, then on your death, no inheritance tax will result. If you jointly own your home, then on death, only your share of it falls into your estate for IHT. Solicitors may advise you to sever a joint tenancy to create what is known as 'tenants in common'. If a joint tenant, on death, your share automatically passes to your spouse or civil partner, for example. If a tenant in common, then you can leave your share to whomsoever you wish, including a trust created in your will. Transferable nil rate bands should give you up to £650,000 IHT reliefs in 2019/20 for married couples and civil partners, plus the RNRB which in 2019/20 is £150,000.

Gifting the family home

The home may be gifted by you to others – for example, your children. This will be a potentially exempt transfer (PET), and the value of the home will be out of your estate after surviving for seven years – that is, provided you have not reserved a benefit to the gift. Staying in the house rent-free after making the gift is seen by HMRC as a reservation of benefit, and the value of the gift will fall back into your estate under GWR (Gifts with reservation) rules. If you gift the home and move abroad, then you may escape the GWR trap. If you return periodically and stay in the house, be sure to pay a market related rent; otherwise you could be paying tax under the pre-owned assets tax regime (POAT) on an assumed rental.

POAT was introduced in the *FA 2004 s. 84* and *Schedule 15*, creating a new tax from the 2005/06 tax year. If you make a lifetime gift and enjoy a benefit from it, you are subject to income tax; otherwise the asset falls back into your estate for IHT purposes. You can make an election not to pay the income tax and for the asset to be liable to IHT on the value instead (in the March 2007 budget the election date has been extended and details are included in the *Finance Act 2007*). There is a *de minimis* exemption of £5,000, so the couple visiting their former home in the UK and staying there (without reserving a benefit to do so), could manage short periods without being taxed under the POAT rules or having GWR rules applied.

For many, though, either paying rent to the new owners for staying in your gifted home, or paying income tax on the rental value, is unaffordable, and gifting the asset and staying there may therefore not work well for them.

Selling the home and staying there rent-free

If you sell your home, there are various options to enable you to remain in it, rent-free.

Home reversions

Here, a portion of your home is sold to a home reversion company in exchange for a cash lump sum. You have the cash to spend on what you wish, and can remain in the home rent-free. The stakes may be high – some home reversion schemes buy 70% or 90% of your home for perhaps 30% of its value. Your share remaining can pass to your heirs on death, to be sold to the same company at that time. You must be over the age of 65 to use this scheme. The value for IHT will only be the remaining value of your house at death. Most schemes have a negative equity guarantee or payout value at death. Most schemes allow for the fact that you may go into long-term care and allow the house to be retained until death of the last-dying.

Lifetime mortgages – equity release

A lifetime mortgage company enables you to release equity from your home and pays you a lump sum, to use as you wish. The mortgage and its interest ramps up against the value of your home and on the last death, the house is sold and the balance of any equity value is paid to your heirs. You may stay in the house rent free for your lifetimes. The value for IHT will only be the remaining value of your house at death. Most schemes have a negative equity guarantee. Most schemes allow for the fact that you may go into long-term care and allow the house to be retained until death of the last-dying.

Selling the house, living there and having IHT benefits

One scheme is that your home is valued and sold to a bank's fund for cash. The cash is then invested into an offshore bond with your children or grandchildren as beneficiaries. The bond also qualifies for a discount for IHT purposes. You must be aged over 65, and can live in your former home without tax penalty until the death of the last dying of the couple (if you are a couple). The house is effectively out of your estates for IHT – the minimum house value is £400,000 to qualify for this plan.

A variation is to take a loan secured against the house and invest that into a DGT (Discounted Gift Trust). A portion is immediately out of your estate (the discount). The investment gives you an income and pays the interest on the mortgage loan. On death the value of the commercial loan reduces your estate as a liability, subject to special provisions where the loan is used to invest in IHT-exempt assets (see below). In addition, the DGT element reduces the estate so that usually the full value of the house is out of your estate. Both schemes avoid the POAT and other GWR and benefit charges.

Secured loans for investment in IHT-exempt assets
From 6 April 2013 special provisions apply to a mortgage taken out on the family home and invested into 100% exempt from IHT assets (farmland, EIS, AIM etc.), where the loan reduces the value of the home subject to IHT, and the assets acquired do not attract IHT. In these circumstances, the amount of the loan must first be deducted from the value of the assets it was used to acquire, not the property it is secured on. The loan and the IHT-exempt assets cancel each other out in the IHT calculation and no tax is saved. This legislation was brought in to limit the deductions from the value of an estate for liabilities owed by the deceased on death. Avoidance schemes included exploiting the current rules that allow a deduction regardless of whether or not the liabilities are paid after death, or how the borrowed funds have been used.

Reducing the value of the home for IHT purposes and staying in it
Equity release using a lifetime mortgage, and home reversion plans where a portion of the home is sold and you stay in it, both reduce the value of the home for IHT purposes. However, they also reduce your asset value base, if the money released is spent. If the money is invested, then it may increase your asset base, but also increase the potential of your new assets falling into your estate for IHT purposes. You should carefully plan your income and expenditure patterns so that income above normal expenditure can be gifted to children or others, thus reducing your estate.

It may also be possible to release equity by borrowing against the property for investment purposes, with a view to creating an estate loss on your death, if the loan is outstanding at that time. The following scheme involves using the equity in the property as security only for a loan that is used to invest into a discount gift trust arrangement:

1. The loan itself is secured on the property and interest is payable.
2. The investment into the DGT provides for an immediate IHT discount, depending on age, gender and state of health.
3. The investment provides an income that is used to service the IHT loan.

4. The income is set from the outset at a level higher than the prevailing loan interest rates to provide for interest rate movements, if a fixed term is not taken.
5. It can also provide additional income for the recipient, if required.

On death the value of the loan itself is a deduction in the estate (but see the section on inheritance tax and loans above – always take professional advice).

Other than the initial discounted gift trust investment which is immediately out of your estate, the balance is a potentially exempt transfer (PET), and out of the estate after surviving for seven years, as well as the growth on the investment.

The investment can continue for beneficiaries, such as children. If the house is sold, the loan arrangements can 'move' with the house, to a new one. It is suitable for people who wish to significantly increase their IHT reduction in as short a planning period as possible. The maximum loan-to-value ratio is usually about 70%.

This route is often preferred to normal equity release or reversion schemes as it creates another deduction – of the loan itself – for inheritance tax planning purposes. You are also in control and do not have to sell your home or have loan interest rolling up against your home (as the interest is paid by you). However, as with any loan scheme secured against property, you may lose your property/capital if loan interest payments are not kept up. A few mortgage lenders will make mortgage loans to the elderly, so these are available.

Other plans and strategies

One can reduce the value of the home for IHT whilst providing an income. Some of the areas you can invest into are:

1. A discounted gift trust. A portion is immediately out of your estate (the discount), the balance of the fund is a PET and you must survive for seven years. The investment can provide you with an income for life. Your house value is also reduced for IHT purposes if equity is released from it.
2. A discounted gift and loan trust – as above but with more flexibility.
3. Buy a purchased life annuity (PLA) with your capital and use the annuity payments to fund a life policy in trust. On your death the annuity ceases with no tax charge and the life policy kicks in immediately with all the value of the asset out of your estate. The income stream is also tax efficient. You do not have to wait for seven years to save 40% on your capital.
4. Purchase of a business either with children or other beneficiaries. On death after two years, the value passes tax free to them (100% BPR).

5. Similarly, the purchase of EIS shares – usually an EIS portfolio to spread the investment risk – will be out of your estate after two years and could give you dividend income.

If you need an income to repay a mortgage or loan secured against property, then choose an option that gives an income; if using equity release to invest to reduce IHT, then no servicing is required for a lifetime mortgage or a home reversion plan, i.e. you do not have to service the capital amount released, and you have more flexible options.

Gifting assets to trust

The gift of the family home to a trust (unless a bare trust) will be a chargeable event and lifetime tax may be payable if over the nil rate band and no other exemptions apply. If the value of your share is within the nil rate band then no lifetime IHT will be payable. However, take into account the GWR rules on reserving a benefit, and the POAT rules on not paying a commercial rent if you stay in the house.

Leases

The taking or grant of a lease can be a useful estate planning tool. The donor would gift a property to the children as a PET or to trustees for them. In return the property would be leased back at full market rent. This way there is no deemed settlement under *IHTA s.43(3)*, and no GWR as full consideration has been paid. Income tax could be payable for leases of less than 50 years under *ICTA 1998 s.34*.

One of the previously-used estate planning mechanisms was to have a lease for life with security of tenure in the property. The donor would pay a cash lump sum for this lease for life and that amount would be out of his estate. Such a lease would be for between 50 and 90 years' 'lease carve-out' or a 'reversionary lease' attaching to your property.

Prior lease carve-outs (where the donor grants a lease to himself and someone else as joint tenants for a term equal to life expectancy plus 5-10 years) have been heavily attacked by the Government. Using leases it had been simple planning to retain a lease over a property with residential rights, after gifting away the freehold and thus avoiding IHT on the property. The lease carve-out worked like this: the lease was for a fixed term; the reversion of the lease was given to the intended beneficiary; on death the full value of the house passed to the donee usually free of IHT, as seven years would have passed since the date of the gift. If some years of the lease remained there would be a very low value for IHT. This type of arrangement was stopped through legislation following taxpayer success at law in the Ingram case.

(*Ingram and ano v IRC [1999] STC 37*). *IHTA 1984 ss.102A-C* has made it a reservation of benefit for gifts of land used in this way. However, if you have exemptions available to you, such as the spouse exemption, or if full consideration has been paid, this type of lease arrangement will still work for you. The only problem is now the pre-owned asset tax (POAT) regime that came in from 6th April 2005, where on retaining a benefit without paying full consideration for it, it could have it fall back into your estate for IHT purposes.

Planning for after death

Usually the value of the family home is a taxable asset in your estate if it exceeds any exemptions you may have.

There is a special dispensation for a family home which is a farmhouse and comprises part of a farm for APR reliefs. Its value should not be subject to inheritance tax, providing the specified criteria apply. The definition of 'agricultural property' in *IHTA 1984 s 115(2)* includes the farmhouse, together with the land occupied with it, if it is 'of a character appropriate' to the property, which will be the relevant agricultural land.

100% spouse exemption and nil rate band trust

UK-domiciled spouses and civil partners may leave 100% of their assets to each other and no IHT is payable. This is known as the 'spouse exemption'. You also have your nil rate band of £325,000, which, under the new rules introduced on 9 October 2007, the unused percentage of the first deceased's NRB can be transferred to your surviving spouse or civil partner. Under the rules applying before 9 October 2007 your NRB would have been effectively lost if the spouse exemption applies, because the nil rate band was not utilised and could not be transferred. Now under the new NRB transferable regime, the parties can ensure that both NRBs are used effectively. However, there is another way to make use of your nil rate band without transferring it to your spouse or civil partner, by bypassing your spouse or civil partner's estate and leaving some assets directly to, say, your children. This is done by creating a discretionary 'bypass trust', also known as a 'nil rate band trust' or a Pilot trust, for the value of the nil rate band at the time in your will and the unused NRB from a deceased spouse or civil partner. Selected assets such as your share of the house can then pass to the trust for the benefit of the children and the surviving spouse can remain in the house without the reservation of benefit or POAT rules applying. You can create this trust during your lifetime, or you can create it in your will (known as a 'will trust').

IHT Spouse exemption if non domiciled

FA 2013 radically changes the IHT treatment where one spouse is UK domiciled and the other (recipient) is not. Up to 5 April 2013, such transfers were subject to a lifetime allowance of £55,000. After 6 April 2013 the IHT exempt amount that can be transferred from a UK domiciled spouse/civil partner to a non UK domiciled spouse/civil partner is increased to the NRB amount, currently £325,000. A non UK domiciled spouse/civil partner can elect to be treated as UK domiciled for IHT. This means assets can pass between spouses without an IHT tax charge. There are rules governing the election. The election ceases to be valid if the individual making the election lives outside the UK for more than 4 successive tax years. So you can be UK resident and live in the UK and retain the non UK domicile, and the election would be valid.

Bypass trusts/nil rate band trusts

Previously it was relatively easy to set up a bypass trust to pass your share of your house to children or grandchildren with an interest in possession to the surviving spouse, ensuring that the value would be removed from the survivor's estate for IHT purposes. However, the rules have been tightened, and unless great care is taken these trusts may now be caught by the new rules introduced in 2006 relating to trust taxation. As a result, wills may now have to be redrafted to take account of the new provisions or to make changes that are more tax-efficient.

Giving away the house on death

Passing your share of the property into a trust for the benefit of your children (for example), where your surviving spouse or partner may benefit from its use, is one way to utilise your NRB without transferring it to a spouse or civil partner. Usually, the trust is set up and on your death your share of the property passes to the trust. Your spouse or partner would retain a 'life interest', or 'interest in possession' (IIP), in the trust asset. This IIP was formerly not taxable for IHT purposes, but after 22nd March 2006, unless the life interest ceases absolutely on the surviving spouse's death, the value of the asset will fall into the life tenant's estate. So, in order to avoid IHT in the survivor's estate, it is now essential that the life interest does indeed absolutely cease on the survivor's death.

If the interest in possession ends on the death or during the lifetime of the life tenant and the assets of the trust pass to another individual absolutely, there are no IHT implications. If, on death of the life tenant, the assets remain in trust, then the value of those assets are included in the estate of the deceased and the new trust is taxed under the discretionary trust rules. It is therefore important that trust's interest in the house passes to the beneficiaries immediately on the death of the life tenant.

Debt and IOU schemes

Instead of giving half the property away on death, many find it more flexible and preferable to have it wholly owned by the surviving spouse. One way to achieve this, and still utilise the first dying partner's NRB, is to establish a trust to receive the first dying partner's share in the house on death, and have the trust transfer (or re-assign) the property share to the surviving partner in exchange for an IOU for the relevant amount. The IOU (for 'I owe you') is a promise to pay in the future – in effect, an open-ended debt. The IOU does not have to be paid during the surviving partner's lifetime, but will be realised on death of the survivor and distribution of their estate (part of the value of which will go to the trust in settlement of the IOU).

The net effect is that the trust accepts an IOU with a charge on the property, and the survivor has complete ownership of the property. The survivor's debt to the trust is deductible from their estate on death. However, *FA 2013* has now introduced restrictions on the deductions of liabilities, and to be deducted *it will have to actually be paid.*

This scheme gives the surviving spouse more flexibility than if the house share remains in the trust. The whole process can be managed without registering an actual sale of the property share so that there is no charge to Stamp Duty Land Tax (SDLT). If not planned properly there could be a liability to SDLT, for example where the survivor buys the interest from the trust for cash instead of the IOU route – this puts cash into the trust, but suffers SDLT.

Planning with IOUs needs to be very carefully considered so as to avoid unnecessary charges. There are two main routes:

1. The personal representatives of the deceased borrow money from the bank (to the value of the property interest) and gift it into the trust. The trustees loan the money to the surviving spouse, who repays the original bank loan in exchange for the property share (i.e. the survivor pays the estate's debt in exchange for the estate's property interest).
2. Alternatively, the will authorises the trustees to accept a debt owed personally by the survivor in lieu of or in exchange for the property share.

There are variations, including the personal representatives imposing a charge on the house in favour of the discretionary trustees.

The debt must be repayable on demand, and interest provided for at commercial rates (although it need not be paid). The IOU or debt scheme will only work if the recipient of the benefit (i.e. the property share) is the same person as the debtor (the party owing money to the trust). This could be a surviving spouse or the trustees of a will trust. It is important that the trustees provide evidence of a trust through their conduct, noting, for example, that they have discussed at regular intervals that interest could be paid or the loan repaid before the survivor's death.

New ruling

In a recent decision (February 2007), the Special Tax Commissioners stated that in certain circumstances the creation of tenancies in common in a jointly owned property is artificial and falls foul of the anti-avoidance rules under *IHTA 1986*. In the case of *Phizackerley* the following occurred. Dr and Mrs Phizackerley severed their joint tenancies and made themselves tenants in common. Their wills allowed for the creation of discretionary trusts and for their respective shares of the house to be left in trust on death. Mrs Phizackerley died and her share of the property duly went into trust. The trust subsequently accepted an IOU from Dr Phizackerley in return for which her share in the property was assented to him. In essence Dr Phizackerley owed £153,000 to the trust set up by his wife to hold her share of the family home. He continued to live in the home until his death.

The HMRC disallowed the IOU as a deduction in the estate of Dr Phizackerley on his death. Their reason was that the arrangement was artificial, that Mrs Phizackerley had not worked, and had therefore not contributed to the purchase of the family home; and that her property share derived from Dr Phizackerley in the first place, so that the return or loan of the property share back to him was circular.

It is believed that the decision will not be appealed. Therefore we now have a strange case law that will affect a number of related areas of estate planning, including: the equalisation of estates (where one spouse gifts assets to the other); the severing of tenancies and leaving the family home or a share of it in trust; the fact that non-monetary contributions to the family wealth might not count in determining ownership rights relating to joint assets.

Future issues will then be:

1. Think before allowing a trust to make loans to a beneficiary for an IOU, and take advice – these schemes are particularly at risk if the money or assets loaned to the beneficiary can be said to have derived from the same beneficiary in the first place (the 'circular' principle).
2. Plan carefully any scheme to equalise estate assets. It seems that a change from joint tenancy to common tenancy might fall foul of HMRC if one party has not contributed financially to the purchase of the property.
3. Plan carefully when placing the family home or a part of it into trust on death. Make sure the trust's ownership is clear and unequivocal.
4. If possible leave liquid assets in the NRB trust rather than the family home – possibly created through life assurance, if you have insufficient assets).

Also, dying in the right order might help! Had Dr Phizackerley predeceased his wife, the situation would not have arisen. Her arrangements were disqualified since she was held to have been gifted the property-share by her husband, so making the transfer or loan back to him circular; had he died first, no-one could have argued that she had gifted her husband his share of the property! In conclusion, when creating a 'nil rate band trust' (or 'bypass trust') to keep certain assets out of the estate of the surviving partner in order to utilise your NRB, select the assets to go into the trust carefully. The house or share of the house as a family home should be a last resort. As well as the Phizackerley issues, there can be other problems. The will clause will usually say 'I leave so much of the nil rate band as it may be, at my death, in trust for the benefit of my children, and my surviving spouse to have the use and income of the asset(s) for his or her lifetime'. The problem with a house (or part of it) left in trust arises when you want to sell it or move home, and say half of it is owned by minor beneficiaries (or adult beneficiaries who cannot agree on a way forward). This can present real practical difficulties.

Other aspects

There are many different strategies available to reduce IHT and remain in the family home whilst doing it. There are ways of using the wealth in the family home for income, to supplement retirement funds, or for the purposes of long-term care costs or remaining in the family home during care. Wills are very important as the mechanism that drives your estate planning and the success of it. Also important are previous Enduring Powers of Attorney (EPAs) and current Lasting Powers of Attorney (LPAs) which enable someone to deal with your affairs should you become mentally incapable.

Note that whilst the emphasis above has been on inheritance tax planning, planning should also involve income tax, capital gains tax, stamp duty land tax, and these cannot be ignored.

The new transferable unused NRB allowance arising on 2nd death should be taken into account for all planning.

If you own then sell your principal private residence, there is no capital gains tax to pay. If you gift your private residence to another there may be inheritance tax to pay in advance at 20% if the gift is worth over £325,000 (the nil rate band), and a further 20% (tapered) if you do not survive for 7 years. If you gift your principal residence to another (or to a trust) but stay in the property without paying commercial rent, this could be a gift with reservation, where the PET rules do not apply and the house is inheritance taxable, and you may also be liable to an income tax charge. On death, the value of the house could be subject to inheritance tax if over the nil rate band.

New rules have changed the way CGT is crystallised when you sell your home. Usually the gain is covered by the principal private residence relief (PPR) to the extent that you have resided in the property. Historically, if you have resided in the property at any point you are deemed to have occupied the property for the last 3 years. This has now been reduced to 18 months for disposals on or after 6 April 2014. The one exception is for disabled people (s225E *TCGA 1992* and sch 1A *FA 2005*) or persons in care homes which retains the 3 year rule subject to conditions. This is important in the context of letting your home then selling it and the amount of capital gains tax payable when it was not your PPR. Timing is critical and advice should be sought to either re-establish the home as your main residence before selling it, or to take into account the new 18 months residency period.

New legislation

Earlier payment of CGT on residential property

Where there is a capital gain, for example on buy to let property, s14 and Sch 2, FA 2019 included enabling legislation to bring the liability to CGT on gains on disposals by UK residents of residential property forward to 30 days after the date of disposal. The change takes effect for disposals on or after 6 April 2020. It essentially strips out the initial computation of gain from the self-assessment system and makes it a standalone report and payment (although self- assessment taxpayers will continue to also report the gain on their tax returns).

Disposals affected

The scope of the changes is set out in paras 1-2, Sch 2, FA 2019.

- Any direct or indirect disposal of land which meets the non-residence condition which occurs on or after 6 April 2019; and
- Any other direct disposal of UK land on which a residential property gain accrues and is made on or after 6 April 2020.

Non-resident disposals have been subject to a reporting regime since CGT became chargeable on residential property disposals by non- residents in 2015. Finance Act 2019 brings all other disposals of UK property of any type within the charge to CGT from 6 April 2019.

The following recent article (August 2015) written for *Tax Insider* considers the planning opportunities following the introduction of the additional nil rate band for passing on the family home and under which circumstances it applies.

"New IHT rules – is the family home really protected?"

Tony Granger covers the new IHT rules relating to the family home and inheritance tax announced in the Emergency Budget.

Inheritance tax is not just for the rich, it may affect middle class families as well. Soaring house values, particularly in London and the South East, have pushed house values up, and with that the prospect of increasing

IHT. Inheritance tax is paid at 40% of the taxable value of your estate after the nil rate band (NRB) of £325,000 has been deducted. The last dying of a married couple has the benefit of two nil rate bands at up to £650,000, if the first dying had not used their NRB fully , and the unused amount can pass to the survivor. However, on the death of the survivor, the family home would be sold or pass to the next generation or a third party and IHT may again become payable.

This issue had become a hot potato for the Government, who had made previous election promises to increase the nil rate band (it has been at £325,000 since 2009 and will endure at this level until 2021 now), but had not done so. The latest Budget announcements changed that position, by adding a further nil rate band amount for married couples (and civil partners) for passing on the family home to direct descendants at a later date.

However, one must consider whether the family will really be protected from IHT for the value of the family home.

New Family Home Allowance
From 6 April 2017 the government will introduce a 'family home allowance' that will raise the Inheritance Tax threshold to £500,000 for an individual and £1 million for couples.

The new main residence or additional nil rate band does not come into effect until April 2017, so for nearly two years taxpayers will only have the existing frozen nil rate band of £325,000.

The additional nil rate band will increase gradually: £100,000 in 2017/18; £125,000 in 2018/19; £150,000 in 2019/20; and £175,000 in 2020/21.

Where it will apply
- *A residential property left to one or more direct descendants on death.*
- *You can leave the property to children and grandchildren only.*
- *Applies to one residential property only. That property can be nominated after death.*
- *Unused portion of additional NRB of £175,000 can be transferred to the surviving spouse.*
- *If the property is sold or downsized the relief could continue.*

Downside
- *The relief is tapered and gradual and not immediate – 6 April 2017 is the earliest to benefit.*
- *Maximum benefit only in 2020/21 tax year.*
- *Only direct descendants can benefit, otherwise the relief is lost.*
- *Childless couples receive no relief at all, losing a maximum of £140,000 in IHT.*

- *Large estates (not only the house value) worth over £2 million net lose the relief through taper on a £1 for £2 basis. At £2.35 million the additional relief is lost completely.*
- *People will stay in their homes and not move, to ensure larger inheritances.*
- *Possible implications if equity is released to pay for care costs (the house is effectively sold) if going in to care, where the reliefs could be lost.*

Tax Tips and Financial Planning

Effectively, if you own your own home and wish to leave it to your children and grandchildren once both owners have died, by 2020 your estate could save an additional £140,000 in IHT. However, immediate savings are negligible. You may not wish to leave the family home to children or grandchildren, or may wish for a trust to be set up to protect a vulnerable beneficiary, or spouse, and in these cases, careful will planning is essential. If your overall taxable estate is worth over £2.35 million, then the additional relief is not available to you, even if your home is valued at £1 million. Consider other IHT planning using life assurance in trust, making bequests to charity, for example to reduce IHT. In certain instances the family home is not fully protected from IHT, as described above.

13

Business and Farming Assets

IHT and business and farming assets. Reliefs available. How business property reliefs can be passed on to family members when you die. Succession planning for businesses and how to avoid future inheritance and other taxes.

Business owners face particular challenges in planning what happens to their businesses after they die or retire: who to pass the business on to and in what format, and how to protect the business and its new owners from inheritance and other taxes – otherwise known as succession planning.

There are different issues arising, depending on the type of business structure involved. The main business structures available in the UK are: public limited companies (PLCs), private limited companies, partnerships, limited liability partnerships (LLPs), and sole traders. Farming may be carried on under any of the structures mentioned above, and is no different to any other business, except that agricultural property reliefs may be available instead of, or in addition to business property reliefs.

There are in excess of 5 million businesses in the UK today, and all would be classed as wealth builders. Creative wealth accumulation and protection strategies are an important component of the thinking of business owners and for those who work in the business. For those without investments or inheritances, the only other source of wealth building may be through their business or employer. Protecting what you have built up is therefore most important for all of them. Succession planning issues must also be considered. Who will replace you when you retire, die or become disabled? Family-owned businesses may wish for their family members to come into the business, and shares and ownership will pass to those siblings in due course. See my *Succession Planning Simplified* book (Management Books 2000) for an in-depth account of succession planning.

Public limited companies (PLCs)

If you have shares in a PLC, whether as an employee or as an investor, these shares could be liable to inheritance taxes. It depends on whether the shares are listed on the AIM stock exchange or not. If shares are listed on AIM then, if they qualify (not all shares on AIM qualify – this depends on the classification and trade of the company and its shares), and if you hold the shares for at least two years, their value will fall out of your estate for inheritance tax purposes. If the shares are listed on a main market, such as the FTSE, then their value will fall into your estate for inheritance tax purposes; these shares will not be subject to business property inheritance tax reliefs (BPR), as this relief applies only to unquoted companies.

On death, shares pass to your heirs or beneficiaries. If shares are left to a spouse or civil partner, then the spouse exemption will apply and there will be no IHT applying on the first death. Unless the recipient spouse or civil partner has remarried or entered into another civil partnership, the value of the shares should be liable to IHT in the second estate. Planning may involve the setting up of a bypass discretionary trust in your will to leave your shares to children or other family members or third parties. If the shares are left to charity, then no IHT is payable on them, as exempt assets.

If the shares are gifted to a discretionary trust, then their value may be subject to a lifetime IHT charge, after deducting annual allowances and other exemptions, and the value of the nil rate band at the time, at a rate of 20%. Dividends will be taxed at 37.5% in the trust. Beneficiaries with a lower tax rate may reclaim tax paid by the trustees.

There may be succession planning opportunities for small PLCs, for a retiring shareholder or one who dies, to pass shares to family members who may be employed in the company.

Private limited companies

Qualifying shares in a private limited company will be unquoted shares. As long as the shares have been held for at least two years, they may be bequeathed to family members and third parties free of inheritance tax, because of business property reliefs attaching. These business property reliefs are usually at 100% of value, and the recipient of the shares will continue to benefit from the reliefs, and their successors on their deaths.

Cash or shares

Shareholders may decide amongst themselves that they would rather their families had cash instead of shares. Small private companies may not have a dividend policy (where cash dividends are paid annually to shareholders), or may have a restricted dividend policy where dividends are only paid on certain types of shares. In general shares in private limited companies cannot be relied on to produce future income streams by way of dividends. Privately-owned companies may also be vulnerable to economic downturns, more susceptible to fraud causing their downfall, or may fail if a key person dies or retires.

There are other reasons too, why it will be better to have cash than shares. Minority shareholdings in a private limited company may have a much-reduced value, and can be hard to sell since the shares are not listed or traded in any established stock markets. Certainly, holding a minority stake in what will becomes someone else's company will not give the holder any control and few rights. In addition, those remaining as owners of the company may not wish to deal with the departed's heirs in the future, and would rather have shareholders who work in the company.

Double option agreement

Passing on private company shares, for anything other than succession planning reasons, may not achieve the income expectations that you require for family members in the longer term.

For these reasons, shareholders in private companies often enter into a 'double option' agreement, whereby they agree that the survivors will purchase the deceased's shares for a pre-determined sum. Life policies are taken out in trust to ensure that the share purchase funds are available on the death of the shareholder. In terms of the double option agreement, on the death of the shareholder, the shares owned by him pass to the surviving shareholders, and cash passes to his estate.

No inheritance tax is payable on the policy proceeds used to buy the shares from the deceased's estate. Under the double option the shares are deemed to be sold post-death, enabling the proceeds to be free of IHT. Note that a simple 'buy and sell agreement' contracting for the future sale of the shares, unlike the option, is seen as an agreement for the sale of shares pre-death and will be subject to inheritance taxes.

Premiums paid by the company for the shareholder protection policies are not deductible to the business, and will be added back to the individual's income for tax purposes and national insurance. Paying premiums will be a dilution of an estate for inheritance tax purposes. However, every individual has £3,000 worth of annual exemptions than can be used (£6,000, if no gift was made in the preceding year), as well as paying out of 'normal income' excess to living requirements, and the payment of premiums will reduce the estate of the payer without IHT penalties in most cases.

Cash received in exchange for shares enables investments to be made that can be income-producing, and also have growth potential. The price of the shares is usually pre-determined in the shareholder's double option agreement, and should be updated each year. Valuing private company shares can be difficult, and the range extensive, with many different valuation options to choose from. Some companies' shareholder agreements optimistically anticipate a surplus from the life policy after purchase of the shares, and stipulate that any excess life assurance cash created on death should be distributed to the survivors, or paid to the business to cover 'keyperson' costs in replacing the deceased at work.

Succession planning

It may be that for succession planning reasons the shareholder decides to bequeath his shares to his children on his death, or his spouse or civil partner, to enable control of the company to remain in the hands of the family. In this case, providing the shares qualify, 100% of the value of the shares will be free from inheritance taxes because of BPR.

Directors' loan accounts

The existence of directors' loans can have a significant adverse impact on the IHT position. Where a director loans money to the company, he is introducing his own capital into the company, and the company owes him the money, which is usually available on demand. A director's loan account is not protected by BPR and its value falls into your estate for inheritance tax purposes. Consider the scenario where a director introduces £100,000 into the business when it is started. Over the years, dividends are declared, but the director does not take the dividend, allowing his director's loan account to increase with tax-paid dividends. He also introduces private assets into the business, such as his motor vehicle and these assets increase his loan account. Over a five-year period, the director's loan account has grown to £250,000. On his death, his estate could be liable for £100,000 worth of IHT, assuming there are no exemptions, such as the nil rate band, available.

It is not unusual to find directors' loan accounts left in a business where the director has retired. In one case on which I was asked to advise, the amount left in a company that had been sold to third parties was £850,000! The amount only came to the notice of his family on his death, and they were unaware of his financial affairs. That oversight cost the family £340,000 in inheritance taxes, and could easily have been avoided. There are ways to remove the director's loan account from the business and to invest the money into an IHT 'wrapped' investment, or to gift it to family members and survive for seven years to have it out of your estate altogether. The director's loan account is replaced with commercial bank finance should the company have been using the money for working capital. Interest on the commercial finance is tax deductible to the company, thus reducing its cost.

Alternatively, a director's loan account can be capitalised into ordinary or preference shares. In this way, shares can become IHT exempt.

Buying back shares

On the death of a shareholder, the company could also buy back the shares, thus providing cash to the estate. This may happen where there is no double option agreement in place and there is no other marketplace to sell the shares, where the surviving shareholders do not have the cash to purchase the deceased's shares, and where the company does not want anyone else to have them. The company would buy back the shares and then cancel them. If this happens there will be an increase in value to other shareholders, and this may have capital gains tax implications for them, and for the seller. Note, however, that capital gains tax dies with you, and if you were deferring a capital gain at death, no CGT arises. The share buy-back should only happen after death and after probate, so that the estate qualifies for BPR on the shares. If it happened before (for example, the share buy-back was at retirement date), then cash is what arises in the estate and this could be subject to IHT, as no BPR will apply.

Own company

It is possible for an investor to set up his own company and to own 100% of the company's shares. The investor introduces capital into the company to buy the shares. These shares should qualify for 100% BPR on death, as long as they have been held for at least two years, and the company carried on a qualifying trade, and met other qualifying criteria. Product providers group together such companies and provide the company trade, sharing in the profits. One can also defer unlimited capital gains using this method and hold the shares until you die, when the capital gain dies with you.

Other companies

If you did not set up your own company, but invested into one or more unquoted companies under the Enterprise Investment Scheme (EIS) and Seed EIS (SEIS), then you would have 100% IHT reliefs after two years, unlimited capital gains tax deferral reliefs and also income tax relief at 30% of the amount invested up to £1 million for EIS and £100,000 for SEIS with 50% tax relief – but you must hold the investment(s) for at least three years to qualify for the income tax reliefs, and you must have an income tax liability to relieve. The new Seed EIS (SEIS) offers income tax relief of 50% on up to £100,000, irrespective of your marginal rate of tax.

Inheritance tax issues

Shares will be fully exempt from IHT on death and will also benefit from a tax-free uplift in base cost value for CGT purposes. It is also possible to transfer shares to individuals or to a family trust arrangement, with a hold-over election for capital gains tax. There is no immediate IHT liability because of the BPR exemption. Shares transferred to an individual will be a PET; shares transferred to a trust will be a CLT. Should the donor die within seven years, the PET will become chargeable; however, if the shares qualified for BPR, they would then be exempt from inheritance tax. Similarly, shares gifted to a discretionary, interest-in-possession or accumulation-and-maintenance trust, will be a chargeable event, as relevant property trusts. However, the business property relief exemption should apply in most cases, and shares will be exempt from the lifetime IHT charge of 20%. Shares not exempt will be subject to the charge, after taking into account the nil rate band and annual exemptions available.

Share transfer will enable the growth in the shares to be outside of the donor's estate. Other issues need to be taken into account, such as losing control through gifting away too many shares, or the need for personal dividends on a particular class of shares.

It is important to note that where a PET of shares has been made, and the donor dies within seven years, thus making the PET chargeable, BPR will only be available where the donee (recipient) has retained the shares until the donor's death, with the shares still qualifying then.

Capital gains tax

Taper relief ceased on 5 April 2008, when it and indexation allowance was replaced with entrepreneurs' relief. Like entrepreneurs' relief, taper relief also distinguished between business and non-business assets, with the capital gains tax due on business assets potentially giving a lowest rate of 10%. You may be able to pay less Capital Gains Tax when you sell (or 'dispose of') all or part of your business.

Entrepreneurs' relief means you'll pay tax at 10% on all gains on qualifying assets.

If you're selling all or part of your business, to qualify for relief, both of the following must apply:

- you're a sole trader or business partner
- you've owned the business for at least 2 years before the date you sell it

Hold-over relief enables the gift to be made free of capital gains tax at the time of disposal under *TCGA 1992 s.165*. The transferor's gain is eliminated. The gain again becomes chargeable when the transferee disposes of the gifted shares. The transferee inherits the transferor's indexed base cost. When the gift is made the recipient transferee's period of ownership begins, and if he holds the shares for two years, then entrepreneurs' relief will again apply.

Since 9th December 2003, hold-over relief cannot be claimed on transfers to a settlor-interested trust (where the spouse or civil partner, and from 6th April 2006, the settlor's dependant children can be an actual or a discretionary beneficiary of the trust). It is important then for hold-over reliefs to apply where they cannot benefit. Shares in trust that qualify for entrepreneurs' relief must be held for two years before being disposed of. There are stringent qualifying criteria for hold-over reliefs to apply, including the position that at least 80% of the company's activities must be in trading.

Gift hold-over relief

You may be able to claim gift hold-over Relief if you give away business assets (including certain shares) or sell them for less than they're worth to help the buyer.

Gift hold-over relief means:

- you do not pay Capital Gains Tax when you give away the assets
- the person you give them to pays Capital Gains tax (if any is due) when they sell (or 'dispose of') them

Tax is not usually payable on gifts to your husband, wife, civil partner or a charity.

Eligibility

The conditions for claiming relief depend on whether you're giving away business assets or shares.

If you're giving away business assets, you must:

- be a sole trader or business partner, or have at least 5% of voting rights in a company (known as your 'personal company')
- use the assets in your business or personal company

You can usually get partial relief if you used the assets only partly for your business.

If you're giving away shares, the shares must be in a company that's either:

- not listed on any recognised stock exchange, or
- your personal company

The company's main activities must be in trading, for example providing goods or services, rather than non-trading activities like investment.

Working out the relief

You do not pay Capital Gains Tax on any assets you give away.

You might need to pay tax if you:

- sell an asset for less than it's worth to help the buyer
- make a gain on what you paid for it

Example

You sell a shop worth £81,000 to your brother for £40,000. It cost you £23,000. Include the £17,000 gain (£40,000 minus £23,000) when you're working out your total taxable gain.

The person you give the asset to will need to include its cost when they work out the gain on the business assets or shares - if they sell them later.
See **https://www.gov.uk/gift-holdover-relief**

CGT rollover relief

You may be able to delay paying Capital Gains Tax if you:

- sell (or 'dispose of') some business assets
- use all or part of the proceeds to buy new assets

Business asset rollover relief means you won't pay any tax until you sell the new asset. You may then need to pay tax on the gain from the original asset. You can also claim:

- provisional relief if you're planning to buy new assets with your proceeds but haven't done yet
- relief if you use the proceeds to improve assets you already own

Eligibility
To qualify for business asset rollover relief:

- you must buy the new assets within 3 years of selling or disposing of the old ones (or up to one year before)
- your business must be trading when you sell the old assets and buy the new ones
- you must use the old and new assets in your business

You can claim relief on assets including:

- land and buildings
- fixed plant or machinery

The alteration of share rights in a company to reduce the value of a shareholder's shares in favour of another shareholder in an unquoted close company, will be treated as a transfer of value from the donor's estate, and may give rise to an IHT charge, subject to reliefs for BPR and the exemption for non-gratuitous transfers. It is therefore important that professional advice is sought when dealing with the gifting of shares to individuals or trusts, or restructuring shares, as the inheritance tax implications may be different, depending on the circumstances.

With entrepreneurs' relief CGT is payable at a flat rate of 10%.

Investment companies

Shareholdings in family investment companies do not qualify for BPR and are subject to inheritance tax. These are companies used for investment purposes and investment income and do not fit the qualifying criteria for a trading company, which would qualify for BPR. If shares are mortgaged then BPR only applies to the net value of the shares, so use non-business assets first if raising money through a mortgage loan secured against shares. 'Excepted assets' do not qualify for BPR – these include substantial cash balances, investments and let properties. However, some companies with a small investment business (not more than 20% of assets usually) may still qualify for BPR.

Controlling shareholders

Controlling shareholders will usually be discouraged from transferring shares before death. They would have 100% BPR from inheritance tax and a tax-free uplift in base value for CGT purposes. BPR is available to you for merely owning the shares – you do not need to work in the business to have the relief. On the death of a spouse or civil partner, where shares are acquired, the previous ownership period of the deceased spouse counts towards the surviving spouse's ownership period for business property relief purposes.

Partnerships and LLPs

A partnership may be either unincorporated or a limited liability partnership (LLP). Where the partnership is unincorporated, all the partners are jointly and severally liable for the actions of the other partners. By becoming a limited liability partnership (LLP), the partners can limit their liability to the partnership assets only. The inheritance tax position for a partner's share of the business is similar to that of a shareholder in a company, in that 100% BPR may apply for qualifying partnerships.

A partner's share of the business includes the value of his capital account in the business. Unlike a director's loan account, the partner's capital account does qualify for business property reliefs, as, even though owned by the partner, it is seen as a business asset.

One of the core objectives of the partnership should be to update the levels of partnership protection life assurance whereby each partner is insured by the other partners in trust, so that on the death of a partner, the surviving partners have the proceeds from a life insurance policy to purchase his share.

Partnership insurance and protection can be designed at an appropriate level to pay out more than just a return of the capital accounts in the business. It is also an additional methodology to increase pre-retirement additional cash for families that is inheritance tax protected. An analysis can be undertaken to determine the current and proposed position, and the proper double option partnership agreements should be put in place.

Double option agreement

It is important that a partnership double option agreement is put into place to govern the relationship between the partners where one partner leaves, dies or becomes incapacitated. These agreements should be regularly updated, and any related life assurance policies should be in trust.

Premiums are not tax deductible on the life assurance policies, and are paid by the partnership (on behalf of the partners). If all the equity partners have an equal share, it is suggested that the premiums be pooled and allocated to each partner on an equal basis.

The proceeds of the policies should be tax free in trust for the benefit of the surviving partners.

The double option agreement is basically a contract post-sale. This means it is inheritance tax effective, and the value of the partnership share would be out of the deceased's estate for IHT purposes. The surviving partners have the option to buy the deceased's share of the partnership, whilst the representatives of the deceased partner's estate have the option to sell his share. If any one party exercises the option, the other party must perform.

What must be decided is whether the life cover thus provided to purchase the deceased's partner's share is in lieu of his capital accounts and current account, or in addition to it, or in partial satisfaction of it.

Wealth creation and succession planning

The partners are in business for profit and individual wealth creation. In the final analysis, this comes from the return, on retirement, of their capital and current accounts, and their property accounts if the partners own property. The partners, through their own endeavours, build retirement plans through savings, investments and pensions derived from their own income, usually after-tax. In addition, the partnership can provide an unfunded annuity to a retiring partner or his dependants (which is deductible to the partners), if required.

The partners also have obligations to each other and this includes paying out a retiring or deceased partner's capital and current account. This can be funded for, or financed, or the partnership pays it out proportionately. Even if the partnership is currently in a healthy cash position with unused banking facilities, in later years this may not be the case, especially if a number of capital account extractions (and current account repayments) occur within a limited time period, as partners retire or die.

It makes sense to strategically plan for wealth creation and succession planning to provide certainty and a level of security to partners for their futures.

It is also important to have the right procedures in place should the business be sold in the future. Not only does this strategy require a group consensus, but each partner will require individual planning to optimise his position.

Issues arising are:

1. For the partnership to be in a position to afford the repayment of capital to the outgoing partner, whether on retirement, disability or termination – particularly in the event of multiple partner exits at the same time.
2. Whether a savings programme should be commenced now by the partnership to buy out the retiring partner's share. This is one route; other routes are to use cash at bank, or to take out loans to buy out an exiting partner's share. Some partnership agreements have a fall-back position whereby buy-outs occur in stages, often over say 5-6 years.
3. That the partnership may consider exit planning as a whole, thereby obtaining a capital payment for the sale of the business; whether this is a possible objective of the partnership; and whether this should be made known to prospective purchasers. If this is the case, then discussion should be on value; valuation and trade pricing.

Succession planning in the event of *death* is important. Surviving spouses may have no wish to take over the partnership; and some partnerships are occupation-specific, such as firms of lawyers, accountants, or doctors, which might prevent a surviving spouse taking over the partnership share. This problem is solved by facilitating buy-out by surviving partners, funded by a life insurance held in trust for this purpose.

Succession planning in the event of *disability* (preventing the partner from working) can be provided through individual income protection policies (PHI), which cover sickness, serious illness and injury. Cover should also be obtained for a dread disease or critical illness such as cancer, where the partner could still work but not at the same pace or level of output.

Succession planning for *retiring* partners should be a core objective, both for the retiring partner, as well as for any new entrants to the partnership. For the latter, the partners would wish to make it as easy as possible for selected new entrants to become equity partners.

Business exit planning needs careful consideration, if the business is sold, for example. If not planned properly, it could be tax-inefficient for the partners.

Large cash deposits at bank may not qualify for BPR on the partnership share, nor will investments made by the partnership if not used in the business, in most cases. There are also capital gains tax issues when a partnership share is sold, or accrues on death to the other partners. There could be an accrual clause in the partnership agreement that states that on the death of a partner, his share accrues to the other partners. The partners' shares in the partnership then increase and so does the value to their estates. This could give rise to capital gains taxes having to be accounted for.

Sole traders

The sole trader is, to all intents and purposes, the business. On his or her death, there is the greatest likelihood that the business will cease, and have no resale value. Sole traders are also the most vulnerable and have no protections from creditors, compared to the limited liabilities offered through a private company or a limited liability partnership. Business assets owned by the sole trader should qualify for 100% BPR in the deceased sole trader's estate. The assets must have been used for at least two years for business purposes, and will include the value of an office owned by the sole trader and other property used by the business.

Many sole traders operate from home, where the home is the principal residence, and relief will only apply to assets used for genuine business purposes. It is unlikely that a portion of the home will qualify for BPR. Cash in business bank accounts or investments will usually not qualify for BPR and will be subject to inheritance tax.

On the death of the sole trader, if there were employees working in the business at the time of his death, they may have a claim against his estate for wages and salaries owing, as well as other expenses. Whilst such claims will reduce his estate for IHT purposes, they can also cause cash-flow problems to the estate, and affect estate liquidity.

Even if BPR did not apply, the sole trader may have other exemptions available, such as the spouse exemption, so that the passing of all assets to the spouse or civil partner will escape IHT in the first estate; however, the second estate could be caught if the survivor has not remarried or entered into a new civil partnership. If the assets were subject to BPR this usually carries through with the asset as a relief in the second estate.

Succession planning

Succession planning for sole traders can be difficult. If there are no family members to pass the business on to, or a third party to sell the business to, then the business will cease. However, it may have been a perfectly good business with valuable clients. Pre-planning is therefore essential. For example, it may that there is a similar business operating in the next county. The parties can get together and take out a double option agreement and insure themselves, so that on death the business passes to the survivor and the cash generated passes to the heirs of the deceased. This methodology preserves the business value, even if the sole trader is no longer there, and where the business may have ceased on his death, for the lack of passing on a business with value. Groups like the Federation of Small Business (FSB) may offer a business marriage service, or the equivalent of Business Link.

Business and agricultural property reliefs

There are generous inheritance tax reliefs applying to businesses. If the assets qualify, they can be exempt from IHT, and in more than one estate.

Business property relief (IHTA 1984, ss103-114)

To qualify for business property relief (BPR), the property must have been owned by the transferor for at least two years immediately before the transfer. It can replace another qualifying property and the properties together must have been owned by the transferor for at least two out of the five years immediately before the transfer. The rates for relief were set on the 5th April 1996 and are as follows:

An interest in a business which is not a company (e.g. a sole trader)	100%
Shares in an unquoted company with over 25% voting control	100%
Shares in an unquoted company with 25% or less voting control	100%
Shares in a quoted company giving control Shares in AIM or USM company	50%
(no matter the level of voting control or controlling interest)	100%
Settled property comprising a life tenant's business, or interest in a business	100%
Land, buildings, machinery or plant in a partnership or in a controlled company or in a settlement	50%

Agricultural property relief (IHTA 1984 ss115-124B)

For full agricultural property relief to apply, the agricultural property must have been occupied by the transferor for agricultural purposes throughout the 2 years before the transfer (death) or owned by him for the seven years before the transfer and occupied by him or another for agricultural purposes throughout that period. The following are the rates of agricultural relief that apply:

Vacant possession or the right to obtain it within 12 months:	100%
Agricultural land let on tenancy after 31 August 1995:	100%
Other transfers:	50%

Ongoing business strategies

There are many different strategies that can be applied to assist businesses in wealth creation, and also to protect the business. It is not uncommon for shareholders to gift their shares or to sell them to family members in order to create multiple income streams from income or dividends for family members. Younger taxpayers and spouses and civil partners will have their own income tax allowances and CGT allowances, and could benefit from such a strategy. Gifting shares to a discretionary trust would be a chargeable event and usually subject to lifetime inheritance tax payable at 20%. However, if the shares qualify for BPR at 100% then no IHT is payable (and if it was, then other exemptions apply such as the value of the nil rate band at the time). However, there may be restrictions in the shareholder's agreement or memorandum and articles prohibiting the transfer of company's shares to a third party, and a trust may be classified as such a third party. It is therefore important to read the small print. The question is often asked whether shares should be gifted to avoid future inheritance taxes. Whilst we have BPR at generous levels currently, this is less of an issue, as shares pass free of IHT if qualifying; however, if BPR was watered down or removed, then gifting considerations will again assume greater consideration.

Assets can also be protected if held in a pension fund. For example, if the business trades from its own property, after A-Day (6th April 2006), the property can be gifted or sold to a pension fund by connected parties. The property may also qualify as an 'in specie' contribution, meaning it can be used as a contribution to the pension fund, and create tax deductions for the contributor. However, there could be capital gains tax considerations to take into account; selling, gifting or contributing will be a disposal for CGT purposes. Once the property is in the pension scheme, it will grow tax-free; if sold, there is no capital gains tax to pay, and any income derived from it will be tax free in the pension fund. Compare this to a company (or partnership or sole trader) owning the property. If sold, capital gains taxes apply and income derived from it is taxable. The pension scheme can derive rental income from the business tax free, and such rental income is deductible to the business. On death of a pension scheme member, the value of the pension fund is free of IHT (although other charges may apply, depending on where the member is in the retirement process).

Inheritance tax planning around the business need not solely rely on business and agricultural property reliefs. Proper planning is essential.

14

Living Abroad

IHT and foreign domiciles. Holiday homes abroad, and retiring abroad. The best structures to protect your assets whilst passing them on.

The concepts of domicile and residence are important ones in our law. Domicile is where you intend to live the rest of your days. This may be choosing a new country (domicile of choice), or acquired because you were born there (domicile of origin) in a particular country, or acquired through a parent moving to another country (domicile of dependency). There is no statutory definition of domicile. You are basically domiciled in the place you consider your home country. This is a matter of intention as well as physical facts. For example, Richard Burton, the famous actor, lived abroad, but wanted to be buried in Wales on his death. He was deemed domiciled in the UK and subject to UK inheritance taxes. Planning to lose your UK domicile is all-embracing. Coming back for periodic visits can also be problematic as indicated below.

You are generally taxed on your worldwide assets except that certain property can be 'excluded' in the following circumstances: if you are not UK domiciled, and if your property was settled outside the UK when you were not domiciled here, the property would not be subject to inheritance tax, becoming an 'excluded property'. You may be 'deemed' to be domiciled in the UK for IHT purposes if you were domiciled in the UK within the three immediately preceding years from the time the question of domicile arises; or if you were resident in the UK in not less than 17 of the last 20 years of assessment ending with the year of assessment when the question of domicile arises. If you are non-domiciled in the UK and you have UK property, then that property could be subject to IHT.

If you are not UK domiciled, or deemed domiciled, and the property is outside the UK, then transferring such property will not give rise to an IHT charge. If you gift property before achieving your 17 years out of 20 years of UK residence, and if you wait for three years before gifting a property after attaining domicile elsewhere, then this should not be caught by the IHT rules.

New rules from April 2017

The following announcement was made in the 2015 Budget with regard to non-domiciled individuals There are extensive changes to the non-domicile status, which will have a significant impact on long-term UK resident non-domiciled people:

From April 2017, anybody who has been resident in the UK for more than 15 of the past 20 tax years will be deemed UK-domiciled for tax purposes and be liable for full UK tax. The tax status remains the same. Non-UK domiciled individuals will be subject to new legislation.

There is therefore potential to remove assets from the UK inheritance tax net by not being domiciled or deemed domiciled in the UK at the time of the transfer.

Transfers between spouses and civil partners

The spouse exemption applies equally for domiciled and non-domiciled spouses and civil partners for lifetime and death transfers, and each spouse or civil partner has the nil rate band of £325,000 before IHT is payable for assets gifted to others. However, where one spouse or civil partner is UK domiciled and the other is not, then restrictions will apply. The previous position before *FA2013* was that if the UK domiciled spouse or civil partner made a transfer to a non-UK domiciled spouse or civil partner then the inter-spouse exemption was limited to £55,000, and this could only be used once (however, the UK domiciled spouse or civil partner also had the nil rate band that could be used for IHT-free gifts, and the PET exemptions – so long as they survived for at least seven years, such gifts would be out of their estate). The **new rule** if the recipient spouse is non domiciled is as follows: *FA 2013* radically changes the IHT treatment where one spouse is UK domiciled and the other (recipient) is not. Up to 5 April 2013, such transfers were subject to a lifetime allowance of £55,000. After 6 April 2013 the IHT exempt amount that can be transferred from a UK domiciled spouse/civil partner to a non UK domiciled spouse/ civil partner is increased to the NRB amount, currently £325,000. A non UK domiciled spouse/civil partner can elect to be treated as UK domiciled for IHT. This means assets can pass between spouses without an IHT tax charge. There are rules governing the election. The election ceases to be valid if the individual making the election lives outside the UK for more than 4 successive tax years. So you can be UK resident and live in the UK and retain the non UK domicile, and the election would be valid.

Double taxation agreements

The UK has double taxation agreements with ten other countries relating to inheritance tax, so that double taxation should not occur on the same assets. These do not include popular retirement places such as Spain and Portugal, but do include the USA, France, Italy, India, Republic of Ireland, Pakistan, South Africa, Netherlands, Switzerland and Sweden.

Income tax and inheritance tax

Income tax depends on your status as to domicile and residence.

Previously (prior to 6 April 2013) you were classed as resident in the UK based on the number of days spent here each year. You become UK-resident if you are physically present for 183 days or more in the tax year in the UK, or if you spend an average of 91 days or more in the UK over a four-year period. Even if you spend less than 183 days of the year in the UK, in certain circumstances HMRC can still designate you as 'ordinarily resident' for tax purposes. The new residency test could make you resident in the UK after 16 days if you have 4 ties or more to the UK.

If you are resident, ordinarily resident and domiciled in the UK, you can be taxed on income arising worldwide. If you are resident in the UK, but not domiciled nor ordinarily resident in the UK, then you are only charged to income tax on foreign income remitted to the UK. If a non-resident and income arises in the UK, you will be liable to UK income tax.

The recent case of *Gaines-Cooper v HMRC SpC 568* is an important one for those claiming they are not resident in the UK. Mr Gaines-Cooper was assessed to income tax on the basis that he was UK domiciled, not domiciled in the Seychelles as he had claimed. For the first time, the days of arrival and departure were not ignored, and the nights spent in the UK were counted. As he visited the UK regularly and his son was being schooled in the UK, it was found that he had not abandoned his domicile of choice in England. He was therefore considered resident throughout the period under assessment, as well as domiciled and ordinarily resident.

On the 14 March 2007 *Citywire* reported that 'Taxman to turn a beady eye on non-domiciled claims'. Until now non-domiciled people had only to confirm their status; now HMRC will challenge them, as UK residents can claim to be non-domiciled even if they have lived in the UK for years and pay no income tax, capital gains tax or inheritance tax outside the UK. There have been new questions on tax returns from April 2007.

It is evident that using the domicile laws to reduce or evade IHT and other taxes is becoming more limiting and specialised planning is required.

In other areas, restrictions are being lifted though. In the March 2007 budget, it was announced that the favourable tax treatment on UK dividends is to be extended to foreign dividends from April 2008, now including the notional tax credit which was previously denied. It was also announced that where UK residents own foreign properties through overseas companies, the benefit-in-kind tax charge for the use of these properties by directors will not apply. This will be retrospectively applied and repayments made where tax charges have resulted. It will only relate to cases where the company is owned by individuals (rather than other companies), where the property is the only or main asset of the company, where the activities of the company are incidental to the ownership of the property and where the property is not funded by a loan from a connected company. Many people own holiday homes and properties through companies, and this relief will be a welcome one to them.

More recently the Government has increased the higher levels of stamp duty (SDLT) where it applies to more expensive properties and also those owned by companies – the preferred route for non-domicilliaries investing into property has been via a company.

The following are the main changes:

- Company-owned residential property – stamp duty liability rises to 15% for properties worth more than £500,000 – the previous threshold was £2 million. The 15% rate does not apply to property bought by a company that is acting as a trustee of a settlement or bought by a company to be used for:
  - a property rental business
  - property developers and trader
  - property made available to the public
  - financial institutions acquiring property in the course of lending
  - property occupied by employees
  - farmhouses

- Annual tax on enveloped dwellings (ATED) – ATED is an annual tax payable mainly by companies that own UK residential property valued at more than £500,000. The rates of ATED in 2019/20 are as follows:

Property Value	Annual Charge
More than £500,000 up to £1 million	£3,650
More than £1 million up to £2 million	£7,400
More than £2 million up to £5 million	£24,800
More than £5 million up to £10 million	£57,900
More than £10 million up to £20 million	£116,100
More than £20 million	£232,350

Rates on your first home

You can claim a discount (relief) so you do not pay any tax up to £300,000 and 5% on the portion from £300,001 to £500,000.

You're eligible if:

*   you, and anyone else you're buying with, are first-time buyers
*   you complete your purchase on or after 22 November 2017

If the price is over £500,000, you follow the rules for people who've bought a home before.

Rates if you've bought a home before

The stamp duty rates on freehold or leasehold sales and transfers in 2019/20 are as follows:

Property or lease premium or transfer value	SDLT Rate
Up to £125,000	Zero
The next £125,000 (the portion from £125,001 to £250,000)	2%
The next £675,000 (the portion from £250,001 to £925,000)	5%
The next £575,000 (the portion from £925,001 to £1.5 million)	10%
The remaining amount (the portion above £1.5 million)	12%

Protecting your assets

Those able to confirm their status as non domiciled and not resident nor ordinary resident in the UK can plan effectively to pass on their assets free of taxes. Those who are domiciled and resident in the UK can still use the normal planning routes of gifting within the nil rate band and other exemptions. Inter-spouse gifts are restricted where one of the parties is UK domiciled and the other is not. Offshore trust and company structures are widely used for asset protection, as are pension funds. However, restrictions apply to a pension fund owning a holiday home abroad, for your own use.

Those retiring abroad

Uppermost in the minds of those retiring abroad will be the protection of their assets from inheritance taxes. Not only will they have UK taxes to contend with, but the likelihood of wealth taxes arising on assets passing in their new countries of residence. Whilst double taxation agreements give some comfort, they may not apply to all countries, and the list of applicable countries is small.

If retiring or working abroad, with no intention of coming back to the UK, it is wise to sever as many links to the UK as possible, to establish a domicile of choice elsewhere. Otherwise on your death, even though you may not have lived in the UK for many years, your assets and those worldwide may be subject to IHT in the UK. Many will set up offshore trusts on departing the UK and stream their income into their new countries of residence. However, they could also be drawing pensions from the UK and may intend to be buried there. They may retain membership of clubs and even a residence for occasional visits. All of these are factors in HMRC determining domicile or deemed domicile.

Specialist advice will always be required on planning your exit from the UK and it could save you thousands of pounds. There are also other factors such as capital gains tax (sell your UK non-principal residence properties after having being abroad for at least five years to avoid CGT); and income tax issues to be aware of. This relates also to the status of beneficiaries of trusts, for example who may be UK resident and domiciled, even if you reside permanently abroad.

Note that since 1 January 2011 France will tax your (otherwise) tax free cash if you retire from your pension scheme and are resident there, and it exceeds 6,000 euros. If thinking of retiring to France (or anywhere else), make sure your planning is up to date.

Non-UK domiciled individuals ("non-doms"): new rules

The rules on domicile changed on 6 April 2017.

- Capital gains on UK residential property are taxable in the UK regardless of the individual's residence or domicile status.
- A UK-domiciled individual is taxable on their worldwide income and gains for any year in which they are UK resident.
- A formerly domiciled resident is deemed to regain UK domicile when they become UK resident again.
- An individual who acquires a domicile of choice abroad remains in the UK inheritance tax net for the next three years.

The remittance basis of taxation is when you choose to be taxed only on your UK income and gains and ONLY foreign income and gains you bring back to the UK. From April 2017, if you were either born in the UK or are a long term resident of the UK (resident for at least fifteen out of the last twenty tax years) you can no longer use the remittance basis and you will be taxed on the arising basis.

The 2008 Budget confirmed there are wide-ranging changes to the taxation of non-UK domiciled individuals and the tax rules of UK residence. The 2011 Budget increased the levy on non domiciled UK residents from £30,000 to £50,000 in certain instances from 6 April 2012 (see page 108).The 2013 Finance Act brought in the new statutory residency test. The Autumn Statement 2014 increased the tax charge for non-domicilliaries using the remittance basis as follows:

Non-domicilliaries who use the remittance basis and resident in the UK

- 7 out of last 9 years charge unchanged at £30,000 per year
- 12 out of last 14 years to increase from £50,000 to £60,000 per year
- 17 out of last 20 years – a new charge of £90,000 to be introduced.

New statutory residence test

Following consultation the statutory residence test has been introduced in FA 2013 and the ordinary residence test is removed from 6 April 2013. How then does the legislation and tax and tribunal cases affect your planning, especially if married to a non-domicilliary, or having moved abroad whether leaving assets in the UK or not? These aspects affect millions of people who have retired abroad, or are contemplating this.

The following is taken from the HMRC SRT Guide December 2013. This is a very complex document and runs to 105 pages. The new statutory residence test (SRT) is in FA 2013 and seeks to codify the law, which was previously based on case law and unsatisfactory HMRC interpretations of what the law should be. There are a series of steps given to consider whether an individual is resident or non- resident in the UK. Residence and domicile are two different things. You may be domiciled elsewhere, but still resident or deemed to have been resident in the UK through periods of visiting the UK, owning a house in the UK, having relatives and dependants who live in the UK and other close ties. If UK resident you could be liable for UK taxes – income tax, capital gains tax, inheritance tax; if non-resident, you could escape these taxes.

Statutory residence test – the basic rule

1. You will be resident in the UK for a tax year and at all times in that tax year (although the effect of this rule is relaxed under split year treatment), if you do not meet any of the automatic overseas tests and:
    *   you meet one of the automatic UK tests, or
    *   the sufficient ties test.

2. You should take the following steps to ascertain your residence status under the SRT:
    *   *Step 1*: Consider whether you spent 183 days in the UK in that tax year (the *first automatic UK test*). If you did, you will be resident in the UK. If not:
    *   *Step 2*: Consider the three automatic overseas tests. If you meet one of these you are not UK resident. If you did not:
    *   *Step 3*: Consider if you meet the second and third UK tests. If you meet one of these, you are UK resident. If you did not:
    *   *Step 4*: Consider the sufficient ties test. If you meet this you are UK resident, if you do not meet this, you are not UK resident.

3. The above steps are shown in the flow diagram on the next page.

The statutory residence test – an overview

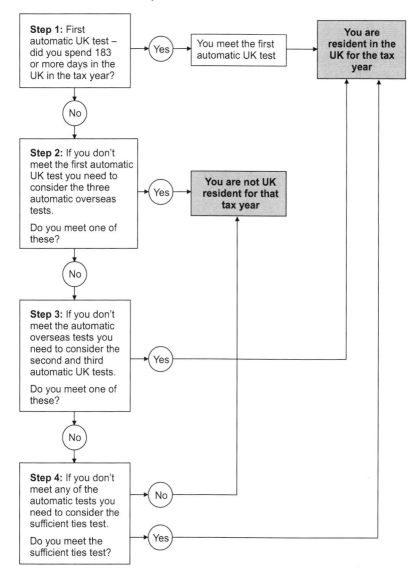

Step 1: First automatic UK test – did you spend 183 or more days in the UK in the tax year?

Yes → You meet the first automatic UK test → **You are resident in the UK for the tax year**

No

Step 2: If you don't meet the first automatic UK test you need to consider the three automatic overseas tests.

Do you meet one of these?

Yes → **You are not UK resident for that tax year**

No

Step 3: If you don't meet the automatic overseas tests you need to consider the second and third automatic UK tests.

Do you meet one of these?

Yes

No

Step 4: If you don't meet any of the automatic tests you need to consider the sufficient ties test.

Do you meet the sufficient ties test?

No

Yes

Automatic overseas tests

4. If you meet any of the automatic overseas tests for a tax year, you are automatically non-resident for that year. You should therefore consider these tests first, as if you meet any one of them, you will not need to consider any of the other parts of the test.

5. *First automatic overseas test*
    You were resident in the UK for one or more of the three tax years preceding the tax year, and you spend fewer than 16 days in the UK in the tax year. If an individual dies in the tax year this test does not apply.

6. *Second automatic overseas test*
    You were resident in the UK for none of the three tax years preceding the tax year, and you spend fewer than 46 days in the UK in the tax year.

7. *Third automatic overseas test*
    You work full-time overseas over the tax year, without any significant breaks during the tax year from overseas work, and:
    *   you spend fewer than 91 days in the UK in the tax year,
    *   the number of days in the tax year on which you work for more than three hours in the UK is less than 31.

8. The third automatic overseas test does not apply to you if:
    *   you have a relevant job on board a vehicle, aircraft or ship at any time in the relevant tax year, and
    *   at least six of the trips you make in that year as part of that job are cross-border trips that:
        *   begin in the UK
        *   end in the UK, or
        *   begin and end in the UK.

9. If you do not meet any of the automatic overseas tests, you should look at the automatic UK tests. If you meet any of the automatic UK tests you are resident in the UK for the tax year. If you do not meet any of the automatic UK tests you will need to consider the sufficient ties test.

Second and third automatic UK tests

10. *Second automatic UK test*
    The second automatic UK test is relevant if you have or had a home in the UK during all or part of the tax year. You will meet this test if there is at least one period of 91 consecutive days, at least 30 days of which fall in the tax year, when you have a home in the UK in which you spend a sufficient amount of time (at least 30 days during the tax year – the 30 days do not

need to fall within the 91-day period), and either you:
- have no overseas home, or
- have an overseas home or homes in each of which you spend fewer than 30 days.

11. If you have more than one home in the UK, you should consider each of those homes separately to see if you meet the test. You need only meet this test in relation to one of your UK homes.

12. *Third automatic UK test*
You work full-time in the UK for any period of 365 days, with no significant break from UK work and:
- all or part of that 365-day period falls within the tax year
- more than 75% of the total number of days in the 365-day period when you do more than three hours of work are days when you do more than three hours of work in the UK
- at least one day which is both in the 365-day period and in the tax year is a day on which you do more than three hours of work in the UK.

13. The third automatic UK test does not apply to you if:
- you have a 'relevant job' as defined by HMRC (essentially jobs involving duties and/or the provision of services on board vehicles, aircraft or ships while they are travelling) at any time in the relevant tax year, and
- at least six of the trips you make in that year as part of that job are cross-border trips that:
  - begin in the UK
  - end in the UK, or
  - begin and end in the UK.

Sufficient ties test

14. UK ties are described as follows:

i) Family tie
You have a family tie for the tax year under consideration if any of the following people are UK resident for tax purposes for that year:
- your husband, wife or civil partner (unless you are separated)
- your partner, if you are living together as husband and wife or as civil partners
- your child, if under 18-years-old. (Children in full time education in the UK are not counted provided they do not spend more than 21 days in the UK outside of term time.)

ii) Accommodation tie

You have an accommodation tie for a tax year if you have a place to live in the UK and it is available to you for a continuous period of 91 days or more during that year, and

- you spend one or more nights there during that year, or
- if it is at the home of a close relative (parent or grandparent, brother or sister, child or grandchild aged 18 or over), you spend 16 or more nights there during the year.

iii) Work tie

You have a work tie for a tax year if you do more than three hours of work a day in the UK on at least 40 days in that year, whether continuously or intermittently. (There are special rules about what constitutes three hours of UK work for people in 'relevant jobs', working on vehicles, ships or aircraft while they are travelling.)

iv) 90 day tie

You have a 90-day tie for a tax year if you have spent more than 90 days in the UK in either or both of the previous two tax years.

v) Country tie

You have a country tie for a tax year if the UK is the country in which you were present at midnight for the greatest number of days in that tax year. If the number of days you were present in a country at midnight is the same for two or more countries in a tax year, and one of those countries is the UK, then you will have a country tie for that tax year if that is the greatest number of days you spend in any country in that tax year. (For the purposes of this SRT test presence at midnight in any state, territory or canton into which a country is subdivided is regarded as presence at midnight in that country.)

15. Once the number of ties has been established, an individual can then refer to the tables in paragraphs 17 and 18 below to determine whether, taking into account the number of days the individual has spent in the UK, the individual is UK tax resident in a particular tax year.

16. If a person is a 'leaver' (having been resident in one or more of the previous three tax years) the rules are as follows:

Days spent in the UK	Impact of UK ties on residence status
Fewer than 16 days	Non-resident
16-45 days	Resident if individual has 4 or more UK ties (non-resident with 3 or fewer UK ties)
46-90 days	Resident if individual has 3 or more UK ties (non-resident with 2 or fewer UK ties)
91-120 days	Resident if individual has 2 or more UK ties (non-resident with 1 or fewer UK ties)
Over 120 days	Resident if individual has 1 or more UK ties (non-resident with no UK ties)

17. For 'arrivers' – defined as individuals who have not been resident in the UK for any of the past three years – only the first four ties are applied (i.e. excluding the 'country tie'). The rules for arrivers are as follows:

Days spent in the UK	Impact of UK ties on residence status
Fewer than 46 days	Non-resident
46-90 days	Resident if individual has all 4 UK ties (non-resident with 3 or fewer UK ties)
91-120 days	Resident if individual has 3 or more UK ties (non-resident with 2 or fewer UK ties)
Over 120 days	Resident if individual has 2 or more UK ties (non-resident with 1 or fewer UK ties)

Capital gains tax

A person is chargeable to capital gains tax in respect of any gains arising for his benefit in any tax year during any part of which he is resident in the UK. Under the new rules proposed in *FA 2013*, if there is a split year, any gain in the overseas part of the tax year is not chargeable.

This does not apply to non-domiciled individuals where they elect to be taxed on a remittance basis, in respect of any gains arising from the disposal of an asset situated outside of the UK, until they bring the proceeds back into the UK.

Persons ceasing to be UK resident for less than five complete tax years will be taxed on any gains arising in the period of non-UK residence in the year they recommence UK residence. (Under new legislation this will be extended to dividends and other income from 6 April 2013).

Days spent

Generally, the ruling confirms that if an individual is not present in the UK at the end of the day, that day does not count as a day spent in the UK – the so-called 'midnight rule'.

However, in order to prevent manipulation of the midnight rule, there is a deeming rule which overrides the basic provision. This deeming rule only applies if:

- The individual was UK resident in at least one of the three preceding tax years (i.e. a leaver).
- Has at least three UK ties in a tax year.
- Is present in the UK in that year for more than 30 'qualifying days' (i.e. days when the individual is present in the UK at some point, but not at the end of the day).

Its effect is that once the threshold of 30 qualifying days is met in a tax year, each subsequent qualifying day in the year is treated as a day spent in the UK irrespective of where the person is at midnight.

There is a concept of exceptional circumstances where an individual may stay for up to 60 additional days beyond the normal day count set out in the SRT. These additional days must arise due to circumstances beyond the individual's control. Whilst these circumstances are not defined, they are likely to include situations such as serious illness of the individual, their spouse or dependent children.

The residency status rules can be particularly harsh. Recently, in a case reported in *International Adviser* (25 November 2013) 'Expats face £600k tax bill after tribunal rules they are UK-resident'. A couple moved to Portugal more than 10 years ago are still classed as UK residents, after the HMRC pursued them saying the farmhouse they owned remained a family home. The couple stated they intended to move permanently abroad. The tribunal ruled that although there had been some "loosening" of the couple's social and family bonds with Northwich, it was not "substantial" enough to make them non-UK residents. The ruling pre-dates this year's Residency Test criteria, and in the court documents, HMRC states that it closely followed the residency guidance "as laid out in booklet IR20" – which relates to the case of the Supreme Court in *Gaines-Cooper*. The *Gaines-Cooper* case also serves to highlight the challenges that expatriate Britons can face when attempting to sever their tax obligations to the UK. After many appeals Robert Gaines-Cooper, a wealthy entrepreneur who moved to the Seychelles in 1976, eventually lost his case in 2011 when the Supreme Court ruled that he was still technically a UK resident. Although Gaines Cooper was careful never to stay 91 days in the UK in any given year – the then widely-accepted measure of residency – the court ruled that his close connections with Britain after decades showed that he was, in fact, still resident – and thus liable for years of back taxes.

Because of uncertainty in interpreting the residency rules, we now have the statutory residency test as outlined above. Whilst residency and domicile are distinctly different concepts, there is no doubt that using the residency rules to establish whether you are UK resident or not will be used to determine intention to support whether you are domiciled in the UK or not. You could claim that your intention was to be non-domiciled and that you had left the UK, but the interpretation of the residency rules could prove otherwise. This will have IHT and financial consequences for many expatriates or those that have retired abroad.

Some issues that may arise, are as follows:

1. Are residence and domicile the same thing? No, you can be resident in the UK, but domiciled elsewhere. If you are a British national born in the UK you will almost certainly still be domiciled there even if you haven't lived in the UK for many years.

2. Marriage to a foreign national makes a big difference. If both spouses or civil partners are domiciled in the UK then transfers between them are exempt from IHT. If one spouse is foreign domiciled then the transfer of assets is now only exempt up to £325,000, the balance chargeable at 40%. If both are non-domiciled then IHT does not arise in the UK unless you have assets in the UK.

3. If you have no assets in the UK but are UK domiciled, then your worldwide assets can be subject to IHT after deducting the nil rate band of £325,000.

4. If you have lived abroad for many years and then die there, but with UK assets, the assets cannot be transferred unless you obtain probate, so it is unlikely you will escape IHT. It may be better to establish a new domicile

elsewhere, however, intention is everything, and if you ever thought of returning to the UK for good (for example to be buried there) then you may still be deemed to be UK domiciled.

5. If you retain a property in the UK that will go some way to proving a connection with the UK. However, you can establish a domicile elsewhere notwithstanding this, but would need professional advice on how to proceed. Whilst residence and domicile are separate things, the new statutory residence test with its 'ties' criteria could influence your domiciliary status.

6. To lose a UK domicile you must establish a connection with another place. For starters, you must be out of the UK for at least 3 tax years. Probably 5 years to be on the safe side. Have you established a main residence abroad and intend to live there for ever?

7. If you do move abroad and establish a foreign domicile, and then return to the UK, this can be done with proper planning, and you can visit the UK when you like, even if you become tax resident. Non domiciled UK residents have many tax benefits. However, recent events will have you adhering to strict criteria and rules to maintain this position and expert advice is essential.

8. If you move back to the UK permanently you will again become UK domiciled. If you set up a discretionary trust whilst not UK domiciled and transferred assets into it, these should remain free of UK inheritance tax. It is about intention – if you intend to stay, or whether you are uncertain – until you decide, the foreign domicile should remain with you.

9. You need to convince HMRC that you have established a new domicile, otherwise you could later find your estate is liable to 40% inheritance tax and/or any transfers you make to a trust could be subject to the 20% lifetime IHT charge.

Life policies under threat

Non-domiciled UK individuals may see their estate hit with an unexpected tax bill on death following a change of stance by HM Revenue & Customs.

Until now, non-domiciled UK clients could take out a UK whole of life insurance policy and arrange it so that the plan was held outside the UK, or "under seal". As the plan was held outside the UK, individuals could save up to 40 per cent on inheritance tax on the value of the life policy, providing they were not living in the UK when they died.

But a change of stance by HMRC means policies set up under seal may no longer be exempt from IHT. HMRC now requires greater tests to be carried out to establish what be considered a non-UK situated asset, including where the insurer is based, where the policyholder is living when they die, and the location of any property where the policy is being used as security. Using trusts could shelter these policies from IHT, and professional advice should be taken.

Deemed domicile

It is possible for an individual to be 'deemed' to be domiciled in the UK for IHT purposes only, while being domiciled elsewhere. outside the UK. This can arise if there is the 'three-year' rule applying to those emigrating from the UK. For example, Fiona who has an English domicile retires to France. She emigrates and takes a French domicile of choice on 31 January 2010. She dies on 1 January 2013 still in France. Under the 'three year rule' she is deemed domiciled in the UK at her death and her worldwide estate is chargeable to IHT. Or, for long-term UK residents, there is the '17 out of 20 rule'. Here, the taxpayer must have been income tax resident in the UK in not less than 17 out of the last 20 years. Note that an exception to this rule is for transfers on death where the deceased's domicile was Italy, France, India or Pakistan.

Without the deemed domicile rules, non-UK domiciled clients could simply hold offshore property in the knowledge that such assets could remain excluded property for IHT purposes even in the face of long-term UK residence (see the update below).

Non-UK domiciled clients with an impending deemed domicile 'problem' may wish to consider an excluded property trust.

This simply requires two tests to be satisfied, that the settlor must be non-UK domiciled at the time the settlement is made (or at the date of any additions, if the added property is material) and the property in question must be situated outside the UK (for example, offshore bond) at the date of the charge to IHT.

Update 6 April 2018

Changes and the current position are noted below. These relate to the taxation of non-domicilliaries (non-doms) and offshore trusts.

The Finance Bill, 6 April 2018, provided revised legislation regard-ing the recycling of benefits from offshore trusts via non-resident beneficiaries and the tax treatment of distributions to close family members of the settlor.

From 6 April 2017

Returning non-domicilliaries
Individuals who were born in the UK with a UK domicile of origin but who later acquire a domicile of choice (returning non-doms) will be treated as domiciled in the UK as soon as they become resident in the UK. Trusts created whilst

a returning non-dom was non-domiciled will be treated as if created by a UK domiciled individual.

Long-term non-doms

From 6 April 2017, individuals who have been resident in the UK in 15 out of the previous 20 years will be deemed to be UK domiciled (deemed-dom) for income tax, capital gains tax and inheritance tax purposes.

Non-dom individuals with less than £2,000 of unremitted income and gains will continue to be automatically entitled to the remit-tance basis of taxation even once they are deemed-domiciled.

Capital gains tax rebasing

The rebasing will only be available to individuals who became deemed-domiciled from 6 April 2017 and who have paid the remit-tance basis charge at least once (a qualifying individual). Returning non-doms cannot be qualifying individuals.

The asset being rebased must have been owned by the individual on 5 April 2017 and must not have been situated in the UK during the period from 16 March 2016 to 5 April 2017. There appears to be no requirement that the individual owned the asset (a qualifying asset) throughout this period.

The rebasing will apply automatically to qualifying assets sold by a qualifying individual on or after 6 April 2017, although an election may be made to disapply the rebasing.

Excluded property for inheritance tax

Non-UK situs assets held by trusts set up before an individual is deemed-domiciled for inheritance tax will remain outside the scope of inheritance tax, subject to the new rules regarding UK residential property held through overseas companies.

Carried interest

Where gains are taxed on an individual under the carried interest rules, they will not also be matched to benefits received from a trust. However, when the proceeds of such a gain are distributed by the trust, they may still be matched to other capital gains real-ised in the trust.

Provisions taking effect from 6 April 2018

The changes which will take effect from 6 April 2018 relate to how income and gains in offshore trusts are taxed when beneficiaries receive capital payments. These rules had previously been an-nounced in December 2016 as part of the consultation into the changes to the taxation of non-doms. However, they were not in-cluded in the first Finance Bill, published in March 2017.

Capital payments received by non-resident beneficiaries
Capital gains will no longer be matched to capital payments re-ceived by non-resident beneficiaries. This means that it will not be possible to 'wash out' capital gains from a trust by making distribu-tions to non-resident beneficiaries. This is already the case for trust income. In addition, capital payments will be disregarded if they are made to a beneficiary who is UK resident when they receive the payment but become non-resident before the payment is matched to a capital gain.

An exception to these provisions is where a capital payment is made to a beneficiary who is temporarily non-resident (ie non-resident for a period of less than five tax years). Such individuals will be deemed to have received the capital payment in the year they return to the UK.

Another exception is in the year a settlement ends when distribu-tions to non-residents will be matched to capital gains.

Capital payments received by close family members of the set-tlor
Where the settlor of a trust is resident in the UK during a tax year and a capital payment is made in that tax year to a beneficiary who is a close family member of the settlor, the capital payment is treated as being made to the settlor. These provisions apply to both income tax and capital gains and will have the effect that the settlor is taxed on any income or capital gains matched to the capi-tal payment. These rules apply to income from 6 April 2017 but will be extended to capital gains from 6 April 2018.

For income tax purposes, the settlor will only be treated as the re-cipient of the capital payments if the actual recipient is either not resident in the UK or is a remittance basis user. For capital gains tax purposes, the settlor will be treated as having received the cap-ital payment regardless of whether, in the absence of this provi-sion, the actual recipient would have been subject to tax in respect of the capital payment.

For these purposes, a close family member includes the settlor's spouse, civil partner, cohabitee or minor child (of the settlor or their spouse/civil partner/cohabitee). Minor grandchildren are not close family members for these purposes.

Onward gifts
If a beneficiary receives a capital payment from a trust which is not taxable and they make an onward gift, the subsequent recipient will be treated as having received the capital payment. These provi-sions apply to both income and capital gains and may have the effect that the subsequent recipient is taxed on any income or capi-tal gains matched to the capital payment.

In order for these provisions to apply, the following criteria must be met:

- The original beneficiary is either not resident in the UK or is taxed on the remittance basis and does not remit all of the capital pay-ment.

- The above provisions in respect of capital payments to close family members of the settlor do not apply.
- The subsequent recipient is resident in the UK when they receive the onward gift.

The rules will only apply where the onward gift is made in the three years after the original payment was made, or before if it is made in anticipation of the original beneficiary receiving the payment. This represents a return to the rule first announced in December 2016, after the three- year timeframe was removed from the Sep-tember 2017 version of the legislation.

The onward gift must be of or include one of the following:

- The whole or part of the original payment.
- Anything that derives from or represents the whole or part of the original payment.
- Any other property, if and only if, the original payment is made with a view that a gift will be made to the subsequent recipient.

This means that gifts made which are not at all connected to the receipt of the original payment should not be caught by these rules. However, the rules are broadly drafted and therefore care must be taken.

Where a series of gifts are made, the recipient of the last gift in the series will be treated as having received the original payment from the trust.

If the subsequent recipient of the gift is a close family member of the settlor of the trust, then this provision will apply in connection with the above provision to tax the settlor as though they received the capital payment.

Planning

- Non-doms who are not already deemed-domiciled under the new rules should consider the creation or further use of foreign trusts to hold investments.
- Non-doms who are not already deemed-domiciled may wish to consider receiving trust distributions whilst they are still able to use the remittance basis.
- Non-doms who became deemed-domiciled from 6 April 2017 should consider whether they can take advantage of the automatic rebasing of non-UK assets for capital gains tax purposes. In par-ticular, individuals who have not previously paid the remittance ba-sis charge may wish to consider if it is worth doing so for 2016-17, or for another year for which they are still in time to make the elec-tion.
- Non-doms with mixed funds should analyse these funds to deter-mine if there is clean capital available that may be remitted to the UK without a tax charge.

- Trustees of offshore trusts could have reviewed any loan relation-ship as a matter of urgency to ensure that steps are taken before 5 April 2018 to avoid the tainting of trusts.

- Trustees of offshore trusts with both UK resident and non-resident beneficiaries could have considered making distributions to non-residents prior to 5 April 2018 in order to 'wash out' stockpiled capi-tal gains.

- Trustees of offshore trusts where the settlor is UK resident could have considered making distributions to close family members of the settlor prior to 5 April 2018.

I am indebted to Saffrey Champness for information used in this section.

15

IHT and Pension Funds

*Strategies on how to pass on pension assets to your heirs.
Pension funds and trusts. How to insure your pension
fund to pass on the whole fund on death, without paying
inheritance tax. The pension regime after the 2014 Autumn
Statement and how it affects your pension assets on death.
Death benefits and ensuring maximum payouts. Death in
service benefits.*

The 2014 March budget changed the pensions' landscape with regard to pension fund flexibility, and also with regard to pension death benefits. This was followed by the 2014 Autumn statement which introduced other measures with regard to pensions passing to others. There is no inheritance tax on pension funds or benefits being inherited by others. However, if you take cash and then die, the cash will be subject to IHT in your estate.

The changes from 6 April 2015 are as follows:

Pension death benefits – defined contribution schemes

Individuals with unused defined contribution pension amounts will be able to pass them to a beneficiary without facing the current 55% 'death tax' charge. Instead, the transfer will happen either tax-free entirely or at the holder's marginal rate of income tax depending on whether they are aged above or below 75 when they die.

- Individuals from the age of 55 with a defined contribution pension scheme will be able to access their pensions on a more flexible basis. This includes the taking of the whole pension fund as cash, after 25% tax free cash, the balance is taxable at your marginal rates of tax from uncrystallised or drawdown funds.

- Sharing of pension funds on death can be generational – funds can cascade down to family members, who would have their own flexi-access drawdown funds.

- If age under 75 at the date of death, remaining funds from a defined contribution scheme can be paid out tax free and the funds are within the member's available lifetime allowance.

- If over age 75 at the date of death, funds received will be taxed at the beneficiary's marginal rate. If a lump sum is paid instead of a pension, then in 2019/20 tax is payable at 45% and marginal rates thereafter.

The ONS projects that only 15% of men aged 65 this year will die before turning 75, so most survivors' benefits from any sort of pension will remain taxable.

Pension death benefits – defined benefit schemes (occupational pension schemes)

The question is asked whether spouse pensions will be tax free where the member dies before age 75. These will not be the same as defined contribution schemes, and the current arrangements will continue. Most spouse income comes from annuities within the occupational scheme and the new arrangements only apply to defined contribution schemes.

However, joint life payments from defined benefit (DB) pension schemes made after the member's death will continue to be subject to income tax. Typically joint life payments are built into DB scheme benefits and an income will be paid to the member's surviving partner.

These payments will continued to be taxed at the surviving partner's marginal rate of income tax, while those paid from joint life and guaranteed annuities will receive income tax free.

Annuity death benefits

Death benefits paid from pension annuities will now enjoy the same tax free treatment as income drawdown. This rule change will only apply where annuity payments are made to beneficiaries for the first time after April 2015. From 6 April 2015, beneficiaries of individuals who die under the age of 75 with a joint life or guaranteed term annuity will be able to receive any future payments from such policies tax free. The tax rules will also be changed to allow joint life annuities to be passed on to any beneficiary. Payments made by guaranteed annuities after the death of their holder will be paid tax free to beneficiaries. Guaranteed annuity payment keep paying income after the holder has died, currently up to a maximum of 10 years from the date the annuity was taken out.

For example, if someone who bought a guaranteed payment annuity died five years after purchase, payments would continue to beneficiaries for another five years.

These payments will now be made tax-free. They were previously taxed on the beneficiary's marginal rate of income tax.

It was also confirmed in the Autumn Statement 2014 that that payments from joint life annuities to surviving partners would be made tax-free after the death of the holder.

ISA death benefits

If an ISA saver in a marriage or civil partnership dies, their spouse or civil partner will inherit their ISA tax advantages. From 6 April 2015, surviving spouses will be able to invest as much into their own ISA as their spouse used to have, on top of their usual allowance, and so, as the government states, "will be better able to secure their financial future and enjoy the tax advantages they previously shared".

Spouses will inherit their partner's individual saving account (ISA) benefits after death. Previously, if someone passed away they couldn't pass on their ISA with its tax benefits to their spouse, even if they have saved the money together. 150,000 people a year lose out on the tax advantages of their partner's ISA when their partner passes away.

From 3 December 2014, if an ISA holder dies, they will be able to pass on their ISA benefits to their spouse or civil partner via an additional ISA allowance which they will be able to use from 6 April 2015.

The surviving spouse or civil partner will be allowed to invest as much into their own ISA as their spouse used to have, in addition to their normal annual ISA limit. The additional one-off allowance is equal to the amount the deceased had in their Isa, which would become available from April 6th.

The ISA allowance is £20,000 in 2019/20.

Previously on death, the inherited ISA became taxable in the hands of the spouse, losing its tax benefits. These tax benefits now remain. However, note that this applies to income tax and capital gains tax and not to inheritance tax. The ISA amount on death could still be subject to IHT if above the nil rate band, or if not passed to a surviving spouse on death.

The previous ISA rules meant that all the benefits of an Isa were lost at the point of death, but the new rules, which come into effect from 3.12.2014, are a welcome addition and allow the tax advantages of married savers to be inherited by their surviving spouse or civil partner

Inheritance taxes can apply to pension fund assets under certain circumstances. Usually, though, there are no inheritance taxes payable until such time as assets have passed to a third party after the pensioner's death. The new pensions' freedoms have created pensions flexibility with how you take your funds and also how you pass your pension funds on to others. From being a Government that previously attacked pension funds, it is now recognized that the UK needs a savings culture that will protect pensions and allow family members to make use of pension assets on death in a benign tax environment.

Having said that, perhaps the new reforms have gone too far in respect of the flexibility offered with unlimited access to defined contribution pension funds after 6 April 2015, which could dissipate funds for the unwary.

Savings culture

People save for pensions both to build funds that will provide them with an income in retirement, and also to provide a pension for their spouses or partners once they have died. This can be extended to providing for dependants' pensions, including children and others financially dependent on the breadwinner. So far, so good – that's exactly what pensions are for. However, most pension fund savers are also building assets within a pension fund, not only to save for retirement, but as part of their capital accumulation. They would like to pass their unused pension assets on to future generations as intact as possible. In the savings culture perpetuated by the Government (encouraging people to save for retirement to cover for the inadequacy of State benefits), we do have an apparently generous tax-based savings opportunity to build protected funds for the future. However, when we lift the veil, the reality is that the current pensions' savings culture is only designed to provide for one or two generations. Beyond that, the State seems determined to decimate the savings so carefully nurtured by ordinary people. The 2014 Budgets have changed that position by creating inter-generational passing of pension funds, and depending on the age of the member at death (above or below age 75), these pension funds can pass on tax-efficiently.

Surely, if the present generation can provide pension assets not only for their own lifetimes, but also for future generations, it will greatly reduce reliance on State funding and alleviate the stress of future generations having to make their own pension arrangements, for many years into the future. People do have alternatives to taking out a pension: they can fund for retirement through investments, savings, building a business and selling it, and many other diverse means. However, pensions' savings are synonymous with a retirement planning culture, and should be encouraged.

Pension term life assurance

This is another important area of pension planning which has recently been under attack by the Government.

Those saving for a pension fund who may die too soon will, in all likelihood, not leave much of a pension fund for their dependants. It is therefore vital that the pension fund accumulation phase be protected with life assurance. On death, the life assurance pays out a lump sum and provides funds that can be invested for income, so that widows and their dependants, in the main, have an income (and are not dependant on the State.) In the past, one has been able to purchase tax-relievable term-based life assurance that will fulfil this need, where the premiums have been tax relievable in some way.

Over the years this tax relief has ranged from 5% to 100% of the life assurance premiums. Even if you did not have a pension scheme, you could buy tax-relievable life assurance that would provide funds in the event of your death before retirement. Was the State giving a meaningful benefit to assist with the generation of pension funding? Yes it was. The Chancellor saw fit to withdraw this benefit in the November 2006 budget statement, another indication of the fact that those in Government do not understand the fundamentals of retirement provision. It's not the withdrawal of the tax relief that's the point. After all, one can always purchase non-tax-relievable life assurance at any time. It was the message inherent in the withdrawal, that whatever your personal provision for retirement, you are more or less on your own – another reason why proper planning is important. Tax relief on pension term assurance was abolished on 14th December 2006.

Funding for retirement

There remain strong incentives to fund for retirement, and there are generous contribution reliefs available to those who do so. There will be an element of compulsion for businesses to ensure that employees have the new minimum compulsory pensions NEST pension account.

Contributions into pension funds are deductible from taxable income, and even if you are a non-taxpayer, you will benefit from these tax reliefs at the basic rate of rate. Children can have contributions made for them, and their parents (or grandparents, if they are the contributors) can have tax relief. Once the contribution is in the pension fund, it will grow tax free, and when you get to minimum retirement age, which is age 55, at least 25% can be taken from your fund in tax-free cash (known as the pension commencement lump sum). You don't even have to retire to take your pension benefits. You can take your tax-free cash and defer the taking of your pension until a later date, if in a private scheme. The rules are different for a company-owned defined benefit pension scheme, where the retirement age is usually 60, and you normally have to take your pension when you take your tax-free cash.

There is no limit to the type of pension funding you may make. However, the following are the tax reliefs and limits for tax purposes. In 2019/20 an individual can contribute up to £3,600 without reference to earnings or 100% of earnings up to £40,000. An employer can contribute an unlimited amount, however the tax limit is up to £40,000 less employee contributions.

There is also a lifetime allowance for the size of pension funds you may have of £1,055,000 in 2019/20.

Inheritance tax and pension funds

With pension reforms announced in 2014 but applicable from 6 April 2015 in the main, there will be situations where the old rules will apply before the new rules become effective. The position with regard to DB – defined benefit pension schemes – remain the same, but those with defined contribution (DC) schemes will have changed over the years.

Pensions commenced prior to 6 April 2011 – USP and ASP

Drawdown options at retirement prior to 6 April 2011 were Unsecured Pension (USP) up to age 75 and Alternatively Secured Pension (ASP) over age 75. The latter applied where you did not wish to purchase an annuity at age 75 and income drawdown was able to be continued. For those in drawdown under these options, different drawdown limits may apply. If in USP and drawing an income, the income limits apply until you reach the first scheduled review date after 6 April 2011. This could be five years from that date, i.e. to the 2016/17 tax year. ASP was reviewed annually and will have moved to the capped drawdown income limits after one year. USP and ASP were fully covered in previous editions of *Pensions Simplified.*

On death, the fund can be passed to a civil partner, spouse or dependant without IHT; it can also be passed to a non-dependant third party, whereupon it would have been subject to IHT.

Inheritance tax

This is payable at 40%, subject to nil rate band provisions.

If ASP assets were not paid to the estate, but to another pension scheme member, the IHT charge will take account of any income tax already paid before the IHT charge arises.

Unauthorised payment charge at 40%

The person inheriting the fund must pay an unauthorised payment charge of 40% – in addition to any IHT due. This unauthorised payment charge cannot be paid from the pension fund itself, and other sources must be found to pay it.

Unauthorised payment surcharge at up to 15%

If the amounts passed from ASP in any one tax year total more than 25% of the ASP fund value, a surcharge of 15% is added. This must be paid by the person inheriting the fund.

Scheme sanction charge on unauthorised payment

The scheme provider must pay a sanction charge of between 15% and 40% on an unauthorised payment, which is not deductible from the client's pension fund. If the recipient of the unauthorised payment pays all the unauthorised payment charges due from him, the amount payable by the scheme provider is 15%. This provides a maximum possible charge on the unauthorised payment of 70% (40% + 15% + 15%).

Effective tax rate

The effect of the inheritance tax liability plus the additional charges, add up to an effective tax charge of 82% on the remaining capital (including the scheme sanction charge paid by the scheme provider). In fact, most of the remaining capital could be wiped out as the scheme administrator could also be subject to charges as well as costs. Note that if the pension funds are left to a charity then no IHT or unauthorised payment charges arise.

Nil rate band

The rules state that the nil rate band will first be applied to the non-ASP part of the estate (i.e. the estate excluding the ASP fund). Any residual amount of NRB left over can then be applied to the ASP fund. Any NRB still unutilised after treatment of the ASP fund can be passed down with the ASP to the inheritor of the fund (to be utilised in their own estates accounting for IHT on the ASP).

In summary, total death tax charges, including IHT could be at 82% on USP and ASP funds. Inheritance tax could apply on death if pension funds are paid to the estate and the estate is above the nil rate band.

Pensions commenced or reviewed between 6 April 2011 and 5 April 2015 – capped drawdown and flexible drawdown

Capped drawdown and flexible drawdown have been the standard methods of drawdown since they replaced the old USP and ASP in 2011. In the 2019/20 tax year, the rules applying to these methods of drawdown for death benefits will remain.

If the member dies while invested through an income drawdown plan, the remaining crystallised pension funds in drawdown can be passed to a spouse or civil partner tax-fee provided that it is used to provide a dependant's pension. A spouse has a number of options as follows:

- Continue with income drawdown
- Take the fund as a lump sum and pay a 55% death tax charge
- Purchase a pension annuity with the remaining fund.

If the spouse continues within income drawdown they can do so for the whole of their lifetime. Any income received from this arrangement would be subject to income tax. By taking the fund as a lump sum the surviving spouse must pay a 55% tax charge. Where the benefits are uncrystallised and death occurs before the age of 75 the pension fund will remain tax-free. The fund is paid free from Inheritance Tax (IHT).

For those individuals that were in ASP drawdown there is a reduction in tax on death from 82% down to 55% and they benefit from the changes from 6 April 2011.

On death before a pension has been taken, the funds available can be paid to the personal representatives of the estate or to any other person. There may also be death benefits payable into trust, where the trustees have the discretion to pay the funds.

If paid to the estate, no IHT is payable if the estate is left to the spouse or civil partner. If paid to a third party, then IHT could be payable.

Note that although IHT may not be payable, there could be income tax payable once benefits pass to another.

The options available are as follows:

1. A return of fund (cash lump sum) less 55% tax for all funds – there is no inheritance tax payable unless it is left to the estate.
2. The remaining fund buys a **single annuity**.
3. The spouse or civil partner can **continue with income drawdown**.
4. If there is no spouse or partner, the fund can be passed free of IHT to dependant children under age 23 or other qualifying dependants for continued income drawdown. However, the fund can only be passed once free of IHT; neither the spouse nor any inheriting dependant can pass the fund on to subsequent heirs or beneficiaries (a 'second passing') without exposure to IHT (if payable and not under the nil rate band).

If there are no dependants, the left-over value of the fund can be passed to a third party, but will be subject to IHT.

In summary, there is no IHT payable on pension funds passing (unless paid to the estate of the deceased for the benefit of 3rd parties), but there is a penal 55% tax charge on taking a 'return of fund' lump sum. The tax recovery charge on death benefits taken as a lump sum will be 55% at all ages once benefits have been crystallised.

Pensions commenced from 6 April 2015 onwards – flexi-access drawdown (FAD)

From 6 April 2015 capped drawdown and flexible drawdown are replaced by flexi-access drawdown (FAD) and new death benefit rules will apply:

*   If age under 75 at the date of death, remaining funds from a defined contribution scheme can be paid out tax free and the funds are within the member's available lifetime allowance.
*   If over age 75 at the date of death, funds received will be taxed at the

beneficiary's marginal rate. If a lump sum is paid instead of a pension, then in 2019/20 tax is payable at 45% and marginal rates thereafter.
- No inheritance tax on pension funds.
- No 55% death tax
- From 6 April 2015 uncrystallised or drawdown defined contribution pension funds can pass to a beneficiary with no 55% death tax charge. Entirely tax free if below age 75, taxable at marginal rate over age 75.
- From 6 April 2015 beneficiaries of individuals who die under age 75 with a joint life or guaranteed term annuity will be able to receive future payments from such policies tax free. The 55% tax charge is abolished. No payments must have been made to the beneficiary before 6 April 2015. If the annuitant dies after age 75 the beneficiary pays the marginal rate of tax or 45% if taken as a lump sum. Lump sum payments are charged at the beneficiary's marginal rate from 2016/17. (Tax treatment of annuities in line with drawdown). One can choose a guaranteed income for life without their spouse being penalised if outliving the annuitant. This does not apply to pensions or annuities from occupational pension schemes.
- Joint life annuities can be passed to any beneficiary. From 6 April 2015, tax rules have been amended to allow people to set up **joint-life annuities**, which will maintain payments for any chosen beneficiary, after the original policyholder has died.

Occupational pension schemes – defined benefit schemes

Benefits received from occupational pension schemes and annuities are free of inheritance tax. These benefits usually cease after the spouse (or civil partner) or dependants die or the benefit period ends, and no funds are available to transfer to third parties.

Value protected annuity

If death occurs and you have a value protected annuity, a lump sum benefit is payable being the difference between the annuity purchase price and the payments made up to the annuitant's death. the annuitant's death. The payment will be subject to tax at 55%, up to 5 April 2015 and tax free thereafter.

Tax-free cash (pension commencement lump sum)

Once you have the tax-free cash, this will fall into your estate for inheritance tax purposes. Any tax-free cash not used up, for example to pay off debts or a mortgage at retirement, and invested into non-protected IHT investments, will be subject to IHT on your death. An IHT-protected investment could be a discounted gift trust investment bond where the discounted portion is immediately out of your estate, or an investment into an EIS qualifying company or portfolio of companies, where the share value falls out of your estate after two years.

FURBS

A Funded Unapproved Retirement Benefit Scheme (FURBS) is a pension benefit scheme set up by employers for a named individual (or individuals), now more commonly known as an 'employer-financed retirement benefit scheme'. Before A-Day (6th April 2006), funds in a FURB on death were inheritance tax free; after A-Day, these funds fall into your estate for inheritance tax purposes. However, they are apportioned for pre and post A-Day, with pre A-Day funds retaining their tax advantages.

Death before retirement

Should you die 'in service' (in other words, before retirement), then the pension fund rules will usually stipulate what sort of death benefits are payable and when.

You may have a pension fund offered through an employer ('scheme pension'), related to your salary and benefits. Alternatively, you may be in a pension fund set up by yourself, such as a personal pension plan.

Employers may have death-in-service benefits arising from the pension fund itself, or the benefits may be provided by group scheme life assurance. The latter is usually available up to retirement age and then ceases. Group life cover is a multiple of salary, for example two to four times final remuneration, or a fixed amount, and is payable to named beneficiaries or dependants. Payments made by the trustees, for tax reasons, are always discretionary, but a letter of wishes is followed, giving direction for lump sum payments.

If there are no additional group scheme or death-in-service benefits, then on death before retirement there would either be a return of current fund value (the better deal), or a return of contributions paid plus say 4% or 5% (worse than a return of current fund value). The differences can be enormous, especially where single premium contributions have been made – return of contributions can be as much as 80% less than current fund values. One can approach the pension provider and ask for a change in how and what death benefits are payable – some will charge you to make this change. This is more likely to be the situation for your own personal pension plans, but could also be the case with some employer-funded schemes.

Such payments on death before retirement are usually tax-free. Partnership group life schemes provide tax-free benefits on death for all partners from 9th April 2003 (not just for the first-dying, which was the previous position).

Dependants' pensions provided on death before retirement will not count towards the standard lifetime allowance. There is technically no limit on benefits that can be provided for dependants on death before retirement. However, aggregate dependants' pensions should not exceed the value of the member's pension to avoid an 'excess charge'. If a pension is paid there can be no guaranteed periods and no provision for value protection. A spouse and children age under 23 will automatically qualify, as will civil partners. If an unmarried couple, you must provide proof of financial dependency to receive a dependant's pension.

Return of funds and pension contributions and death-in-service life assurance (including pension term assurance) can be paid tax-free so long as the payments overall are within the standard lifetime allowance (SLA), which is £1,055,000 in 2019/20. Above the SLA, there are tax charges. Where the excess is taken as income, the tax charge is 25%; where taken as a lump sum, the tax charge is 55% (unless funds were protected under your own purchased life annuity (PLA) – i.e. an annuity not from a pension fund but purchased using your free capital – when the higher limits will be paid without penalty).

A registered group life scheme's life cover benefits will be accumulated with the value of your pension fund for lifetime allowance purposes. You can instead have excepted group life benefits that do not count towards the lifetime allowance.

Death after retirement

Once you have retired, you will be receiving your monthly pension or annuity or income drawdown. Your pension funds will have been invested by the pension's provider to produce an income, and this is generally known as an annuity or pension income. Unless there is a guarantee operating, the main pension itself will come to an end on your death. However, dependants', spouses' and civil partners' survivor pensions may be payable until their own deaths.

The type of death benefits, if any, will depend on the type of annuity or pension's contract, or other arrangements, such as drawdown, in force at the time.

The most common types are as follows:

Occupational pension schemes

If single, the scheme pension will merely cease. Some schemes have a guaranteed period of payment, and pension payments will continue to the estate of the deceased, or nominated beneficiary or dependant for that period of guaranteed payment.

If married or in a civil partnership, usually a reduced pension is payable to the spouse or civil partner, until his or her death, depending on the scheme rules. 50% widow's or widower's pensions are common, but the range could be from less than that to up to 2/3 of the member's pension.

Personal pension schemes and schemes where annuities are payable

Much depends on the type of the scheme. A scheme with a 'term certain' guarantee will pay out for that term and then cease. For example, if the annuity is payable for two lifetimes, but for a minimum of 10 years, and both annuitants die in, say, year eight, then the annuity continues paying for another two years (to the estate or dependants) before it ceases.

If a single life annuity, then the annuity will cease paying out on the member's death, or after the expiry of any guaranteed period if later.

If a joint and survivor annuity, then on the first death, the annuity continues paying to the survivor (usually a reduced amount) until the death of the survivor, when it ceases – unless within the term certain guarantee period, if there is one attached. If the spouse dies before the member, then on the death of the member, the annuity will cease unless within a term certain guarantee period.

If a single-life nil-guarantee annuity is taken, to achieve the highest level of income option, and the underlying pension fund is insured, then on the death of the annuitant, the annuity itself ceases, but the insurance proceeds are paid out in trust outside of the deceased's estate, free of all taxes. This may then be reinvested for income, or for a voluntary purchase annuity that is more tax efficient.

Planning areas

1. Review pension planning at least from age 55.

2. Decide on how much income you wish to take from your pension funds (you may wish to diversify and build up alternative IHT-protected funds) or to enable you to gift excess income to children and grandchildren), and for what purpose. You now have greater flexibility on how to use your defined contribution pension funds.

3. If you have no dependants, leave pension assets through your estate to charity (assets left to charity are an allowable deduction in the estate).

Phased retirement

Many people prefer to take all of their pension benefits at once. Others prefer to take pension income and lump sums as they see fit, and according to their needs.

If the funds have been phased (where pension segments have been taken as the individual requires them), then the position is as follows.

Death before retirement

On death before retirement, the full fund can be paid to dependants free of tax.

If the transfer was originally from a company scheme to say a personal pension scheme, then only up to 25% may be taken as tax-free cash and the balance as income from an annuity or as drawdown income. One of the annuity options may be the purchase of an impaired life annuity, if you qualify through ill-health or being a smoker. This type of annuity is medically underwritten, and could result in a higher income. For example, Mrs Smith has cancer and her life expectancy is shortened. She could qualify for enhanced income of 50-75% higher than a conventional annuity. People with more than one pension fund may wish to stagger the retirement dates to provide income as well as tax free lump sums when they need them. Phased retirement also enables you to take a tax free lump sum from your pension scheme, but to defer the taking of income or an annuity until much later. You therefore have more flexibility with greater options.

There is no difference in how the various pension funds are treated whether you phase your retirement benefits or not. The same rules will still apply.

Death after retirement

It is unlikely that any death-after-retirement life cover benefits will be available from a pension fund or group life scheme, or death in service benefits scheme, unless provided independently by the annuitant.

In most instances, it would be in the interests of all parties to have death benefits paid in trust outside of the estate, to avoid probate before being paid out to beneficiaries. This means that such death benefits in trust will escape IHT.

Life assurance in trust

The use of life assurance is a powerful inheritance tax planning tool. Life assurance underwritten in trust is free of inheritance tax. It is most useful to provide immediate liquidity in a person's estate, which may require cash to pay inheritance taxes, to fund trusts or to provide an income for dependants, supplanting or supplementing pension or annuity income.

The concept of life assurance can also free up your thinking with regard to increasing your income in retirement – particularly when it comes to the choice of annuity-type. One of the major reasons why people wait until they are as old as possible before taking an annuity is because at younger ages, annuity rates are very low. These annuity rates increase generally rate for age. As a result they get better when you get older. The more guarantees you have with an annuity, such as guaranteed periods, paying an annuity for two lifetimes, taking income in advance, escalating your income – the lower the annuity income – in fact annuity costs can take up over 65% of your annuity income. By reducing the guarantees, and perhaps limiting the annuity to single-life you increase income, but reduce inheritable value; and that's where the life assurance policy comes in.

The best deal for you, in terms of income received during your retirement, would be a single annuity with no guarantees. That will pay you the highest income possible at a given annuity age. However, it will cease on your death. To get the best income later, it is possible to insure your life for the required inheritable fund value as early as possible. Then on your death, the full value of your fund pays out to your dependants, free of inheritance taxes. It can then be invested tax-efficiently to provide an income.

If this strategy is adopted, it could significantly increase your income in retirement, provide for and protect your beneficiaries and financial dependants and pass capital free of taxes to whomsoever you want. Your pension from your funds will cease on death, but be replaced by more efficient funding – for both income and tax reasons. It is important to have a whole of life policy to do so and many companies have a guaranteed premium and sum-assured whole-of-life policy on offer. The younger you are when you do this, the cheaper it will be for the rest of your life.

Pension benefits generally

Pension benefits are payable to the member of the pension scheme. The default position for all schemes is that on the death of the member of the pension scheme, pension assets and options pass to a spouse or civil partner, with children as dependant beneficiaries (usually pensions may be paid to a dependant child up to the age of 23, but different funds have different rules). If you are a cohabitee, but not married or in a civil partnership, you will not automatically receive the pension benefits of the member on death. You may have lived with the unmarried partner for 25 years, and even had children by them, but you may still not be entitled to receive their pension benefits. It is therefore important that a letter of wishes be left with the trustees of the pension fund to indicate where the member wishes the benefits to go on their death. Unfortunately this is a discretionary position. What if the member left a former spouse, now divorced, who was financially dependant on him? The trustees may have difficulty with this one, especially where multiple claims may be made by other financially dependant people.

However, there is nothing to state that when you retire you cannot name anyone as your co-annuitant for a joint and survivorship annuity. Note that once this election has been made it is irrevocable, and cannot be changed once you start taking your benefits. This is because the annuity has been calculated on the age of your partner as well as your age. This also causes problems if your spouse or partner has died before you – you cannot add another person later, once the annuity is in payment. Proper planning is essential to maximise annuity and pension options and to avoid paying unnecessary taxes.

Future changes

Current Government thinking is definitely focused on short-term rather than long-term incentives to pension provision. While they concentrate on providing immediate tax incentives to get you funding into pension plans, and equally generous incentives to keep your current pension plan arrangements going, they have become more flexible after April 2015 in what you do with your pension fund – to the extent that the whole fund could be taken as cash. Pensions and annuities could also be passed to future generations.

In summary, it is evident that there is still much work to be done to ensure a smooth flow of pension assets to succeeding generations. This will reduce the burden on families (as well as the State) who could then fund for more generational pensions. There is still the issue of the reduced value of pension scheme protection plans through taking away tax incentives to life cover providing for death benefits where funding has been poor due to not enough time to fund (early death), or reduced lifetime funding.

All in all, the pensions' landscape is showing some signs of improvement, with positive reforms welcomed. It is said that those entering work now from school will probably not retire before they are age 70 from the state pension fund. This is even more reason to build up private pension funding. With people living longer, the principle is that the state pension pays out for 1/3 of your adult life.

16

Life Policies and Investment Bonds

Moving unprotected life funds into trust to avoid IHT and the implications around setting up new trusts.

Significant changes to trust law were introduced in the *Finance Act 2006*, and these may affect life assurance policies placed into trust, as well as investment bonds made into trust. The chargeable event legislation now applies to all trusts except for certain bare or absolute trusts. There is therefore a position to be considered for policies written before 22 March 2006 and after that date.

Personal life policies in trust

Position for policies written before 22 March 2006

A life policy underwritten in trust does not fall into your estate for inheritance tax purposes and therefore matures income tax free if a qualifying policy and inheritance tax free. This is the case even where premiums continue to be paid to the policy after 22nd March 2006. You may make allowed variations provided for in the contract, such as exercising an option to increase premiums without bringing the trust into the new regime.

Position for policies written After 22 March 2006

If underwritten in trust after the 22nd March 2006, then there could be a tax charge. However, there are certain exemptions:

1. Bare trusts are not affected by the changes
2. Policies in trust to pay off a mortgage on death are outside the rules and exempt (and the proceeds of such a policy will not fall in to your estate)
3. Policies providing life cover for families on death will be exempt where there is no value in the trust to tax – which is what happens in most cases, especially where the proceeds have paid out, or if the value is below the nil rate band at the time of death. Any excess in value

above NRB is subject to IHT at up to 6% after 10 years on the excess amount. There may also be an exit IHT charge.

There is a difference between life policies arranged to provide family protection or to pay off mortgages, underwritten in trust, and investment bonds underwritten as life policies (see next section). With the former, the position is usually a bare or absolute trust that 'wraps' the proceeds of the policy until paid to the beneficiaries. The 'investment' element of such policies in any event is usually small. These policies are mostly exempt both before and after the budget.

Where the policy is underwritten under a flexible gift trust from the outset, the premiums will typically be exempt under the normal expenditure or annual exemptions. Larger premiums may not be exempt. There may be CLTs to consider and to be reported. However, if under the nil rate band, there should not be any immediate lifetime tax charge. At the ten-year anniversary, if the life assured is not in bad health, the policy will have little or no value. There will therefore be no periodic IHT charge at that time. If it's a whole-of-life policy with a significant surrender value or large ongoing premiums, this may give the policy a value for periodic charges. A periodic IHT charge could arise at the tenth anniversary, if the value of the trust property exceeds the nil rate band. Death proceeds kept in the trust and not distributed could give rise to periodic charges in the trust. The maximum charge at the 10th anniversary is 6% of the trust fund. If not in trust, the claim value would be 40% inheritance taxes payable.

Your best strategy for larger policies and bigger premiums is to have separate trusts created on different days where each has its own nil rate band. The minimum value will be the total premiums paid under the policy when valuing a transfer of value under a life policy. (*IHTA 1984 s 167*).

Large premium and surrender value policies used in IHT whole-of-life policies need careful planning to ensure that the incidence of trust charges is kept low.

Investment bonds

Bonds underwritten before 22 March 2006

Investment bonds are single premium whole-of-life policies. They are mainly for investment purposes and widely used in inheritance tax planning and in trusts to provide 'income'. The investment bonds can be underwritten in trust, in which case they can avoid IHT. They can also be split by the establishment of a discounted gift trust (DGT), where a portion of the investment can be designated as a discounted income stream, and immediately taken out of your estate, with the balance of the investment gifted to a class of beneficiaries or named beneficiaries as a potentially exempt transfer (PET). That balance and the growth on it would be out of your estate for inheritance tax purposes after seven years, and is treated as a PET – a potentially exempt transfer. On death within the seven-year period, taper relief applies to reduce the amount falling back in to your estate for inheritance tax purposes. These investment bonds are hugely popular and provide a set income on which the discount is based (along with age and state of health). Existing investments prior to 22nd March 2006 are exempt from the new legislation. (See also Chapter 19 "Discounted Gift Trusts".)

Bonds underwritten after 22 March 2006

If the discounted gift trust approach is used (see previous paragraph), and the discounted portion is made into a bare or absolute trust it would be exempt from the new rules. The gifted portion, if it exceeds the nil rate band, would be subject to IHT as a CLT since the type of trust would now be an interest-in-possession trust. The inheritance tax is only payable on the amount above the current NRB.

Thus a new insurance product (after 22nd March 2006) is not affected unless the investment element has reached the NRB in a seven-year period, when it could be subject to the periodic charge of up to 6%.

Whilst some life assurance companies use bare trusts for the PET exemption, this is inflexible, and most will use flexible trusts which are discretionary in nature. This will give to a chargeable lifetime transfer, if exemptions such as the nil rate band have been used previously. If the gift is higher than the nil rate band, there will be an immediate charge to IHT at 20%. If the settlor pays the IHT, this charge will be 25%. Periodic and exit charges will also apply and these are described elsewhere. One could gift up to the nil rate band every seven years; or gift assets to spouses to invest to use up their nil rate band allowances as part of your planning.

Business policies held in trust

Policies underwritten before 22 March 2006

Life or term policies held in trust for the benefit of surviving partners, shareholders or LLP members to fund their purchase of the deceased's business share will be exempt from IHT; the proceeds of the related sale of the deceased's business share will also be exempt from IHT if a suitable double option agreement governing the sale and purchase of the business share was in place before death.

Where there is a firm 'buy and sell' agreement in place, instead of a double option or cross option agreement, this is viewed as an agreement entered into pre-death and the proceeds of the sale of the deceased's business share will not be exempt from inheritance taxes.

Policies underwritten after 22 March 2006

The changes after 22 March 2006 affect the tax position on interest-in-possession and accumulation-and-maintenance trusts only (they do not affect bare or absolute trusts). Since the majority of business policy trusts are set up as bare or absolute trusts, designed to pay out policy proceeds soon after receipt, rather than hold or accumulate, these trusts are not affected by the changes, and periodic and exit charges would not apply. The policies themselves, if term policies, have no investment value; if whole-of-life, they would usually have a small investment value (below the £325,000 NRB threshold in 2019/20), and would therefore be exempt from the new legislation.

It is even more important now to ensure that trust provisions are in place for business protection and shareholder purchase policies, to ensure that the policy proceeds remain outside of the estate, because the individual nil rate band is becoming an increasingly precious commodity and should not be wasted (for example used up by life policy proceeds provided for partner, shareholder and LLP member protection as opposed to pure family protection.)

Where business partners, shareholders and LLP members have effected life cover intended for the purchase of their shares, and where this life cover is not underwritten in trust, the proceeds could potentially be payable to their respective estates on death, and therefore be subject to inheritance tax. This is the case where the partners agree to insure themselves, for example, for the benefit of the surviving partners, but there are no agreements or trusts in place to state what the money is for on death. This position can be avoided by subsequently writing the policies into trust. Policies of little or no value (term or whole-of-life), or policies being 'wrapped' into a bare or absolute trust, would be exempt from the new legislation. In this case, in any event, the trust is merely a conduit of the proceeds to the surviving partners, LLP members or shareholders, and will not make investments.

Interest-in-possession trusts (IIP)
Accumulation-and-maintenance trusts (A&M)

Trusts created before 22 March 2006

Both IIP and A&M trusts have been widely used to protect vulnerable beneficiaries as well as to bypass generations for assets which would otherwise be subject to inheritance tax. Assets held in these trusts went in to trust without an inheritance tax charge. During their time as a trust asset the investment was not subject to periodic or exit IHT charges. A discretionary trust on the other hand, could have assets taxed at 20% going in to the trust on assets worth more than the nil rate band of £325,000; a periodic investment charge of up to 6% every ten years following the date of creation of the trust and an exit IHT charge of 10% on capital leaving the trust.

Trusts created after 22 March 2006

New rules apply from 22nd March 2006. The rules bring the inheritance tax treatment of IIP and A&M trusts onto the same basis as a normal discretionary trust. The only exemptions for new trusts are (i) for interest-in-possession trusts created on intestacy or by will (ii) accumulation-and-maintenance trusts created on the death of a parent where beneficiaries take the trust assets at the age of 18 (iii) trusts for disabled people (iv) regular premium life assurance policies written into trust.

Most controversial are new rules to reduce the age when a beneficiary receives income or capital from the age of 25 to 18 for a trust benefiting a child to escape the IHT penalties.

Existing A&M trusts will be treated as ordinary discretionary trusts from April 2008 (unless the trust deed provides for the absolute transfer of assets to the child at the age of 18). Trustees have two years to change the terms of a will trust following death.

For existing interest-in-possession trusts, the current rules continue until the interest in possession ends. If the IIP ends on the death or during the lifetime of the life tenant and the assets of the trust pass to another individual absolutely, there are no further inheritance tax implications. If, however, the interest in possession ends on death and the assets remain in trust, then the value of those assets are included in the estate of the deceased and the new trust is taxed under the new rules (unless exempt). If the IIP ends during the lifetime of the individual, and the assets remain in trust, then the new rules apply (IHT entry charge if above the nil rate band threshold, periodic charge and exit charge).

As referred to on page 123, the two-year transitional period for IIP trusts to be amended to avoid them falling under the new discretionary trust regime was extended to end on 5th October 2008; however, this extension did not apply to A&M trusts,

Moving policies into trust

As part of the estate planning process, you may be advised to move existing policies into trust to protect them from future inheritance taxes. This is possible and the life assurance company can provide forms to do so. The size of the policy and its value will determine whether future trust charges may be applied. Term policies have no investment element and therefore no value until they pay out the death proceeds of the policy, and should not therefore be a problem; policies with value may involve a transfer of value but this should still be fine if the value transferred is under the value of the nil rate band, or if the transfer is exempt as a PET to a bare trust, for example (where you have to survive for seven years for it not to affect your estate for IHT). Most trusts are flexible trusts and discretionary and there could be potential for CLTs to apply. Careful planning is required, including possibly changing the ownership of the life policy through gifting it first.

Endowment policies

Although no longer sold, most people have them. If you are the owner, the policy proceeds pay out tax-free on death for qualifying policies. If not in trust, the proceeds will fall into your estate for IHT purposes and you could lose 40% of their value. If you have purchased a second-hand with-profits endowment policy, on maturity it could be subject to capital gains tax, after your personal exemptions for CGT (currently £12,000 in 2019/20). If you die as owner of a second-hand policy, then the surrender value would fall into your estate for IHT purposes.

The latest on life policies

Non-UK domiciled individuals may see their estate hit with an unexpected tax bill on death following a change of stance by HM Revenue & Customs.

Until now, non-domiciled UK clients could take out a UK whole of life insurance policy and arrange it so that the plan was held outside the UK, or "under seal". As the plan was held outside the UK, individuals could save up to 40 per cent on inheritance tax on the value of the life policy, providing they were not living in the UK when they died.

But a change of stance by HMRC means policies set up under seal may no longer be exempt from IHT. HMRC now requires greater tests to be carried out to establish what be considered a non-UK situated asset, including where the insurer is based, where the policyholder is living when they die, and the location of any property where the policy is being used as security. Using trusts could shelter these policies from IHT, and professional advice should be taken. While it is still possible for policies to be taken outside the UK, they may no longer be exempt from IHT.

Life assurance qualifying policies

From 6 April 2013 there is an effective **£3,600** annual limit on the total premiums an individual can pay (£300 per month per person) into qualifying life assurance policies such as MIPS and other endowment policies. (If the limit is exceeded policies will cease to be qualifying and there may be a tax charge on gains.) Transitional provisions applied to qualifying policies from 21 March 2012 to 6 April 2013. The limit of **£3,600** p.a. only applies to new policies with premiums paid before 6 April 2013 and up to the limit on or after this date.

17

Wills and Estate Planning

IHT and intestacy and achieving IHT reduction. Will trusts. The position of the surviving spouse or partner and life interest or interest-in-possession trusts. Using the nil rate bands as well as the spouse exemption – effective strategies. Probate changes.

The will is the mechanism that ensures that the bulk of your estate planning will work. The better and more effective your will, the greater efficiencies will be achieved. These will be efficiencies in planning as well as saving inheritance and possibly other taxes.

On death, assets are pooled and liabilities subtracted from your estate. You have certain exemptions and allowances as well as deductions from your gross estate before an inheritance tax calculation is done. Reducing the incidence of taxes is part of estate planning, and not using available exemptions and deductions will cost you dearly.

If a couple, each party should have a will. If you die without a will, your estate is intestate and the order of who inherits from you is decided for you, according to a laid down scale. Having a will therefore helps you to decide who will benefit from you, even if you have very few assets, on your death.

Nil rate band

If single, you have the nil rate band (£325,000 in 2019/20) to reduce your taxable estate, as well as exemptions for owning business and agricultural property. If married or in a civil partnership, in addition to these exemptions you have the spouse exemption. The spouse exemption is at 100%. Assets left to a spouse or civil partner by will, will be 100% free of IHT in the estate of the first to die. You cannot have more than 100% worth of exempt assets so you lose the value of other exempt assets, such as the nil rate band and BPR and APR exemptions.

To plan effectively, so that you use the nil rate band and your other exemptions, assets can be left to third parties, such as your children, for the BPR and APR exemptions and the nil rate band amount can be left to a discretionary trust for the benefit ultimately of your children or other beneficiaries. The surviving spouse or civil partner can have the use of the trust as a life tenant and enjoy its income. On the death of the spouse or civil partner, the capital or assets of the trust pass to the beneficiaries. If this is not the case, then if the assets remain in trust for another life tenant or are passed to another trust, such assets will be subject to the entry, periodic and exit charges applying to discretionary trusts.

What goes into trust

Planning what goes into the trust is important. Most are inclined to sever a joint tenancy and pass say half the house into trust for the benefit of the children as ultimate beneficiaries. Whilst you may remain in the house rent-free, and it will not fall back into your estate for IHT purposes, it should pass from the trust to the beneficiaries, when you, the life tenant, dies. If not, the value of the asset could fall back into your estate as it has remained a trust asset. There may be problems with the house in trust, especially if it needs to be sold and the other trust beneficiaries are minors, for example. You may need to apply to Court for permission to do so. The same is true on intestacy when statutory trusts are set up and the house falls into trust. Some prefer investments and cash going into the discretionary trust, or the proceeds of a life policy, as opposed to 'hard assets' such as a house. It is common for the IOU or debt charge to form part of the trust if this is used in your trust planning to create greater flexibility in dealing with your house or other fixed assets. So take advice before acting.

Spouse exemption

It is important, then, to make use of the spouse exemption. However, this may be restricted if one spouse (or civil partner) is not UK domiciled (to £325,000 presently). The UK spouse exemption exempts lifetime and death transfers between spouses from IHT, but is limited to £325,000 on transfers from UK-domiciled spouses to non-dom spouses. The £325,000 nil rate band (NRB) is also available, meaning the maximum a UK domiciled individual can leave to a non-dom spouse without IHT consequences is £650,000. There is also the RNRB IHT exemption to be considered where your residential home is left to a direct descendant. In 2019/20 this is £150,000.

Unmarried couples/cohabitees

If a couple is not married or in a civil partnership, but living together, there is no spouse exemption. All they have is the nil rate band for each estate, and other exemptions like BPR and APR on business assets and agricultural assets. Their planning will therefore need to make full use of the nil rate bands for each of them. Unfortunately, the balance of their assets are taxed faster than if they were married. The estate of the first-dying is taxable (not largely exempt, as with the spouse exemption) and they are treated as two single people. The second-dying's estate is then also subject to IHT. There may be 'deaths in quick succession' relief if the surviving partner inherits too soon and tax has been paid on the estate assets already, and taper reliefs will apply to any PETs made in the last seven years.

Other exemptions

The main additional estate exemptions are for business property relief (BPR) at 100% for business shares and agricultural property reliefs (APR) at also up to 100%. Certain investments qualify for these reliefs, and can be left separately to non-spouses, and still be exempt in your estate.

Dying without a will, or with a will that needs changing – deed of variation

After your death, whether you have a will or not, one can effectively be written for you, under what is known as a deed of variation. All the beneficiaries and potential beneficiaries must agree to this variation. It is usually proceeded with to make use of IHT exemptions, such as bequeathing the nil rate band, or using the unused portion of the first-dying's nil rate band if a married couple or civil partners.

Wills not only direct where you want your assets to go, but also give your trustees wide investment powers and the power to make loans and repay debt on your behalf, amongst other functions. The cost of a will can be as cheap as one from a stationer's or off the internet; solicitors charge on average around £150 (some may be cheaper, others more expensive, depending on what your need requirements are). Ensure that you have a lasting power of attorney (LPA) completed at the same time so that your financial affairs may be dealt with if you become mentally incapable. Lasting powers of attorney (LPAs) took the place of EPAs from October 2007.

Transferable NRBs

From 9th October 2007 civil partners and married couples are able to transfer the unused portion of the first-dying's NRB to the second-dying's estate. This is calculated as a percentage of the unused NRB. If, say, 50% of the 1st dying's NRB had been used in his estate, then on the death of the second dying in 2019/20, £325,000 is uplifted by (50% of £325,000 = £162,550) to £487,500 in the second dying's estate.

Probate changes

Probate Fees

The government is proposing to change the current probate fee structure from a flat rate fee to one based on the value of the estate.

To get probate the person dealing with the estate must first submit an Inheritance Tax account to HM Revenue and Customs (HMRC).

Probate registries won't normally accept an application for probate until HMRC has confirmed that it has processed the Inheritance Tax account.

However, while the process for introducing the new fee structure is ongoing, probate registries will accept applications for probate before the account has been processed by HMRC. The application must include a note to say that the appropriate Inheritance Tax forms will follow shortly.

April 2019 was set to see the new probate fee structure, but the changes have not yet been implemented at the date of writing (October 2019). Once the draft is approved in the Commons, the new probate fee regime comes into effect 21 days later. In England and Wales, probate is the process of applying for the legal right to deal with the deceased's property, money and possessions.

The current fee structure is a flat probate fee of £215, or £155 if the application is made by a solicitor. No probate fee is charged if the estate value is under £5,000.

The new fees will apply on a sliding scale linked to the value of the estate as follows:

Estate Value	New Fees
£50,000 or exempt from acquir-ing probate	£250
£50,000 - £300,000	£750
£500,000 - £1m	£2,500
£1m - £1.6m	£4,000
£1.6m - £2m	£5,000
Above £2m	£6,000

Lifting the fee threshold to £50,000 means an extra 25,000 estates per year will not pay fees at all. For estates over £2 million this is a 2,700% increase in cost expected to net £155 million a year.

Whilst business relief (BPR) can provide 100% IHT mitigation, it does not take assets outside of the estate. BR qualifying shares will still be subject to probate fees. Taking assets outside of the estate and into trust would reduce both probate fees and IHT. Shares that qualify for BPR reduce the lifetime charge to IHT applying to assets settled into trust (in excess of the NRB) from 20% to 0%. These shares are also not liable to periodic or exit charges.

18

Life Assurance Funded Trusts

How to create estate liquidity on death to ensure your liabilities are covered and your trusts are filled with cash to provide an income and capital for your heirs.

A funded life assurance trust (FLAT) will give you the peace of mind and assurance that your estate has sufficient liquidity or cash to be able to do the following:

- pay estate debts and liabilities
- pay any inheritance taxes
- provide trusts that have been set up by you with cash for investment purposes, sufficient to meet your objectives
- provide for bequests to children
- provide for bequests to charities
- for general funding purposes, to provide an income for dependants.

Many estates comprise 'hard' or fixed assets such as properties that are difficult to sell, or have investments, such as private company shares, where there is no market for them, or have very few assets but very big need requirements. The FLAT is the most appropriate vehicle to provide the necessary cash exactly when your estate and dependants may need it the most – on your untimely death.

A FLAT is nothing more than a life policy underwritten in trust at the necessary sum assured to provide the benefits you are seeking. Your circumstances will change over your lifetime. When younger, with a growing family, the need is for family protection and large levels of life cover. As you get older and accumulate wealth, the need is then for estate liquidity and IHT payments, funding trusts and other need requirements.

There are strategies you can undertake to fund the premiums: for example purchasing an immediate annuity (reduces your estate) that is used to fund the premiums, or investing into a discounted gift trust bond and using the income for premiums (thereby obtaining IHT reliefs on the investment as well as the life assurance); or plain funding the premiums individually or through the business.

Life policy proceeds paid into trust escape probate and will be immediately available free of inheritance taxes, as written into trust. The FLAT becomes your after-death cash pool. The premium costs obviously vary according to age and state of health, but the costs are usually low in relation to the benefits provided.

Examples

Assume male and female non-smokers at various ages, with single whole-of-life policies on maximum-cover basis for £500,000, underwritten in trust.

Age	Male/Female	Whole-of-life Maximum Cover – Premium per month	With Waiver of premium
35	Male	32.43	33.09
35	Female	32.43	33.09
45	Male	51.87	52.92
45	Female	51.87	52.92
55	Male	130.61	133.23
55	Female	130.61	133.23

The above illustrations are for single whole-of-life policies, where a specific adult wishes to underwrite a FLAT, at various ages. Waiver of premium benefit is usually only payable to the age of 65. It provides for the premiums to be paid for you should you become sick, ill or disabled in terms of the definition, so that you cannot work, and therefore become unable to afford the premiums. Note that the equalization of premiums for males and females of the same age, has meant that premiums are the same cost.

If proceeds are to be directed to a joint estate, payable on the second death, then the premiums are much cheaper. Take a couple older than the examples above, Roger and Emily Newhouse. They were both born in 1958 and are aged 61 this year. They have a need for a joint-life second-death policy to pay an amount of £400,000 into trust on the second death. They choose maximum cover as the cheapest option now, with the premiums and sum assured guaranteed not to change for the next ten years. Thereafter, on review, they are aware that premiums may go up.

The premiums are £49.71 per month, and with waiver of premium included to the age of 65, will rise to £53.08 per month for £400,000 cover paid into trust on the second death.

Example

Michael lives with Nancy, and has two children from a previous marriage. He wishes to give Nancy an income when he dies, meet his expected IHT bill and start his two children off on the housing ladder. He is advised to take out a whole-of-life policy with waiver of premium for £500,000.

FLAT

Michael age 45 pays £52.92 per month to a maximum cover whole-of-life policy, written in trust for £500,000	£500,000 is paid into a Funded Life Assurance Trust (FLAT) to meet the IHT liability of £150,000 and to produce an income for his Partner Nancy of £12,500 per annum after leaving legacies of £50,000 each to his two children from a former marriage.

On Death

IHT Liability of £150,000	£100,000 to two children	£250,000 to provide an income of £12,500 p.a. (invested at 5%)

19

Discounted Gift Trusts

*DGTs and investment bonds for immediate IHT reduction.
The implications for income planning and removing
investment growth out of your estate.*

The discounted gift trust (DGT) is one of the prime products available to investors today to reduce their potential inheritance tax bill immediately. The investment is essentially in two parts, where a portion of the investment can be designated as a discounted income stream, and immediately taken out of your estate, with the balance of the investment gifted to a class of beneficiaries or named beneficiaries as a potentially exempt transfer (PET). The DGT allows the gifting of a lump sum into a trust whilst retaining a lifelong 'income' from the money (which are actually withdrawals of capital), with the aim of reducing IHT on death.

HMRC continue to examine trusts and to consult on changes that could be made to counter tax avoidance. However, on 22 July 2015 it was announced that 'HMRC spares 'non-aggressive' trusts from IHT avoidance scheme crackdown'. HM Revenue & Customs has proposed strengthening the 'hallmarks' it uses to identify inheritance tax planning arrangements but has excluded certain types of trusts used alongside life assurance policies.

A scheme will fall under the disclosure of tax avoidance schemes regime if its main purpose is to obtain an IHT advantage and if it is 'contrived, abnormal, or unlikely to have been made if there were no tax advantage'. However, the legislation specifically exempts Discounted Gift Trusts used with a life assurance policy as well as Loan Trusts, as they are accepted by HMRC as non-aggressive planning opportunities.

Discounted portion

The first part is an allowable discounted income stream, and the proportion of an investment which can be so designated is based on your age, state of health, whether you are a smoker or not and whether investing singly or as a couple jointly. It is also based on the future income yield selected. The higher the income yield, the higher the proportion of the investment which can be designated allocated as the 'discounted portion'. The potential future stream of income is valued as being spent from your estate and this provides an immediate discount from future inheritance tax in your estate. This is the open market value of the regular withdrawals. Whilst alive the stream of income to you is from a trust (often a bare trust) and the income ceases on your death. Its value is then worth nil, as it was held for the settlor absolutely. As this was not a CLT there is no exit charge.

Invested portion

The balance of the investment is gifted into a trust, specially set up for this purpose. For trusts set up before 22nd March 2006, this investment was seen as a PET and was out of your estate should you survive for seven years. It was an interest-in-possession or life-interest trust. Most life assurance companies prefer a more flexible trust arrangement. Since 22nd March 2006, you can select a bare or absolute trust which will still be a PET, or a more flexible discretionary trust, which will be a CLT. IHT is only paid in advance at 20% if the investment actually made into the trust is above the nil rate band. The nil rate band is £325,000 in 2019/20.

In later years, if the investment performs strongly, it could be above the IHT threshold. The trust could then be subject to periodic and exit charges. However, with proper planning and even multiple trust arrangements, set up on different days, most of this extra charging or taxation could be avoided.

On your death, the discounted income stream ceases, and if, under schemes set up *before* 22nd March 2006 (or bare trust schemes), you have survived for seven years, then the capital beneficiaries of the invested portion receive their share, and this is out of your estate, with the growth on it.

If you have effected a DGT *after* 22nd March 2006, then depending on the kind of trust used, there could be potential for IHT to be paid (at the lifetime rate) if the amount invested is over the available nil rate band at the time £325,000 in 2019/20) – the IHT would be charged at the lifetime rate, and on your death a calculation would made to pay the balance of the IHT then due. The capital passes to your beneficiaries, as being the investment value of the trust.

There are many different kinds of trust planning devices available to you, and the structure depends on what you want from a trust.

Do you wish to make a gift, but require an income?
If the answer is yes, then the following trusts and investments are possible:

- **Estate transfer trust:** for access to original capital and future growth
- **Gift and loan trust:** for access to original capital, but not to future growth
- **Retained interest trust:** for access to some capital, whilst making a PET
- **Discounted gift trust:** no access to capital, but an immediate IHT saving

If you wish to make a gift, but do not require an income

- **Gift trust bond without life cover:** no income, for a gift of capital and no specified sum paid on death
- **Gift trust bond with life cover:** no income, a gift of capital and a specified sum paid on death

Where an income is required to fund premiums

- **Gift trust or gift trust bond:** funds a regular premium whole-of-life

The above are the more common structures, although the names may differ from one product provider to another.

Getting the best discounts for IHT from a DGT

The allowable 'discounted portions' can range enormously, depending on age, health, and the chosen income levels. The highest discounts are where high levels of income are withdrawn, where ages are young, and you are in good health. The worst discounts for IHT are where you are in advanced age, with poor health, and taking a low income. If your health is poor you may not even get underwritten for the discount.

Prior to 1 December 2013, rates were gender-specific and favoured females. However, in 2013 HM Revenue and Customs (HMRC) stated that from 1 December 2013 discounts calculated for new discounted gift schemes have to be gender-neutral. The same rates must be offered to both males and females. It is possible to set the DGT up on a single or a joint-life basis. If the income is to continue until both partners are deceased the value of the withdrawal (the discounted portion) obviously increases.

At present, different product providers may publish different discount tables, but the HMRC have recently announced their intention to publish their own discount tables to be used by product providers. The following table gives examples of the sort of rates that might currently apply:

Age	Health	Smoker	Income yield	Discounted portion
55	Good	Yes	5%	57.44%
55	Good	No	7.5%	88.30%
65	Good	No	7.5%	73.54%

85	Reasonable	No	5% esc at 5%	26.57%
65 & 62 (joint)	Good	No	5%	79.28%
85 & 82 (joint)	Reasonable	No	5% esc at 3%	46.08%
58 & 55 (joint)	Good	No	5%	87.11%

You can have a low starting income and then add an escalating income; the increase income withdrawals will be reflected in an increase in the discounted portion (i.e. reducing the value of the gift to the trust's beneficiaries).

The higher the level of discount, the smaller the gifted portion. It is the gifted portion that has to be within the nil rate band level when made, therefore the following will give you an idea of how much the overall investment could be without becoming subject to chargeable event taxation.

Example

Age	Health	Smoker	Income yield	Discounted portion
55	Good	Yes	5%	57.44%

On a £100,000 investment, £57,440 (i.e. 57.44%) is immediately out of the estate, and £42,560 (42.56%) is the gifted portion.

To calculate the maximum investment possible without taking the gifted portion over £325,000 (the present nil band rate), divide £325,000 by 0.4256 = £763,627.

Check

* The discounted portion is £763,627 x 57.44% = £438,627

* And the gifted portion is £763,627 x 42.56% = £325,000 (the nil rate band)

* Total: £763,627

This person could then invest a total of £763,627. Of this, £438,627 would immediately fall out of her estate, with IHT savings of £175,451. After seven years, the balance of the investment drops out of the estate with IHT savings of £130,000 on the investment in trust of £325,000. If the investment had grown to £425,000 over the next ten years, then the growth would be outside of the settlor's estate as well, another £40,000 in IHT savings. However, if the investment grew beyond the nil rate band at the periodic review stage it could be subject to a tax charge, if more than the nil rate band at the time, and if there was entry charge payable.

The calculation must therefore show the discount available as well as the amount for the nil rate band trust.

Income is calculated on the whole investment, not just the discounted portion and 5% of £763,627 would be £38,181 per annum for life at 5% of the amount invested. This income cannot be changed and must be taken once selected. It is also not taxable at the time it arises if at 5% or less.

Single or joint lives?

There are a number of discount options available. The usual options are for single or joint investments and options. However, one spouse may be in poor health, or you may wish for joint income arising from a single life case, and this may be possible. It would be preferable for the income to continue to the other spouse should one die (and not cease).

Bare trust or flexible discretionary trust?

This is for the gifted portion, where there will be beneficiaries. The bare trust is seen as being inflexible, the discretionary trust more flexible. The gift to the bare trust is a PET, and you must survive for at least 7 years for it to be out of your estate. The gift to a discretionary trust is a CLT and will be subject to lifetime IHT if made above the nil rate band.

On death, the PET made into the bare trust could be out of your estate after seven years or subject to IHT, but with taper reliefs applying. The gift as a CLT to the discretionary trust would now be subject to the death rate of 40% less lifetime tax paid (but no refund on tax if overpaid). There is no ongoing IHT payable where the bare trust is used, but the discretionary trust could be subject to periodic charges every ten years up to a maximum of 6% of the then trust fund. There is no periodic or exit charges applying to the settlor's fund on the regular withdrawals.

If using a bare trust, then the beneficiaries must be named from the outset and they are absolute beneficiaries and cannot be changed. The settlor is excluded as a beneficiary. Under the discretionary trust regime, there are no named beneficiaries and these can be flexibly appointed at any time to benefits and removed, if desired. A spouse or civil partner can be a beneficiary under both trusts.

If using a bare trust and a named beneficiary dies, then the capital value of the beneficiary's interest forms part of his estate, even if the settlor is still alive. This is not the case with a discretionary trust.

On death of the settlor, the trustees pay out the proceeds of the bond to the beneficiaries, or assign the bond to beneficiaries, or maintain the bond subject to the original trust. During the settlor's lifetime, the bond can be surrendered. If using a bare trust, then the named beneficiaries must consent to this; if using a discretionary trust then only the settlor's consent is required.

The bare trust route does give certainty, but is inflexible with regard to adding beneficiaries and other changes. The discretionary trust has wider options and powers and beneficiaries do not need to be named. This could be important for the passing of assets down the generations in the future.

Full underwriting

For HMRC to accept the discount in the future, it is important to have full underwriting at the outset. Poor health cases may result in lower revised discounts. This an area where HMRC may actively contest the discount, and already one or two product providers have adjusted their discount rates to lower levels. Underwriting the client provides for greater certainty if ever challenged.

Gift and loan arrangements

This type of trust and investment arrangement suits a person with an IHT liability who has substantial capital. The plan enables the investor to freeze the growth of the investment in his estate, or to reduce the potential IHT liability. A nominal gift is made to a trust, and at the same time a more substantial amount of capital is loaned to the trust. You can retain control over your capital and have access to loan repayments through tax-efficient withdrawals. Beneficiaries can have IHT-free benefits built up for them outside the settlor's estate. The interest-free loan made to the trustees is repayable on demand. The trustees invest the loan (say into an investment bond) and there can be 5% tax deferred withdrawals taken from the trust's investment. Essentially the investment growth is frozen in the settlor's estate and the use of the loan reduces the estate by the loan value. Any loan outstanding at death could be taxable in the settlor's estate.

There is no gift when setting up a loan trust, so there is no CLT and no IHT payable on the loan element, no matter how large the loan is. The nominal gift made is covered by an exemption such as the annual exemption of £3,000 (£6,000 if no gift made in the preceding year) or the nil rate band. The value of the trust fund at the ten-yearly periodic charge is reduced by the value of the outstanding loan. Only the value of the investment growth will be subject to any charges. Capital payments can be stopped or started at the settlor's request; the settlor could decide that no further repayments of capital are required and waive his right to the outstanding loan and so convert it to a gift at that time. Be careful with your choice of arrangements and trustees as you do not wish the 'gift with reservation' rules to apply.

Some may wish to combine the discounted gift trust with the loan and gift trust arrangement, and the two IHT mitigation regimes can be very useful in estate and inheritance tax planning.

20

Insuring for IHT liabilities

Decreasing term assurance for PETs, and whole-of-life second death policies. Explaining how maximum and standard coverages work, and the optimal structure to reduce premium costs. Policies written in trust to escape IHT on the policy proceeds.

In conjunction with other IHT planning, insuring for the IHT liability is an option used by many. Estate liquidity is important and to provide much needed cash at the point when it is required, is vital. This is especially the case where assets are difficult to sell, or where you may not wish the assets to be sold. For example, the family home could make up the bulk of your estate, and you would not wish to sell it to pay for inheritance taxes. You may have earmarked cash and investments for other purposes, and may not wish it to be used to pay for estate liabilities. Inheritance taxes are not the only things insured for – you may wish to pay off a mortgage or loans and other debts on death.

There are different types of life assurance policies which can be used, depending on the purpose. If the purpose is to make a gift to another where the potentially exempt transfer rules apply, and you survive for seven years, then the value of the gift is out of your estate. However, if you die within the seven-year period, then a portion of the gift falls back into your estate for IHT purposes. Here, the most appropriate life policy is a decreasing term insurance. If you wish to cover an IHT liability generally, then the best type of policy is a whole-of-life.

Decreasing term assurance

This type of life policy decreases in value as the liability reduces. At the end of the investment period there is no value and the policy ceases. If Cyril makes a gift to his nephew Charlie which is worth £100,000, and he survives for seven years, then the value of the gift is left out of his estate for IHT purposes. However, if he dies during the seven -year period then a portion of it will fall back into his estate. His nephew, as recipient of the gift, would have to pay the inheritance tax arising, and could insure Cyril for the amount of the liability and pay the premiums on the policy. Assume Cyril is aged 57 on his next birthday, and has used his available estate exemptions, including the value of the nil rate band for other purposes. The proportion that falls back into the estate for IHT within the seven-year period, and taxable at 40% is:

Years before death	Tax	Taxable Reduction Amount	Tax to Pay
0-3	0%	£100,000	£40,000
3-4	20%	£80,000	£32,000
4-5	40%	£60,000	£24,000
5-6	60%	£40,000	£16,000
6-7	80%	£20,000	£8,000
7+	100%	£0	£0

The policy should be able to meet the IHT liability at any of the stages during the taxable period. The premium for £40,000 worth of decreasing term cover with guaranteed premiums is £10 per month. For comparison purposes, a level term premium would be £12.15 per month.

If his wife Penelope, who is aged 68, had made the gift, her premium would be £21.91 for £40,000 worth of decreasing term cover, and level cover would be £33.44 per month for comparison purposes. Although Penelope is more than ten years older than Cyril, the difference in premium cost is not that great.

Whilst decreasing term cover meets the exact liability, level term cover remains constant at £40,000 for the full seven years, and some may prefer it, to provide for contingencies, such as increasing IHT liabilities in the future.

All term cover has no investment element, and at the end of the term, the cover ceases.

The total premium costs for Charlie, Cyril's nephew, over the seven-year period is £840 for the decreasing term assurance starting at £40,000 and decreasing to nil at the end of the seven years.

Whole-of-life assurance

If the IHT liability needs to be funded for, how the policy is set up depends on your circumstances. If single, then a whole-of-life policy on a single life is used. If married or in a civil partnership, then more commonly a whole-of-life policy on joint lives, payable at the second death is used. This is because of the 'spouse exemption' where assets passing to a spouse or civil partner on death are exempt from IHT. The estate value is compounded in the hands of the second person dying and therefore the policy required must pay out on the second death.

If you are married or in a civil partnership and you leave your estate to another who is not your spouse, then there is nothing for the spouse exemption to apply to and your estate will be taxable, if over the nil rate band, and other exemptions applying. In this case, you may wish for two single policies to be taken out, each payable immediately on death.

If you are not married or in a civil partnership but cohabiting, there is no spouse exemption, and assets passed to the cohabitee will be subject to inheritance tax. Again, single policies should be used.

There is much said about joint-life first-death policies. Avoid these if at all possible. They cover two lives, but will only pay out once, on the death of the first-dying. The survivor will then have no cover in place. It is always better to have two separate whole-of-life policies, where both will pay out, even if the premiums are more expensive.

Why whole-of-life? Some providers used to provide an open-ended term policy, with guaranteed premiums and a sum assured that would not change, or would write a term policy to the age of 120, to ensure that you would be covered over the period. However, these types of policies are costed each year at your age for that year and could become prohibitively expensive. Whole-of-life is exactly that – it will cover you over your lifetime, ensuring the funds are available when required at any time should death occur.

The problem, though, has been that after the first ten years on all whole-of-life policies, the premiums are reviewable, and may increase. There has not been certainty in the process with regard to premiums payable and levels of coverage going forward after that period. Recent innovations by life assurance companies have now produced a whole-of-life product that provides guaranteed premiums throughout the life of the client, as well as a guaranteed sum assured, which may be escalated, if required. This innovation provides a half-way house between the certainty of term cover and premiums, but over a whole lifetime.

Whole-of-life cover can be very cheap or expensive, depending on the type of contract used. The two main products available are *maximum cover* whole-of-life and *standard cover* or *balanced* whole-of-life policies.

Maximum cover whole-of-life

This is the cheapest form of whole-of-life cover available. There is a very small investment element in the policy and premiums are therefore more likely to increase after the first ten years. In the first ten years, premiums and cover levels are guaranteed, thereafter, they are reviewable, and the review process is usually every five years after the first review, and even more frequently, for some product providers.

Standard or balanced whole-of-life cover

This type of policy is much more expensive. The reason is that your premiums and the investment returns earned on your money build up a policy reserve. After the initial ten-year period, the value of the policy reserve will determine the extent of premium increases, if any. The bigger the policy reserve, the less likelihood of premium increases in the future. However, the life assurance company has the choice to say whether that policy reserve belongs to you or not. Let us assume that you have a whole-of-life standard cover policy with a sum assured (the amount that is payable on death) of £1 million. Your policy reserve through premium accumulation after ten years is £350,000. What would you get on death – £1 million or £1,350,000? The answer is only £1 million as the sum assured only is payable. The policy reserve goes to the life assurance company.

As a result, many people cash in or surrender their policies to get at their 'investment' in the policy, losing the valuable life cover benefits. It is possible to choose a premium more suited to affordability, which will be between the maximum cover premium and the standard cover premium offered to you. You will therefore build up a smaller policy reserve and take a risk on future premium increments being lower than they would be under a maximum cover policy. You need to choose a life assurance company with solid investment performance and work out the possible future premium increases at review periods. This exercise can save you on cash flowing throughout the period and give you the cover, but there is a risk of premiums increasing at review periods.

Guaranteed whole-of-life

The guaranteed whole-of-life policy does not have a review period, and premiums and sum assured are guaranteed. Whilst the policy reserve builds up in the normal way, this is unable to be accessed by the client. However, you have certainty and can plan your cash flows accordingly.

Examples

Brian and Tessa have recently completed an estate planning analysis and find that after using all exemptions there will be an IHT liability in the second death's estate of £600,000. Brian is aged 57 next birthday and Tessa will be aged 55.

They decide to cover their IHT liability with a whole-of-life second death policy written in trust for the benefit of their three children, who will inherit from them and could pay the IHT using the proceeds of the life policy. Premiums and surrender values are illustrative only and will be different depending on your personal circumstances.

Option 1
Whole-of-life second death, maximum cover
Sum Assured: £600,000
Premium: £41.18 per month
Annual cost as % of cover: 0.08%
Total premiums first ten years: £4,941.60
Total premiums as a % of cover at 10 years: 0.82%
Surrender value year 10: £530
First ten years: sum assured and premium guaranteed not to change
Thereafter: expect premium reviews and increased premiums
Waiver of Premium: to the age of 65.

Option 2
Whole-of-life second death, balanced or standard cover
Sum Assured: £600,000
Premium: £460.83 per month
Annual cost as % of cover: 0.92%
Total premiums first ten years: £51,840
Total premiums as a % of cover at 10 years: 9.21%
Surrender value year 10: some plans have no surrender value, others do
First ten years: sum assured and premium guaranteed not to change
Thereafter: expect premium reviews and possible increased premiums
Waiver of Premium: to the age of 65.

Option 3
Whole-of-life guaranteed cover
Sum Assured: £600,000
Premium: £707 per month
Annual cost as % of cover: 1.41%
Total premiums first ten years: £84,840
Total premiums as a % of cover at 10 years: 14.14%
Surrender value year 10: £0
The premiums and sum assured are guaranteed not to change over the life of the policy. There are no premium reviews.
Waiver of premium: to the age of 65

From the above, Tessa and Brian have a number of choices and flexible options. They can select a number of options, for example, 50% of their cover at the maximum cover level and 50% at the guaranteed cover and premium level. The annual cost of the premiums when viewed against the amount of cover provided in the three scenarios above range from 0.08% to 1.41% for £600,000 worth of cover. Against this must be viewed the full IHT liability of £600,000 heading in the Chancellor's direction at 40%. In the final analysis, much will come down to affordability and monthly cash-flow. The costs must be weighed against not having the benefits available.

Premium payment periods

Whilst a whole-of-life policy continues for your lifetime, many life assurance companies do not charge a premium after a certain age is reached, using the policy reserve to sustain the cover. This varies from one life assurance company to another, and the range is between the age of 85 and 100 years old in most instances. Premiums may be paid monthly, quarterly or annually. If a single premium payment is made, this could render the policy non-qualifying and any gain may be subject to tax. However, investment bonds could be single premium life assurance contracts and often pay out up to 101% of value on death.

Writing a policy in trust

Policies underwritten in trust escape IHT on the policy proceeds and it also means that they do not have to be taken into account for probate purposes. It is pointless not to underwrite in trust as 40% of the policy proceeds could be lost in further inheritance taxes, thus greatly reducing the benefit of the cover in the first place. If your existing policies are not in trust, you can have them moved into trust – however this may be a potentially exempt transfer (PET), and you need to survive for seven years for the proceeds to be out of your estate.

Paying premiums and IHT

HMRC view the payment of premiums as a mechanism to reduce your estate for the benefit of another. You may make annual premium payments of at least £3,000 under the annual exemption limits (£6,000 if no gifts made in the preceding year), and anything above that should be surplus to your normal living needs requirements for that exemption to apply (expenditure out of revenue, not capital, surplus to your requirements). Keep proper records, in case this issue arises, to show your income and expenditure patterns. See below under changes to life policy rules.

Waiver of premium benefit

This add-on to the premium for the life cover provides a mechanism whereby if you become sick, ill, injured or permanently disabled so that you cannot work, that the life assurance company will pay your premiums for you. The benefit is usually only available up to the age of 60 or 65 (depending on the life assurance company), but is a valuable benefit and should be considered. The age limitation is to cover your work period before going into retirement, when your retirement income becomes available.

Planning cash flow

Premiums easily affordable whilst you are working can become more onerous in retirement. It is therefore important to obtain a cash flow of future premiums early on in the process to check future affordability.

The use of life assurance in estate planning and inheritance tax funding is most important. The younger you are when policies are taken out, the cheaper the premiums will be. You may not have a liability to IHT now, but may have one in the future, and protection policies should be part of your planning, as well as the review of existing covers.

Changes to Life Policy Rules

Life assurance qualifying policy rules have changed. New policies issued after 6 April 2013 will have their annual contributions limited to £3,600 p.a. This legislation will affect contributions to MIPs (monthly investment plans) seen as an alternative to pension funding. Restrictions will apply on tax relief available to the proceeds of regular premium life assurance policies. This will usually only apply to policies with a large investment element. Those policies where the investment element is small or non-existent will not be affected. There could be an effect though where large premium IHT policies are required that have an investment element that grows. The premiums on these policies can be substantial and for new policies issued after 6 April 2013, if in breach of the £3,600 p.a. premium rule, could make the policy non-qualifying with a taxable gain on death.

If covering an IHT liability with life assurance, it will be better to have a whole of life policy with a guaranteed sum assured and no investment element, or one where the level of premiums paid will be greater than the investment element. It will not then matter if the premium limit of £3,600 p.a. is exceeded as there will be no gain to tax. [The gain would be the difference between the premiums paid and the surrender value of the policy, not the difference between the premiums paid and the policy payout, or proceeds on death]. Always take professional advice before acting.

21

Investments

Investments that are fully taxable on death; investments that give IHT tax relief. Wrapping investments to protect them from IHT and other taxes. Death-bed planning with investments. Pensions, annuities, EIS and other investments.

Most investments will fall into your estate on death and may be subject to inheritance taxes, depending on your personal circumstances. These include ISAs (unless a part is invested through the ISA into EIS qualifying shares), investment bonds, property, works of art, wine and stamp collections, cash in bank and building society deposits, national savings, and anything you may own. If you own an asset jointly, then only your share of it falls into your estate at death.

A number of investments will have inheritance tax exemptions, or be 'wrapped' in such a way that part or all of the investment will qualify for IHT reduction or relief. Generally, though, the rule is that all assets held worldwide fall into your estate if you are domiciled in the UK (or deemed domicile). It may be that your assets are taxable in another jurisdiction (for example your holiday home abroad), and in that event, a double taxation treaty should ensure that the same assets are not taxed on death twice.

Below is an outline of current inheritance tax planning mitigation and reduction schemes and strategies that are legislated for or in general use.

Enterprise Investment Scheme (EIS)

An EIS investment can be fully out of your estate after holding qualifying shares for two years. The investment must be made into qualifying unquoted companies, and these can include certain AIM stocks. Single EIS companies are more risky than investing into a portfolio of qualifying EIS companies, where your investment risk can be spread. This is not to say that companies invested into will not fail; some will, some should perform satisfactorily, and one or two companies in your portfolio may be stars. The hope is that with proper funding the EIS company invested into may be listed on the stock exchange and bring the investor significant gains. There are generous IHT, income tax and capital gains tax deferral reliefs available.

You can set up your own company and own 100% of the shares, or you can invest into someone else's company. You may qualify for business property reliefs (BPR) as well as EIS IHT reliefs, but will only get one relief. Up to £1 million may be invested per person in 2019/20 for income tax relief of 30%, but IHT relief is unlimited. The Seed EIS (SEIS) allows £100,000 to be invested per person for 50% tax relief in 2019/20. Back-dated SEIS relief is available for 2018/19. For any back-dated tax relief – to a previous tax year for EIS or SEIS contributions made in the current tax year – the rate that applies is the rate for that previous tax year (i.e. 2018/19 in this case).

Company shares

Setting up your own company

You can invest into your own company, where you own 100% of the shares, or into other companies that qualify. As long as the company carries on a qualifying trade, under the EIS (Enterprise Investment Scheme) rules, the value of the shares will be out of your estate for inheritance tax purposes after two years. EIS qualifying shares can be used to defer a capital gain at 10% (up to basic rate limit) or 20% (over the basic rate limit) or 28% if a property sale causes the gain. Product providers manage portfolios of trading companies that have been set up for individuals who own 100% of the company shares. The profits are shared between the company owners and the promoters. The minimum investment is usually around £50,000. After 3 years, the nature of the 'trade' may be changed, retaining the qualifying CGT and IHT reliefs. Similar qualifying partnership activities are available for the development of pubs, childcare centres and other investment possibilities. The company and the activity are managed for the investor. On death, after two years, the shares are out of your estate for IHT purposes, and any capital gains tax liabilities die with you.

Example

Philip has made a capital gain of £100,000 after disposing of a property. The capital gains tax payable is 28% (20% plus 8% for property), which would leave Philip with £72,000 after tax (assuming the gain is a net one after available reliefs).

Philip invests £100,000 (the gain) into his own company, carrying on a qualifying trade under the EIS rules, and managed by a large bank's management company. Profits will be shared 50/50 after costs.

Philip does not have to pay the capital gains tax which is deferred through making the investment – a saving of £28,000 – and he has a company with

£100,000 invested into it, which will participate in the construction of residential properties, along with 100 other similar companies. This is a qualifying trade. After two years, the value of the company shares has risen to £130,000. Philip dies. There is IHT relief of 40% not having to be paid on the investment (£52,000), which would have been paid had he not made the qualifying investment. Capital gains tax dies with you, so no CGT is crystallised on his death, saving another £28,000. Philip has saved £80,000 in taxes on his money, and has an investment worth £130,000.

Had he paid the capital gains tax he would have been left with £72,000. Had he invested this into ISA's and unit trusts, or bonds, on his death, the value after two years would be say £79,380 at 5% capital growth. On his death, he would lose 40% of this, i.e. £31,752 – leaving a balance of £47,628 for his heirs.

Could Philip have done better?

Investing into EIS companies generally

He could have invested into other EIS qualifying companies, and one that was not owned by him. He cannot have more than 30% in any one EIS company in order to qualify. If you invest into an unknown EIS qualifying company, such shares may be considered high risk and very volatile, and you could lose your capital. To diversify risk, it is better to invest into an EIS Share Portfolio – a holding in differentiated EIS qualifying shares. The investor invests into a portfolio of qualifying (usually AIM) stocks. This gives a spread to reduce investment risk through diversification. After two years, the value of the shares and the growth on them is out of your estate for inheritance tax purposes. Losses qualify for loss reliefs against either capital gains and/or taxable income. You can defer a capital gain through such an investment; income tax relief is available at up to 30% of the investment made capped at £1 million in 2019/20.

Philip, through investing into the EIS Portfolio now has income tax relief of 30% of his investment made (£30,000 off his tax bill), in addition to his capital gains tax deferral relief and inheritance tax reliefs.

For income tax relief, the investment must have been held for at least 3 years. This type of relief is given in the tax year when made and is equivalent to a guaranteed investment return of 10% p.a. (30% divided by 3 years), for the first three years.

Under this scenario, had Philip lived for 3 years rather than 2 years, he would have the benefit of income tax relief of £30,000, worth £12,000 at his marginal rate of 40%, on top of the CGT and IHT savings of £80,000 referred to in the previous illustration.

Moreover, if he lives longer, sells his shares after three years and immediately reinvests them, his position is even better. Assuming the shares were now worth £145,000 (the average return on most portfolios was around

15-16% p.a. up to 2006, but this has fallen considerably over the past two years to low single figures), there is no capital gains tax on the sale of the shares. Philip picks up further income tax relief of 30% x £145,000 = £43,500, worth £17,400 at a marginal income tax rate of 40%. He continues to defer his capital gains through the EIS investment; but the clock has started again for his IHT relief – he now has to wait for two years before the value of the investment and the growth on it is out of his estate.

Should a company fail in his portfolio, Philip would have loss reliefs against both income tax and capital gains tax for the amount of the unrelieved loss.

Portfolio investment returns have been good for some managers, poor for others. Some have high charging structures, others are more reasonable. One can go for sector diversification as well as company diversification. Venture capital returns have been as high as 20% in the past; however, falling stock markets during the past few years have severely affected values in AIM stocks, some of which have fallen by 50% or more. It is always better to seek investments with asset backing for more stable returns.

This type of investment may be better for IHT death-bed planning as the holding period is only two years to be fully out of the estate. The amount that can be invested is unlimited both for IHT mitigation and CGT reinvestment reliefs. It is only subject to a limit for income tax relief (£1 million per person). These investments must be considered high risk and you could lose your capital.

Life policies in trust

Life policies underwritten in trust are free of inheritance taxes. The premiums that you invest into a life policy should be reasonable and within certain limits, otherwise HMRC may regard paying them (on your own or on third parties' policies) as a depletion of your estate. However, everyone has an annual IHT allowance of £3,000 that is exempt (£6,000 if no gifts made in the preceding tax year), and as long as premiums are payable out of normal expenditure that does not reduce your standard of living, you should be within allowable limits.

Policies entered into after 22nd March 2006 and in trust could be subject to a tax charge, but there are exemptions that apply, such as policies paying off a mortgage on death or where providing for families on death.

Proceeds that continue to be held in trust above the level of the nil rate band, and invested, may then be subject to the trust taxation rules on periodic and exit charges. If a bare trust is used, the proceeds vest directly in the beneficiaries and no tax charges result. The advantage of life assurance as a means of future IHT-free money for your heirs, is that being underwritten in trust produces tax-free proceeds that are then reinvested by beneficiaries in a tax-efficient or IHT-efficient manner.

Investment bonds

Investment bonds are single premium whole-of-life contracts. They are non-qualifying and the gains on the bonds are subject to income tax (not capital gains tax), depending on whether you are a taxpayer or not. One may extract up to 5% 'income' per annum (strictly speaking, this is a return of capital and not income), and these 5%'s may be accumulated if not taken in any one year and then taken as a lump sum. If you invested into an investment bond and did not take 'income' for say 5 years, the cumulative effect is that 25% of the original investment can be taken as 'income' and there is no immediate tax charge. On their own, these bonds fall into your estate for inheritance tax purposes. However, you can elect to have a version of the bond that is 'wrapped' for IHT purposes, and an amount is immediately out of your estate for inheritance tax. This type of investment bond is known as a discounted gift trust, or DGT. *Note that any trail commission payable from your investment bond reduces the amount of the tax free withdrawal by that amount. So if on 0.5% trail per annum, the amount available to you is 4.5% of the 5% non taxable withdrawal.*

Discounted gift trust bonds (DGT)

Your investment is divided into in two parts. One part is set aside as a discounted income stream (the 'discounted portion') which gives you an immediate reduction from IHT. The second portion is a potentially exempt transfer (PET), where you are gifting the investment to children or grandchildren, or others. If you survive for seven years after making the gift, it will be out of your estate (plus the growth on it), for inheritance tax purposes.

The investment is made into a DGT with an immediate IHT saving on the 'discounted portion'. The younger you are, the greater the discounted portion, and hence the greater the immediate IHT saving. The discount is medically underwritten to avoid disputes with HMRC later. If the discounted portion is part of an absolute trust, it is not caught by the new trust taxation rules; the balance is gifted as a PET (potentially exempt transfer) to beneficiaries and is out of your estate after you have survived for 7 years (falling back in to your estate on a tapered basis if you fail to survive 7 years). This balance should be within your nil rate band for exemption purposes. Depending on ages, you could make investments of up to £400,000 that will be under the new tax regime for trusts. The DGT gives a fixed income to the settlor for life; it can be for joint lives or joint incomes. The higher the level of income chosen, the greater the discounted portion for inheritance tax purposes. Grandparents can pay for school fees using this income, for example. (See also Chapter 19 "Discounted Gift Trusts".)

Example 1

Mrs Cooper is aged 71 and wishes to invest into a discounted gift trust bond to provide her with an income for life. She wishes her grandchildren to benefit from the investment after she has died. She is a non-smoker. Mrs Cooper is currently invested into ISA's and has cash in a current account at a local bank. She can invest £100,000 and is concerned about inheritance tax and how to mitigate it.

Her health is good. She requires 5% income from her investment, fixed at that level for life.

Discounted portion for immediate IHT relief:	£50,280
Balance as a PET (to survive for seven years):	£49,720
Total:	£100,000
Immediate IHT savings of: 40% x £50,280 =	£20,112
Further IHT savings after 7 years:	£19,888
Full IHT savings after 7 years	£40,000
Income per annum	£5,000

Example 2

Rodney and Helen are aged 59 and 56 respectively. They are both smokers and require 3% income per annum, escalating at 3% per annum. They have a £100,000 to invest and are in good health (apart from smoker's cough!).

Discounted portion for immediate IHT relief:	£57,770
Balance as a PET(to survive for seven years):	£42,230
Total:	£100,000
Immediate IHT savings of: 40% x £57,770 =	£23,108
Further IHT savings after 7 years:	£16,892
Full IHT savings after 7 years	£40,000
Income per annum	£3,000p.a.
	+ 3% p.a.

Had they been non-smokers, the IHT discount is £67,930, as opposed to £57,770.

Example 3

Wilfred is aged 81 and requires 7.5% income per annum. He has £100,000 to invest and is in good health and is a non-smoker. He is single.

Discounted portion for immediate IHT relief:	£40,670
Balance as a PET(to survive for seven years):	£59,330
Total:	£100,000
Immediate IHT savings of: 40% x £40,670 =	£16,268
Further IHT savings after 7 years:	£23,732
Full IHT savings after 7 years	£40,000
Income per annum	£7,500 p.a.

As shown in the above examples, the amount of the discounted portion applicable depends on your state of health (better discounts the healthier you are), whether a smoker or not (better discounts if a non-smoker), on your age (better discounts the younger you are), and on the level of income you take (better discounts the more income you take) – see Chapter 19 for further details. The plans are flexible to suit your circumstances. Some investors may already be in an investment bond that is not IHT protected. You would need to encash the investment and transfer the proceeds to a discounted gift trust bond to qualify for the IHT protections. There may be a tax charge arising, but this could be offset through higher allocation amounts in your new investment policy, depending on which product providers are used.

For more risk-averse investors, the DGT route can be lower risk. However, you are also locked in to the investment and its income. Income taken above 5% from a bond will be 'taxable' at the amount over the 5% of the original investment made. In Wilfred's case above, 2.5% of his income will be taxable. He has no other income and at the age of 81, his income allowance is £12,000 in the 2019/20 tax year, and no tax would be payable on the £2,500, if he had no other income. His state pension income would be fully taxable less any unused allowances – in 2019/20 Wilfred can expect £129.20 per week (£6,718.40 p.a.). The state pension and additional bond interest will be within his personal allowance and therefore tax free to him (£2,500 plus £6,718.40 = £9,218.40, which is less than his £12,000 personal allowance).

Discounted gift trust bonds on death

For older bonds issued before 22 March 2006, the discounted portion is out of your estate and on your death, assuming HMRC accepts the discounted value. The balance of the investment made will be a PET – a potentially exempt transfer if made to bare, A&M and IIP trusts before 22nd March 2006. If you have survived for seven years, the value of this portion of your investment should fall out of your estate. If not, then the taper rules apply, and a proportion will fall back into your estate and be subject to IHT at 40%, if over the nil rate band of £325,000 in 2019/20). Your beneficiaries receiving the value of the investment will have to pay the IHT, if any, unless you stipulate that your estate is liable for it. If a new trust arrangement, then the new rules will apply after 22nd March 2006. The discounted portion will be out of your estate in the usual way, the balance may become a chargeable transfer (if a trust other than a bare trust was used), and if over the nil rate band and other exemptions will be subject to IHT at the death tax rate of 40%. CLTs where the lifetime rate of 20% will be taken into account, however no refund is made if tax has been overpaid.

Gift and loan trusts

Where you have a gift and loan trust arrangement, on death the value of any loan outstanding will fall back into your estate. However, the value of any investment made and the growth on it will be out of your estate for IHT purposes, and can accrue without tax in the hands of the beneficiaries.

Investments in trust

Where you have previously made gifts to trusts, (and where now invested in that trust), the structure and type of trust will determine whether you will be subject to IHT, as well as the manner in which the gift was made. If the gift was made before 22nd March 2006, different rules will apply than those applying if the gift was made after that date, and there are also transitional arrangements for interest-in-possession (IIP) and accumulation-and-maintenance trusts (A&M).

Before 22 March 2006, both IIP and A&M trusts were outside the discretionary trust regime and gifts made to these trusts were PETs. You had to survive for seven years for the gift to be out of your estate. After 22 March 2006 these trusts generally fall into the discretionary trust regime and after 22nd March 2006, could be subject to a lifetime IHT tax charge of 20% with the balance payable on death (if over the nil rate band at the time, going in to the trust). The only exemptions for new trusts are for (i) IIPs created by will or on intestacy, (ii) A&M trusts created on the death of a parent where beneficiaries take the trust assets at the age of 18, (iii) trusts for disabled people and (iv) regular premium life assurance policies written into trust.

Existing A&M trusts created before 22nd March 2006 will be treated as ordinary discretionary trusts from 2008 (unless the trust deed provides for the absolute transfer of assets to the child at the age of 18). Trustees have two years to change the terms of a will trust following death.

For existing interest-in-possession trusts, the current rules continue until the interest in possession ends. If the IIP ends on the death or during the lifetime of the life tenant and the assets of the trust pass to another individual absolutely, there are no further inheritance tax implications. If, however, the interest in possession ends on death and the assets remain in trust, then the value of those assets are included in the estate of the deceased and the new trust is taxed under the new rules (unless exempt). If the IIP ends during the lifetime of the individual, and the assets remain in trust, then the new rules apply (IHT entry charge if above the nil rate band threshold, periodic charge and exit charge).

An interest in possession is where, for example, you give the right to an income (and sometimes capital) to an individual, arising from the trust assets. This is more commonly a spouse or civil partner being provided for from investment assets in the will, or a third party. On death of the spouse or civil partner receiving the income (known as the life tenant), the capital will then usually pass to beneficiaries (known as remaindermen), or be recycled to provide income to others. Where the right to income ends and the assets of the trust pass absolutely to another, there is no IHT implication. It is where the assets remain in trust that IHT may be payable in the estate of the deceased, and the new rules will apply. The essence of the new legislation is that a new discretionary trust is created if the assets remain in trust and will be taxed under the discretionary trust regime.

It is therefore most important to regularly review trusts and wills to maximise your position and to plan accordingly.

PETS – potentially exempt transfers

It is still possible to reduce your estate by gifting assets and surviving for 7 years after doing that. The amount gifted will be totally out of your estate after 7 years, as well as any growth on that asset. There is no IHT or capital gains tax payable on the gifted asset by the recipient or the donor (unless the donor first realised the asset and paid CGT on it before gifting it).

Investments made into a bare trust (absolute trust) will remain a PET. However, if the child beneficiary is under the age of 18, the parent settlor will be taxed on trust income above £100. If the child beneficiary is over the age of 18, and the child is taxed, which is more favourable, as income tax and CGT annual allowances will be available to the child.

If a gift is made to another individual, this will be a potentially exempt transfer (PET) and no IHT is payable when the gift is made, of unlimited amount. If you, the donor, die within seven years, then the gift may become chargeable as a CLT (chargeable lifetime transfer) and subject to IHT, reduced by the nil rate band and taper reliefs.

Investments made by the donee (recipient of the gift) would then be for their benefit. Assuming the donor has survived seven years, there are no further IHT implications for the donor. The donee should ensure that the investment is itself protected from IHT.

Wealthy individuals can reduce their estates through gifting assets to children and grandchildren with no IHT arising, provided they survive for seven years. Generation skipping by a grandparent in favour of grandchildren will ensure that no IHT arises in the hands of their children, as assets pass to the grandchildren for their use and not the children, who may be wealthy in their own right.

Discretionary trusts

The position is different if the gift is made into a discretionary trust for an intended beneficiary, and the quantum of the gift is above the nil rate band (£325,000 in 2019/20). Then IHT is payable in advance at 20% on the amount over the nil rate band exemption. Note that you also have the annual exempt amount of £3,000 (£6,000 if no gifts made in the preceding year) to deduct in addition to the nil rate band).

Making gifts for investment into a discretionary trust will be subject to IHT, unless the nil rate band and other exemptions, such as BPR apply. There are also periodic and exit charges to contend with, and trust taxation at up to 45%.

Woodlands

The ownership of woodlands is treated as a business for IHT purposes and can attract 100% business property relief. Income derived from the sales of timber will not be subject to income tax or capital gains tax. The minimum investment is £5,000 if you invest through a syndicate and £50,000 if you invest directly.

Membership of Lloyds

Membership of Lloyds is treated as a business for IHT purposes. You could receive 100% business taper relief on syndicate business value attributable to the Lloyd's member.

All underwriting income is deemed trading income. The sale of syndicate capacity is subject to capital gains tax, but rollover relief and business taper reliefs apply.

Residential property

An investment into residential property is subject to inheritance tax. People owning their own homes feel most affected by inheritance tax, and naturally tend to seek IHT mitigation strategies. Some of these strategies involve equity release or home reversion plans, where you reduce the value of your home through either releasing equity or selling a portion of it. Other schemes involve selling your home and remaining in it, thus saving IHT. There is a new RNRB where leaving your residential property used as a home to direct descendants, which in 2019/20 is £150,000.

Getting your home out of your estate and still living there

This scheme was purportedly cleared by the HMRC and marketed by Close Brothers at the time. Your home is valued and sold to a bank's fund for cash. The cash is invested into an offshore bond with your children or grandchildren as beneficiaries. The bond also qualifies for a discount for IHT purposes. You must be aged over 65, and can live in your former home without tax penalty until your death or the death of the last dying of the couple if you are in a marriage or civil partnership. The house is effectively out of your estates for IHT. The minimum investment value is £400,000. A variant is to take a loan secured against the house and invest that into a Discounted Gift Trust (DGT) – see Chapter 19 for further details. A portion is immediately out of your estate (the discounted portion), and the investment gives you an income and pays the interest on the mortgage loan. On death the value of the commercial loan reduces your estate as a liability (but it must be repaid under the new rules, on death). In addition, the DGT element reduces the estate so that usually the full value of the house is out of your estate. Both schemes avoid the POAT and other GWR and benefit charges.

Gifts between spouses and civil partners

Gifts made by one spouse or civil partner to another have no tax implications during lifetime or death, provided the spouse receiving the gift is domiciled in the UK (otherwise the gift is limited to £325,000); and a strategy may be to 'equalise' your estates by making such gifts. That recipient spouse could make gifts, but it must not be conditional on the spouse to make such gifts, otherwise HMRC could apply the 'associated rules' and this will have tax implications.

In addition, if one of the parties is a higher-rated taxpayer and the other a lower-rated or non-taxpayer, it makes sound commercial sense to shift taxable investments to the lower-rated taxpayer, thus reducing the incidence of tax. There would be increased allowances for tax-reducing investments, such as

EIS investments, that are not only income tax relievable, but also provide inheritance tax protection.

Every individual has a nil rate band of £325,000 in 2019/20 and could make gifts to others within the NRB, that would be IHT exempt. You also have annual allowances of £3,000 p.a. each (£6,000 if no gifts made in the preceding year), and can make gifts in contemplation of a child's marriage and other IHT reducing allowances. Spreading assets and taxable income amongst multiple taxpayers is a good strategy for reducing taxes all round, and ultimately IHT.

It may be that couples are on their second marriage or civil partnership and decide not to make full use of the spouse exemption at 100% of assets left to a spouse or civil partner, but rather to benefit children or even former spouses. If that is the case, then they could increase their exposure to IHT, as one of the main IHT exemptions – the spouse exemption – is not being fully utilised. In these circumstances, it is particularly important to maximise utilisation of both partners' nil rate bands. If one spouse or civil partner has insufficient assets to make use of their nil rate band, and the other partner has assets that take them over the nil rate band, then by passing assets from the second to the first, they could use that extra nil rate band amount. Advance planning is therefore essential. For example, if one spouse or civil partner is in poor health, and the other is not, a higher discount for IHT could be obtained for a discounted gift trust investment (DGT) for the healthier spouse. The spouse or civil partner in ill health could gift assets to the other to make the investment. Alternatively, NRBs are now transferable between spouses and civil partners and planning can take this into account. For example, the need to equalise estates is less if the unused portion of the NRB is available to either estate.

Investing in your own business

Investing in your own business could be a good investment for you and your family. You could qualify for 100% business property reliefs from IHT. Assets used in the business can qualify, but not investments or large cash holdings.

Non-UK domiciled individuals ("non-doms")

If domiciled outside the UK you may hold an authorised unit trust or share in an open-ended investment company (OEIC) with no IHT implications. In addition, if not domiciled, resident or ordinarily resident in the UK, there is no IHT on foreign currency accounts held in the UK.

There are new rules for non-UK domiciled individuals who are resident in the UK. For many with more than £2,000 p.a. arising foreign income from investments and using the remittance basis, there is a flat rate of tax of £30,000 per annum. The new rules in the Autumn Budget 2014 are:

- 7 out of last 9 years charge unchanged at £30,000 per year
- 12 out of last 14 years to increase from £50,000 to £60,000 per year
- 17 out of last 20 years – a new charge of £90,000 to be introduced.

As a direct consequence, trust investments and offshore investments are affected, especially if income producing. This may present opportunities for planning to reduce the incidence of taxation (i.e. investing into bond wrappers so that income does not arise, and consequently further IHT mitigation planning as well). This area is complex and expert advice is required. Also see the new statutory residency test discussed in an earlier chapter and its impact on domiciliary status. See the section on non-doms, Chapter 14 'Living Abroad'.

Pension benefits

Investments into authorised pension schemes, by making pension contributions, will not attract inheritance tax. These investments grow tax-free and are not subject to capital gains tax. At retirement (unless protected for a higher amount), a tax-free cash portion of 25% (now known as the pension commencement lump sum) can be paid to you income tax free. There are three main aspects to the pension fund. These are the fund itself, the tax-free cash on retirement and the pension or annuity arising from the pension fund as income.

The pension fund itself

If you die before retirement, your pension fund will be transferred to or used by your dependants for annuity or pension income without any IHT charge

If transferred to, or used for the benefit of a third party, who is not a financial or other proved dependant, there will be an IHT charge, less any exemptions that may apply, such as the nil rate band. If gifted to charity, there is no IHT charge.

If, on death, the pension fund is used by a spouse or civil partner, there is no IHT payable, (there will be a tax charge on the fund passing of 55%, but this is nil after 6 April 2015); on their death, the fund will be subject to IHT over the usual exemptions.

The tax-free cash

Unless invested into IHT protected investments, any tax-free cash not spent will form part of your estate for IHT purposes.

The pension or annuity

Once you are retired and in receipt of a pension or annuity, and you die, the pension or annuity dies with you (unless 'guaranteed') and will not be subject to inheritance tax. The underlying fund producing the pension or annuity is not subject to IHT. See Chapter 15 "IHT and Pension Funds" for further details.

Pension contributions made

These are not generally subject to IHT, even if made on behalf of another, such as a grandparent making a contribution for a grandchild. The PET rules could apply where you have to survive for seven years after making the contribution; however, the contributions are limited to £3,600 gross (£2,880 after income tax at 20% in 2019/20). It could be argued that you only make a net contribution of £2,880, which is within the annual exemption of £3,000 per person (£6,000 in the first year if you have not used your annual allowance in the previous year). Otherwise the 'expenditure out of surplus to normal income' allowance should apply. Make sure you keep records and document fully your income and expenditures, as HMRC are hot on the trail of possible chargeable transfers that could be subject to IHT.

Pension investments, if properly structured could have IHT reduction benefits for you and your family.

Moving your pension fund offshore

Strategies are currently being promoted whereby, with HMRC approval, you can move your pension fund to another EU jurisdiction, and when you die, there will be no IHT payable on pension funds, even if they pass to third parties. It is always wise to consult with leading tax planners before embarking on this type of planning.

HMRC has issued extensive guidelines on QNUPS and QROPS (qualifying pension transfers abroad). See **www.gov.uk/government/publications/list-of-qualifying-recognised-overseas-pension-schemes-qrops**.

For more information on IHT and pension funds, see Chapter 15.

Voluntary purchase annuities or PLAs

For this type of investment you invest your cash into an annuity for a period or for your lifetime. The annuity is made up of a capital and interest element, and when you receive income, a portion of it is not subject to income tax (the capital portion returned with each annuity payment). A voluntary annuity is also known as a purchased life annuity (PLA), and has nothing to do with annuities arising from pension funds. On your death within the guaranteed period, a portion of your capital may be returned to your estate. This is not exempt from IHT and may be subject to IHT if you have used your available exemptions, such as the nil rate band.

Gifts with reservation (GWR)

If you make a gift to a third party and you retain a benefit in or from the asset, then the value of the gift could be added back to your estate for IHT purposes. Suppose that you make a gift to a child or third party, such as your house, and you continue to live there without paying a commercial rent – such a gift retains a benefit to you and will be added back to your estate for IHT purposes. The donee (recipient) is liable to the tax arising and there may be other implications. For example, if you died without a will, the gift with reservation cannot be used in a deed of variation after death. Where the GWR has been made and the donor ceases to enjoy the benefit, the gift then counts as a PET from that date, and the donor must survive for seven years for it to be out of his estate.

There are exemptions to the GWR rules. For example, gifts out of income, annual IHT exempt gifts, gifts for the benefit of a spouse or civil partner without conditions, gifts involving excluded property, gifts into a settlement where the settlor is a trustee, gifts of business property and family company shares (but criteria apply).

Investing into farming

Agricultural property reliefs (APR) may apply, and 50% to 100% of the business and assets may be relievable in your estate. The business need not be in the UK to qualify. There are qualifying rules for 'relevant business property' and the amount of time you have held the assets that qualify – usually a minimum period of two years. If you inherit the property on the death of a spouse or civil partner, then your period of ownership can include the deceased's, otherwise, the period of ownership starts again.

The assets must have been used in the business for at least two years. For example, farm land not used in the business, but for personal use, should not qualify. However, farm land that is let would qualify. IHT, if payable, can be paid in annual instalments over a period of ten years. Where APR does not apply, it may be possible for BPR to apply. The rules are complex, and need careful consideration. For many, investments into farming are not a profitable exercise, so tread warily.

One strategy to reduce IHT is to take a mortgage against your home and invest into a farming partnership that buys land used in the business. Immediately the mortgage loan would reduce your IHT bill and after 2 years, you could have APR/BPR reliefs as well at up to 100%. You do have to service the mortgage loan though!

Death-bed planning

There are very few opportunities available for death-bed planning. Gifting of assets to others means you have to survive for seven years, and is hardly appropriate if you are at death's door. The three major effective areas are in EIS investments, where you need only survive for two years for the value of the shares to be out of your estate; using a discounted gift trust (DGT) has immediate effect for a portion of the investment coming out of your taxable estate – however this is subject to health underwriting and age and may not work, as HMRC could deny you the discount if you died too soon. Investing into businesses or farming with BPR and APR reliefs could be effective – but you must have owned the assets used in the business for at least two years. Excluded property trusts are possibly no longer effective (you basically sell your investments or properties to someone else's trust); however some versions may still work, according to tax experts. Gifting to charity is 100% effective and reduces your estate by the amount of the gift.

The choice and scope of investments that benefit from IHT reliefs are many and varied. Some investments are very high risk, such as EIS investments, even though they offer many tax breaks; with others the risks can be controlled (EIS own-company shares, or investing into low risk DGT bonds), or are lower risk. If there is a potential for IHT payable on your assets always at least consider 'wrapping' the investment for IHT purposes. For example, if you wished to invest into an investment bond for 5% income per annum, why not consider a discounted gift trust version that has immediate IHT reliefs as well?

Transferable NRBs available from 9th October 2007 may relieve IHT on smaller estates – those in total worth £650,000 and less in 2019/20 plus the RNRB of £150,000 – where the first NRB has not been fully utilised. This only applies to married couples or civil partners and their widows and widowers.

22

IHT and Tax Planning

Deaths in quick succession. The cumulative effect of the 7 and 14 year rules. Set up multiple trusts on different days to get more nil rate bands applying.

Deaths in quick succession

To avoid inheritance tax being paid twice on the same property, where two transfers of the same property occur with a five-year period, and both are chargeable to IHT, then relief operates through IHT being payable on the second transfer being reduced. (*IHTA 1984 s.141*)

The gifts can be lifetime or death gifts. IHT charged on the second transfer is reduced by quick succession relief.

The tax relief actually given is calculated as a percentage of the IHT paid on the first transfer, and then deducted from the IHT paid on the second transfer.

The relief is not relevant when the gift is received from a spouse or civil partner in lifetime or on death; or where received otherwise and no tax was paid on the first transfer.

Relief can be claimed even if you no longer retain the asset. It can also be claimed on trust assets where the person entitled to receive the income dies and there have been successive IHT charges to trust property. Relief is given as follows:

Period between transfer and death	Percentage Relief
Less than 1 year	100%
1-2 years	80%
2-3 years	60%
3-4 years	40%
4-5 years	20%

Example

William died on 28th October 2014, leaving an estate of £450,000. He had received a gift of £75,000 from his mother on 12th May 2012, on which he had paid IHT of £30,000, following his mother's death on 30th June 2013.

William died in the two to three-year period after the gift was made, and tax in his estate will be reduced by quick succession relief as follows:

Net transfer	£45,000
Tax paid £30,000 x 60% =	£10,800
Tax payable is reduced by	£10,800

Exempt and taxable gifts made – the 7 and 14 year rules

Gifts made during your lifetime could be exempt, potentially exempt (could fall back into your estate within seven years – PETs), or a chargeable lifetime transfer (CLT).

On your death, your estate may be subject to additional taxes. If you died within seven years of making a gift, be it chargeable or potentially exempt when made, then the value of such gift could fall back into your estate for IHT purposes.

All PETs made in the previous seven years become chargeable transfers. These are added to your other chargeable transfers in the last seven years (CLTs), and charged to IHT at the death rate of 40%.

Taper relief applies to reduce the IHT payable, if you died within three and seven years of making the gift initially chargeable, or now chargeable. This taper relief is not to be confused with deaths in quick succession relief, which is over a five-year period.

The IHT liability first has taper relief applied, and then any IHT paid during your lifetime is reduced. If the IHT paid during your lifetime exceeds the remaining liability it is not reclaimable.

Taper relief

Period between making the gift and death	Percentage reduction at death rates
0-3 years	100% – no reduction
3-4 years	80% – 20% reduction
4-5 years	60% – 40% reduction
5-6 years	40% – 60% reduction
6-7 years	20% – 80% reduction

On death, a calculation must be made to see whether any previous PETs now become chargeable, and also whether the balance of any lifetime tax is now payable.

Example

Christopher has made various gifts in the past, to his wife and son, as well as to a discretionary trust. Both he and Angela, his wife, are domiciled in the UK. He died on 5th August 2014. Calculations must be made to establish what falls in to his estate and how any chargeable transfers will be taxed. Over the whole period, one must go back over the past seven years. It may be that reference has to be made another seven years before the previous seven years (as you would look back seven years from the gift made seven years ago, making it 14 years altogether).

Christopher made the following gifts during his lifetime:

30.10.2005 – to wife Angela (exempt)	£1,200,000
11.11.2006 – to discretionary trust (CLT)	£200,000
3.3.2012 – to son Andy (PET)	£40,000
20.10.2012 – to discretionary trust (CLT)	£300,000

Both the CLTs were subject to annual exemptions of £6,000 – i.e. £3,000 for the year of transfer plus £3,000 unutilised from the preceding year.

At the time of his gift to the discretionary trust in October 2012, the tax position would have been calculated as follows:

Nil rate Band 2012/13:	£325,000
Add up CLTs of last seven years (£200,000) less the annual exemptions applicable (£6,000):	<u>£194,000</u>
Balance nil rate band available	£131,000
Gift to discretionary trust	£300,000
Less annual exemption applicable:	<u>–£6,000</u>
Chargeable lifetime transfer	£294,000
Less available nil rate band 2012/13	<u>£131,000</u>
Chargeable transfer	£163,000
IHT if payable by trustees at 20% (gross transfer)	£32,600
IHT if payable by Christopher at 25% (net transfer)	£40,750

On his death on 5th August 2014 the IHT position is recalculated. The time line is as follows:

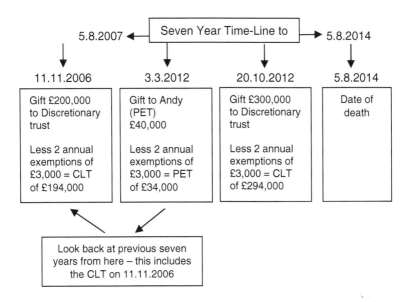

Because the PET to Andy has now become a CLT, we have to look back seven years from this date, and this will include the CLT on 11th November 2006. This is outside of the seven years from the date of death, and now into a 14 year period.

The nil rate band available to offset against the discretionary trust created on 20th October 2012 is as follows:

Nil rate band in the 2019/20 tax year (date death)	£325,000
Less CLTs in previous seven years	£194,000
Balance	£131,000
Less PET charged	£34,000
Balance	£97,000

The IHT due on the gift to the discretionary trust on 20th October 2010 is calculated as follows:

Gross chargeable transfer	£294,000
Available nil rate band 2019/20	£97,000
Chargeable transfer	£197,000
IHT payable by trustees at 40% (gross transfer)	£78,800

Less taper relief (0-3 years): 0% x £78,800	£0
Tax to pay	£78,800
Less lifetime tax paid by trustees	£37,600
Additional tax to pay (if trustees pay)	£41,200

Survival by the donor or settlor for as much of the seven years as possible will give greater tax discounts than Christopher achieved above. He died within three years of his last CLT, so no taper relief was available to him. Planning with the nil rate band determines whether lifetime taxes are payable on making gifts. Every settlement has its own nil rate band. Note the effect of a transferable NRB available that can be used to reduce chargeable transfers.

Multiple trusts

It is better to set up a number of smaller trusts on different days, than to create one large trust. As each settlement has its own nil rate band, significant tax planning can be done, using multiple trusts on different days. If used on the same day, HMRC could say that the intention was to create one large trust and not several smaller ones. However, be careful if gains accrue in one trust only. The exemption for capital gains is half the CGT personal allowance at £6,000, but this is divided by up to 5 trusts in existence with the same settlor. This means only £1,200 is available to each trust. Whereas, with multiple trusts, where gains are only experienced by one trust, the balance of the trust exemptions for capital gains allowance for the settlor will be lost. To use the multiple trust route would indicate significant values to be gifted above the nil rate band.

Note that the 2013 Autumn Statement introduced the concept of only one nil rate band per person of £325,000 (from 2015), and to not allow individual ones for each trust, as is the current system. This is a major attack on trusts that could see the periodic 10 year charges escalate as there will be fewer nil rate bands available to reduce their affect, whilst at the same time the new rule to treat undistributed income as capital for valuation purposes will provide more 'capital' to trusts to be taxed at the periodic review. The Autumn Budget 2014 reversed the above decision, so we still have the concept of multiple trusts set up on different days (Pilot trusts) each with its own nil rate band.

Order of gifting

The order of gifting is important and affects how your estate will be subject to IHT on death. Anyone can make a gift of up to the nil rate band £325,000 in 2019/20, and even if chargeable, no lifetime IHT will be paid. A gift to a discretionary trust will have immediate IHT payable at the lifetime rate of 20%

if made over the nil rate band and no other exemptions apply. A gift to a person or bare trust made of any amount will be out of your estate after seven years, as well as the growth on it, as a PET.

The following order is most effective for overall tax reasons:

1. Exempt gifts – for example, gifts between spouses or civil partners who are both UK domiciled, premiums paid on regular premium policies, use of the annual exemptions of £3,000 per annum, marriage gifts and others.

2. Gift and loan arrangements – here the trust used where the gift is exempt through the use of annual exemptions. The loan is not a CLT or a PET.

3. CLTs – chargeable lifetime transfers – for example, gifts made into a discretionary trust.

4. PETs – potentially exempt transfers – for example a gift to your children, or into a bare trust.

23

Case Study 1

Individual High Net Worth Planning

Ken and Amy Brossard are typical of many 'Middle England' families. They own their own home, have some investments, and cash in the bank, life assurance policies, credit cards and a mortgage. Both are employed, Ken (age 57) in consulting and Amy (age 44) as an NHS physiotherapist. Ken earns £46,500 per annum and Amy £22,184. Ken has a works money purchase pension scheme and Amy is in the NHS Superannuation pension scheme. They have two children, Toby aged 7 and Nicholas aged 10.

Ken and Amy are most concerned about their financial futures, especially with having two young children. Normal retirement age is 65 for both. Amy is particularly concerned about having to work even harder to pay for school and university fees for the children, as most of her income pays for education provision, and as a couple they are committed to this.

As an only child, Amy should inherit a substantial amount from her parents over the next ten years – in excess of £500,000. They are both concerned about their IHT positions. Amy's parents are elderly and not in good health.

Ken does not have a will. He would like a will where assets are held in trust for the children and with a life rent to Amy. Amy does have a will leaving assets in trust to the children to the age of 21.

There are no living trusts onshore or offshore. No gifts have been made to others.

Amongst their objectives are the following, with '1' being most important, and '4' being least important.

1. Family Protection in the event of death of a parent [1]
2. Improving mortgage arrangements [1]
3. Regular savings [1] for Ken [2] for Amy
4. Planning for retirement [1] for Ken [2] for Amy
5. Inheritance tax planning and Wills [1]
6. Planning for school and university fees [1]
7. Income tax reduction [1]
8. Cash flowing improvement [1]

The above is mostly for background information, so that you can get a 'feel' for Amy and Ken's personal situation. In our case study scenario, only the inheritance tax and estate planning issues are being dealt with.

The following is the estate position, should death occur in 2019/20. The house is jointly-owned.

Assets	Ken	Amy
House (joint)	£300,000	£300,000
Contents	£25,000	£25,000
Life policies in trust	£250,000	£216,400
Life policies not in trust	£455,425	£243,000
Motor Vehicles	£15,000	£7,000
Other assets	£0	£0
Equities – ISAs	£20,866	£0
Bank accounts	£10,000	£11,250
Total Estate	**£1,076,291**	**£802,650**
Liabilities		
Mortgage	£130,000	£130,000
Credit cards	£11,000	£500
Last expenses (funeral and hospital)	£5,000	£5,000
Net Estate	**£930,291**	**£662,650**

Assume death in service benefits in trust, outside of the estate.
Pension benefits pass directly to widow/widower.

Inheritance tax position if Ken dies intestate

Under the **rules of intestacy**, if the deceased was married and there are issue alive at death, the surviving spouse takes absolutely the deceased's personal chattels and the first £250,000. The remainder is held on statutory trusts and is divided equally among the surviving spouse and the deceased's issue, where the spouse takes only a life interest in their half- share, and the remaining half-share is held in trust for the deceased's issue. On the death of the surviving spouse, the first half-share will also pass to the issue. The surviving spouse may redeem the life interest in the estate. This may be appropriate when the beneficiaries are all adults as the whole estate may then be distributed. On redemption the surviving spouse receives the capital value of the life interest.

IHT liability, first death

If Ken dies first

Ken has no will and his estate passes intestate. After £250,000 and personal chattels have passed to the spouse, Amy has a life interest in a half-share of the residue. The children share the other half of the residue and also take the surviving spouse's share on the spouse's death. The value of the house automatically passes to the survivor if jointly owned.

Net Estate	£930,291
Less assets under the Spouse exemption	
Assets to or for benefit of the spouse	£250,000
House	£300,000
Contents	£25,000
Less policies in trust	£250,000
Less Nil rate band*	£325,000
(*residue in statutory trusts)	
Taxable Estate	£0
IHT payable	**£0**

If Amy dies first

Amy's estate is as follows (leaving everything to her children):

Net Estate	£662,650
Less policies in trust	£216,400
Less nil rate band	£325,000
Taxable	£121,250
IHT at 40%	**£48,500**

IHT liability, second death

The cumulative position (i.e. total taxes paid on both deaths) will be as follows:

Joint estate:	£1,592,941
Less life policies in trust	£466,400
Less 2 nil rate bands	£650,000
Taxable	£476,541
IHT at 40%	**£190,616**

Position after wills rectified

In this scenario, both would actually use their nil rate bands if they were the first-dying. Ken made use of his nil rate band for the residue of his estate going into statutory trusts on intestacy and the spouse exemption at 100% for those assets going to Amy, such as the first £250,000, personal chattels and the house held as joint owners. Amy did have a will and left everything in trust to the children. She did not use the spouse exemption.

After reflection, Amy and Ken decided to leave their estates each to the other, and on death of the last one, to their children in trust to the age of 21 (notwithstanding the tax charge on a trust for assets left beyond the age of 18, which they feel is too young for their children to inherit fully from them).

This strategy saves £48,500 in inheritance taxes in Amy's estate through being able to use the spouse exemption at 100%. In their wills, the value of the nil rate band is bequeathed in each estate to a discretionary trust for the children, with the survivor having a terminating life interest in the trust. The trust will be to the age of 21 and will have wide investment powers, unlike the statutory trusts on intestacy. They also decide to sever the tenancy of the house, becoming tenants in common, as opposed to joint tenants. This gives them more flexibility with regard to passing on the house.

It is also recommended to ensure that the life assurance that is not in trust is passed into trust to save more in inheritance taxes.

The new position after making the estate planning changes:

IHT in Ken's estate if he is first dying: Nil
IHT in Amy's estate if she is first dying: Nil

IHT in joint estates on death of last dying who has not remarried:

Joint estate:	£1,592,941
Less life policies in trust	(£1,164,825)
Less two nil rate bands	(£650,000)
Taxable	£0
IHT at 40%	**£0**

If each leaves assets one to the other, using both nil rate bands, then to the children in trust, and put the policies not in trust into trust, then the joint estate is reduced to nil, with a total IHT saving of over £190,616.

Note that the RNRB could also apply where the family home is left to direct descendants.

Planning scenarios

1. Ensure that both have changed their wills to reflect the new position, making use of the spouse exemption as well as the nil rate band for each estate.

2. Sever the joint tenancy to give more flexibility for leaving the house.

3. Take out a 'lasting power of attorney' for both Ken and Amy to deal with their assets and financial affairs if they become mentally incapable.

4. Use of discretionary trusts for the children to the age of 21 (as this is more suitable for them).

5. Write life policies in trust so that they do not fall into their estates for IHT purposes. They would lose 40% of the value of their life cover through not doing this. It will be recommended to take out life assurance in trust and to then discontinue most policies not in trust, or unable to go into trust at this time.

6. Planning through the use of wills changed the direction of their assets and estate flows on death. Just through changing wills clauses and writing life policies into trust, they have saved the estate over £190,616 in inheritance taxes.

7. Had they not made the changes, they would have had sufficient estate liquidity to pay off their liabilities, including paying inheritance taxes. However, £190,616 in additional capital from saved IHT can provide income of at least £10,000 per annum for life on the capital, if invested at 5% for income.

Note that only the IHT and estate planning issues have been dealt with and not the other objectives at this stage. However, it could be that pension funds eventually fall to inheritance taxes after the spouse dependant has had their use of them, and suggestions may have been made for future investments to be IHT 'wrapped' if at all possible.

24

Case Study 2

Business Property Reliefs and Succession Planning

Kathy and Bronwyn Kelly are in a farming and business partnership with their parents, Hamish and Frances. Kathy is aged 36 and runs a horse and equestrian centre on the farm, whilst Bronwyn (aged 38) looks after the dairy and other farming interests. Before any single farmers out there read this and get excited at the prospects, unfortunately for them both Kathy and Bronwyn are married and have young families. Their parents Hamish and Frances are aged 65 and 64 and have been farming in partnership with their daughters and wish to retire in the near future. Hamish had inherited the farm as a going concern from his parents. As yet, neither daughter has identified any of their children as being interested in farming, but there is always the chance that one or more of them will wish to do so, and they wish to keep their options open.

Their farmhouses are both integral to the farm and are surrounded by farm land. The two sisters share their business dealings 50/50 and have recently taken over their parents' share of the family business. The business is a farming partnership with farm assets of 500 acres worth £3,000 per acre, farm buildings and machinery, as well as livestock. There is also a company, which directs and owns the equitation business on the farm.

After a family discussion, the sisters decide that on the death of one of them, the other will buy out the share of the deceased sister for cash. They enter into a double option agreement and each takes out a life policy in trust for £1 million, with the proceeds payable to the other on death, in exchange for their share of the businesses. In their wills, they leave their assets not covered by the double option agreement to their husbands, and then into trust for their children.

Bronwyn dies on 1st May 2010. Bronwyn's assets are left to her spouse Thomas, after a £325,000 nil rate band trust for children (the NRB applicable in the year of death). Estate representatives exercise the double option agreement to sell the shares and receive the cash.

Inheritance tax position, 1st death

(assuming assets and liabilities identical)

50% share of farming partnership	£1,500,000
including farm house and assets used in farming	
50% share of Horses R Us Limited	£100,000
Loan account in company	£50,000
Investments	£350,000
EIS shares held for 3 years	£160,000
Life assurance in trust	£1,000,000
(as payment for shares and partnership £1,000,000)	
Life assurance not in trust	£230,000
Gift to discretionary trust 6 June 2005	£200,000
Other assets	£175,000
Total Estate	**£3,765,000**
Less liabilities	
Loan	(£50,000)
Net Estate	**£3,715,000**
Less exemptions	
100% agricultural property and business reliefs	£1,500,000
including farmhouse	
100% business property reliefs on company shares	£100,000
100% relief on EIS shares	£160,000
100% relief on life assurance in trust	£1,000,000
100% spouse exemption	£955,000
Taxable Estate	£0
Add back CLT within the last seven years	£200,000
Less the two annual exemptions	£6,000
	£194,000

No tax paid as within the nil rate band at the time

The nil rate band available to offset against the discretionary trust created on 6th June 2005 is as follows:

Nil rate band in the 2009/10 tax year	£325,000
Less CLTs in previous seven years	£194,000
Balance nil rate band	£131,000
Less balance of nil rate band available 2009/10	£131,000
	£0

Last dying – Thomas – estate position

His estate is worth, say	£450,000
Her estate (net of the loan of £50,000 and £1m farm assets sold through the double option agreement)	£2,515,000
Joint estates	£2,965,000
Less agricultural property reliefs (APR) (as £1m worth has been sold for £1m life assurance)	£500,000
Less business property reliefs (BPR)	£100,000
Less EIS reliefs	£150,000
Less life assurance in trust	£1,000,000
Less balance of nil rate band to children	£131,000
Total joint estate (Net)	£1,084,000
Less his nil rate band	£325,000
Taxable	£759,000
Inheritance tax at 40%	**£303,600**

Those inheriting farming and business assets carrying agricultural and business property reliefs will continue to be able to pass these assets with their reliefs on to succeeding generations. The EIS shares continue to benefit from IHT reliefs, relating back to the original period of ownership. Life assurance in trust falls out of the estate for inheritance taxes and probate. Whilst the farming partnership and assets used in the business were valued at £1.5 million, the life assurance only provided for £1 million worth of assets to be sold to the surviving sister, the unsold portion passing by will to her husband (£500,000). This part included the farmhouse where the family live. It may not qualify for APR in the future, if not connected to farming.

Note that the loan account in the company does not qualify for business property relief (BPR), and falls into the estate for IHT purposes.

Note that the balance of her nil rate band after accounting for the earlier CLT, has been left to the children in her will, thus effectively reducing her estate to nil.

As Thomas is the second-dying, his combined net estate with Bronwyn's, even after exemptions and reliefs is still liable for IHT of £303,600. There is sufficient liquidity in the estate to cover the IHT liability. Alternatively a joint-life second-death policy for say £300,000 should cover the IHT liability in the second estate, at a cost of £15 per month, being the minimum premium at this age.

Note that if a main home residential property is left to direct descendants, there is a further nil rate band available (RNRB) which in 2019/20 is £150,000.

25

Financial and Estate Planning

Where are you on the financial planning cycle? Comparing different schemes and arrangements before selecting the best ones.

Often guidance is needed to decide on what level of estate planning is required now and in the future. A certain level of awareness is required at all levels. For example, you may know what the current position is regarding your level of inheritance tax payable, but what will it be should you inherit from your parents on their deaths?

There are different stages of estate planning, and much has to do with your family and marital status, as well as your age and work profile, on the one hand, and your preferred investment profile on the other. The latter may be totally unconnected to age, and high or levels of investment and assets may be held at any time.

The typical financial planning cycle

Birth >>> School >>> University >>> Adulthood >>> Work and earnings >>> Retirement >>> Long-term care >>> Death >>> Passing of assets

Sometimes, this scenario is referred to as the 'Seven or Eight Stages of Man':

Birth, School, University:	usually no earnings or asset accumulation
Work and earnings:	asset accumulation; debt accumulation; IHT mitigation through wills and trusts; some mitigation through investments; some through gifting; insuring against IHT; cheapest time for IHT mitigation through second-death whole-of-life assurance policies; new wills.

Retirement:	asset consolidation and accumulation; debt free; income from assets and pensions; IHT mitigation through wills and investments; some IHT reduction through gifting; insuring against IHT is more expensive; review wills; take out LPAs.
Long-term care:	usually in retirement as above; possible increasing debt against assets; equity release; increasing costs; IHT mitigation through loans, equity release; insuring against IHT probably impossible.
Death:	asset distribution; debt reduction; paying of IHT; IHT mitigation through wills and trusts; IHT mitigation through investments and reliefs being passed on; cost of gifting reconciled if PETs before seven years, or CLTs where the balance of IHT is payable; insurance payouts in trust are tax-free; if not in trust policy proceeds add to the IHT burden.

Wherever you or a family member may be on this cycle, you can plan effectively. Earlier planning during the accumulation phase, is usually aimed at protection of the family, and providing for IHT through life assurance. As you get older and your children move off your hands, you are focusing on building investments or making contributions to pension funds. You may feel that you have sufficient assets to cover IHT payable, or have made use of all necessary exemptions and allowable IHT deductions, and do not need the life assurance option – or as much life assurance as you previously thought you needed.

The estate planning cycle can involve more than one generation of the family, and this should be encouraged. If the family is directing its assets, it is pointless to have them end up in the wrong place at the wrong time. I have convened many family conferences involving grandparents, parents and children (who sometimes act for their own children) and even remoter relatives. We always have an agenda and everyone can put their point of view on how they see things or would like to happen. We then draw up an action plan that is agreed by all of those present.

Often the family conference starts because the parents wish to gift their house to the children or make contributions of house deposits to grandchildren to get them on to the housing ladder. Questions are then asked around how this is going to happen, and what are the consequences? These include, 'What if the child marries someone and then gets divorced, whilst owning part of your house?' Or, 'What if you benefit a child and he goes bankrupt and takes part of your assets with him?' All contingencies need to be covered. The peace of mind that flows from having done the right thing is enormous. People often agonise about what to do; the solution is sometimes to let someone else decide for you.

Comparing different schemes

You may be advised to take a certain course of action or make an IHT-saving investment, or change your will, or add to a trust or settlement. If you do not have a snapshot of what the overall planning universe looks like, you will not be able to identify where your particular part of the jigsaw sits. If you have educated yourself in these matters, or have the benefit of a financial plan prepared for you, you will be able to identify those areas most appropriate to your circumstances and take the necessary actions.

It is most important that you are aware not only of what the scheme will do for you, but also what the costs will be; what the risks will be now and in the future; what the consequences of your actions will be.

For example, suppose you decide to release equity from your home. Not only will this reduce your IHT bill, but it will also provide a much-needed top-up to your retirement income. However, suppose that what you were planning to do was to leave the house to the children on your death, and the particular equity release scheme stipulates the house must be sold and if anything remains thereafter, this residue can go to your children. You feel you have lost control of your asset (your home), and would have preferred a different option – possibly a simple mortgage against your house to release capital to be invested into a plan that pays the mortgage interest as well as gives you an income and IHT relief. The plan works in cycles and every 10 years is recycled, repaying the previous borrowing and starting again if you wish to do this.

Having options to consider is important, and your financial planner should cover all of the bases, giving you the option to say yes or no to any proposal. Some schemes and investments are irreversible, so it is important to make sure that what is being offered to you is what you wish to go ahead with. This may sound like ordinary common sense and it is – however, you would be surprised by how many people say after the event 'I wish I'd never done that!' Planning is therefore most important. You should not wait until retirement to begin your planning. The earlier you start, the better.

A prime example of how to use the same product for different financial planning objectives is as follows. Whilst you are young and possibly just starting out in married life or with young children, your prime concern is family protection. You need as much life cover as you can afford. If you die or become disabled or critically ill, there will be a pay-day when a lump sum will pay out and can be invested for your income for your family – often for life. You also want the income to increase over time. The fact is that you probably have very little pension funding either at that stage (as all your money goes in to the mortgage and raising a family), and your life assurance covers your pension fund as well.

However, as you get older, and accumulate assets, pay off your mortgage and other liabilities, fund a pension scheme to have enough to retire on, and look forward to a heavy inheritance tax bill, that large life policy which you took out many years ago to protect your family can now be used to protect your estate. All you are doing is shifting the emphasis as your objectives in life change. Another piece of advice that will save you thousands: that same life policy will protect your pension fund until you retire and beyond. It will enable you to select the best retirement options, because your fund will be covered. You can control much of your estate planning lifestyle through having the right protections in place. Possibly no one has shown you how before. It is therefore important for parents to ensure that their working children follow in their footsteps and adopt cheaper strategies when they are younger. It will save them hundreds of thousands of pounds in the long run.

26

The Challenge of Living Longer

How to prepare for life in retirement, taking into account your changing circumstances as you get older; providing for increasing income from investments, pensions, equity release. IHT mitigation strategies.

It's official – there are more people aged over 65 than there are under the age of 16. No amount of priming the pump will get that baby boomer feeling back again! More and more people will be eligible for their Saga correspondence as they turn 50, and as we go forward, less and less people in work will be supporting those in retirement, as they do now. It is said that for every person in retirement, there are around 1.8 people paying in their national insurance to ensure the pensioners continue to receive their state pensions. By 2024, this figure looks set to drop to around 1.4 people working to support those in retirement. Result – massive rises in national insurance contributions over the years to come.

Low retirement earnings from the state pension

The problem is that there is no state pension scheme. Those people in work pay in national insurance contributions until they retire, and once a week the pensioners receive the old age pension. The current state pension for a married couple at the age of 65 works out at approximately £10,475.40 per annum or £201.45 per week (£6,718.40 per annum for a single person). The state pension is increased each April using the increase in earnings, prices or 2.5 per cent, whichever is the highest. In April 2020 retirees on the New State Pension will receive £175.35 a week, while those on the Basic State Pension will get a weekly income of £134.35. The long and the short of it is that the Government knows it has a monumental job on hand to provide for ongoing state pensions, even at the levels they are at now. Our UK state pensions are amongst the lowest in Europe, and should never be seen to be anything other than something to be topped up by you. From December 2018 the State Pension age for both men and women will start to increase to reach 66 by October 2020.

Living longer

With changes in medical advances and life expectancy, many thought it would go on for ever, that people's life expectancy would edge up to beyond the age of 100 on average. The reality is that females may live to the age of 88 and males to 86, and we seem to be level-pegging at around that age range. Some magnificently, no doubt on a diet of alcohol and regular habits, surpass the age 100 barrier, and more of us look forward to that event. However, sadly, in the local newspaper I continue to be amazed at those who leave this life relatively early, in their 50's and 60's, whilst others continue resolutely to receive the Queen's congratulatory telegram on attaining the age of 100. So, for some, they may live longer, but for the vast majority, the nineties are about it, if not before.

Retirement risks

Research into the risks people fear in retirement shows that the majority are worried not so much about how their capital is invested or specific investment risks faced in the stock markets, as about the risk of outliving their capital and its failure to provide an income which keeps pace with inflation. Outliving your capital is a serious proposition, and escalating retirement incomes are important, and become more so as you get older. There is also an inverse risk ratio that in general the older you get the more cautious you become with your money. So, as you get older, you become more risk averse. This is entirely understandable as you cannot afford to lose capital or to put capital at risk. For inheritance tax planning amongst the elderly, the preferred structure is likely to be something guaranteed not to lose capital, whilst providing a reasonable, escalating income to deal with the risks of inflation. It would obviously be most helpful if, at the same time, their investment could reduce their IHT bill now and in the future. These needs are fully understood by product providers who design low risk products for the IHT-planning target market, such as discounted gift trust bonds.

Stretching your income to make it last

So, you will live longer. On average, you may spend more than your working life in retirement. If you started work at the age of twenty and worked for 40 years to the age of 60, you may be in retirement for another 40 years and live to be 100. Just thirty years ago, the average time you would draw your pension after retiring at the age of 65 was just 5-6 years. Your dependant pension may have gone on for a bit longer. However, you had spent your life saving up to retire and then had less than ten years in retirement to enjoy it. Having to provide for lengthy ongoing pensions was not as great an issue then as it is now. People are determined to live longer and they do. This has a knock-on effect for estate planning and IHT. We would like our assets to stretch for far longer and if they could help other generations down the line that would be fantastic. It's just a pity that what we want and what the Government is prepared to give us are miles apart.

Long-term care

Two major issues have come to the fore. Firstly, the longer you live, the greater the chances are that you will have some requirement for long-term care, and there is a cost associated with that (25% of those aged over 80 will go into care). Secondly, it is a growing challenge to increase your income in retirement, when savers' incomes barely cover inflation and real returns can be poor – especially if you have a very low investment risk profile. It is most important that annuities, pensions and investments provide, or are able to provide, for increasing income. It is equally as important that you realise that some of your capital may have to provide for you to go into long-term care at some stage and that merely planning for an income in retirement is not good enough today.

Increasing income requirements

Your income requirements will be more closely linked to your IHT planning, and you will require flexible options going forward. You would not wish to be with a product provider that may be flexible on the face of it, but charge you enormous exit penalties for the flexibility. This is typical of some equity release providers, should you try to change or reverse a scheme that you have entered into. Billions of pounds will be released from home equity this year and will continue well into the future. It is seen as a growth market, but very few advisers have taken the additional examinations required of them. Many therefore remain ignorant of the stringent advice features that should be used with their clients. Others, not wanting to pay the fees for advice, go ahead and make the most dreadful mistakes which they cannot get out of. Releasing equity will always reduce your home value for IHT purposes. However, there are many different equity release schemes available, so proceed with caution. You could lose valuable pension credits and council tax rebates if income is increased on the one hand, but benefits lost on the other. Get your current income portfolios checked to see if they could do more.

IHT planning need not be complicated or costly

IHT planning strategies can be as simple as changing the clauses in your will. The setting up of a discretionary nil rate band trust can save your estate £130,000 in inheritance taxes – for the cost of around £150 for a full will's review from a solicitor. Some are more expensive, depending on the level of planning required. Other planning could be a bit more complicated and involve tax and investment planning. Whatever is planned for – it is most important that realistic timelines are used.

27

Building an Income Fund

Learn how to best build your own super-charged income fund that is also IHT efficient – strategies for the best funding options; getting the best value with lowest charges. Learn about the different investments to provide tax efficiency and higher levels of income in a risk – protected environment.

It is a common fallacy that to yield a decent income, an investment must be a high-risk one. Some low risk investment instruments can produce an income that provides decent returns. To find products that produce income as well as having IHT advantages is key.

There are a number of different aspects to consider, and this involves planning around the person, as much as planning around the products available.

In planning around the person, there are a number of key IHT exemptions available. These are the nil rate band, valued at £325,000 in 2019/20, and the spouse exemption, which is 100% if both parties are domiciled in the UK.

Our investment planning would be IHT acceptable if it was an investment within the nil rate band amount, although not itself IHT protected.

Investments within the nil rate band or spouse exemption

These exemptions would apply to any investment made. The upper limits for the investment not to be subject to inheritance tax (along with other assets), would depend on how much of it would fall within the nil rate band available. If a couple, then the value of the nil rate band can be doubled. If the couple leave their assets each to the other after using the value of the nil rate band, then the spouse exemption at 100% would apply. However, there could be IHT payable in the estate of the second-dying.

Investments that are specifically exempt

There are a number of investments that have a discount from IHT payable, or fall out of IHT after an investment period, usually two years, sometimes seven years. These are described below:

1. Discounted gift trust investment

An amount is immediately out of your estate (the 'discounted portion'), the balance falling out after seven years (the gift). An income provided is fixed at the outset, and may range from say 3% to as much as 10%. You could have an income of say 3% with 3% escalating annually. Any payments of income from an investment bond are tax deferred (essentially tax free when you take the income) up to 5%. Above that figure, tax is paid on the amount over 5%.

2. EIS/SEIS investments

The Enterprise Investment Scheme (EIS) provides for investments into unquoted companies, sometimes singly, more often in investment portfolios. Stockbrokers in the main offer EIS portfolios. Income returns are probably around the 1-2% mark for young portfolios, that are more interested in capital growth than income. Income that comes to you is dividend income and that is taxable in the usual way, with tax credits being added back for dividends. The EIS/SEIS investment itself is out of your estate after 2 years (and any growth on it). You can also invest into your own company for 100% of the shares and produce an income from a qualifying activity. One such activity is property construction and returns to you are around 5% per annum.

3. Investment in business or farming

Invest into a business or farming and qualify for BPR or APR at 100%. These investments, if properly structured could give you 100% IHT relief on the investment, with the investment reliefs continuing down through the generations if the business activity is continued. The level of income that may be earned is debatable, and some may well incur losses from their activities. Income could be uncertain.

4. Woodlands

Ownership can attract 100% BPR for inheritance tax purposes. Income is not taxed and losses are not allowed for income tax. This could be a long-term business. Income can arise from the sale of timber and using the timber resource for recreational purposes. The most successful ones are where you buy into a syndicate and all of the activities are done for you. Income could be uncertain.

5. Personal annuities

Term-certain or purchased life annuities can provide a set income, some of which may be tax efficient, as a portion of it is a return of capital to you. If the annuity dies with you, it will not be subject to inheritance tax. If there is a capital guarantee and you die within the guarantee period, a proportion could fall into your estate.

6. Equity release

These plans provide capital for investment, with no interest to pay directly. Interest either ramps up against the value of your house for a lifetime mortgage, or is not paid because you have sold a portion of your house, as with a reversion scheme. The equity release reduces the value of the house for IHT purposes. How best you invest for income is your concern.

7. Loan release

A mortgage loan is secured against your house and the capital raised is invested to provide an income return that repays the mortgage income and gives you an income. This is usually achieved through a plan with internal gearing and you need a higher risk profile for it. You do, though, have more control and flexibility than with a pure equity release. The income return is probably around 2-3% after allowing for the mortgage interest payments. The loan reduces the value of the house for IHT purposes. Note however, that geared loan investments with, for example, a basket of traded endowments, to repay the loan, where a lender provides an ongoing loan facility to provide income (which is repaid from the maturing endowment policies) are to be avoided as unstable and very high risk. It is far better to arrange for a 'cheque book' drawdown facility from your house equity, when you can access the equity on a regular basis, without any gearing. Always take professional advice before acting.

8. Trust investments

You can gift assets to trust where they are invested for the benefit of beneficiaries. You would aim to have the value of the gift to trust out of your estate, as well as the growth on it. You would wish for the income arising in the trust and any gains to be for the benefit of individual beneficiaries, who would have lower tax rates, if at all possible. If a trust may appoint beneficiaries to capital, then 'income' from investment bonds is not taxable in their hands when made, so long as it is 5% or less.

9. Buy to let

This strategy enables you to take non-taxable capital from your growth investments and not pay tax on the amount taken. House inflation has averaged over 5.9% over the last ten years, though more recently, as readers will be aware, house values fell by 20% over 2008-9, but are increasing in 2019/20. Current rental yields are in the order of 4-5%. If you take an optimistic (or neutral) view on the future of property prices, investing in a buy-to-let property and then drawing down 5-6% tax-free from the capital value of the property is the equivalent return for a 40% taxpayer of 9-10% taxable, with the hope obviously that you will also see some capital gain in the future. However, as well as the current uncertainty regarding property prices, there is also some uncertainty regarding the letting market itself, with certain areas showing a surplus of supply over demand. Take advice before proceeding on this route.

Buy-to-let landlords can offset their mortgage interest payments and some of their costs against their income. Higher and additional rates of tax relief on mortgage interest is being phased out and will be restricted to 20% for all landlords by April 2020.

The above is a *sample* of the main products that can provide income as well as provide for IHT mitigation or reduction.

Much therefore depends on whether you plan around yourself (and your family members) or around the product set. You should always plan around yourself and your objectives first. The type of product should be secondary to your specific need requirements, such as the ability to give up control of an investment, the ability to take a fixed income, or the requirement for a variable income; and what to do if circumstances change, such as having to go into long-term care, where more funds are required.

Need requirements will usually be for:

* an income sufficient for need requirements
* an income able to increase with realistic inflation
* an income produced off a secure capital base
* the capital base to have guarantees if possible
* tax-free income for higher rated taxpayers; lower rated taxpayers may do better in taxable investments to use up their allowances
* utilisation of capital gains tax allowances are £12,000 per person in 2019/20
* utilisation of special offers and discounts on investments for those of a certain size, or possibly an age discount or extra allocation for the elderly.

Asset allocation

Modern portfolio investment theory is concerned with asset allocation. The principle is to spread your assets in such a way that when certain assets are performing well, others are not, and when the non-performers begin to perform, the previous performers are not. All things occur in cycles and when equities are up, the likelihood is that gilts or bonds may be down, and vice versa. The proponents of investment allocation believe that risk spreading through suitable asset allocation allows for a portfolio to be balanced from time to time and for changes and corrections to be made.

Within the asset allocation mix, there are those who prefer investments that have a very low level of volatility but still perform reasonably, and others who wish to have investments that are not correlated at all to the investment markets.

Investment selection depends on the level of investment risk you wish to undertake. This may mean diversifying into cash, fixed interest, bonds, equities, property and other asset classes. Some investments offer so-called guarantees – such as structured products – to return your capital intact at the end of the investment period. Always diversify and always consider liquidity issues, and how accessible your cash will be when you need it.

Within the asset allocation mix would also be found your 'diversifiers' – extra elements including higher risk investments which provide special tax reliefs such as EIS investments, for example, which give income tax, CGT and IHT reliefs.

Building your super-charged income fund

People invest either for capital growth or for income, and often for both. For example, a building society or national savings investment may give an income return, but no capital growth; an equity investment such as an NSA could give both tax-free income and tax-free capital growth.

The challenge is always to achieve the best possible income without depleting your capital. In the past 40 years the level of annuity rates has been poor and better incomes from annuities are only obtainable if medically underwritten and you qualify for higher rates; savers' rates have been dire for the past ten years or more, and since late 2007 have been decreasing as the Bank of England rate decreases. The bank base rate is currently 0.75%, amongst the lowest in over 300 years. The outlook for savers at present is bleak. Shop around for the best interest rates.'

You can obtain income from the product as an interest rate, or you can take a capital gain from it, tax-free up to £12,000 per person in 2019/20. Good performing shares would enable you to take the profits in this way. If £100,000 was invested and provided a tax-free growth of 3% that could be taken as income, this is a good deal, when the average interest rate on short-term deposits is around 1.0%. The investment does not have to be one that produces savings or investment income only – it can produce growth that can be encashed. A couple with a large investment portfolio can take out £24,000 in capital gains tax exemptions between the two of them tax free, just through using their capital gains tax allowances of £12,000 each for the tax year. Your children also have the same allowances, no matter what their ages. So, if you have no other income, you will have income tax free bands and capital gains tax free allowances to consider. You have your tax-free personal allowances from income tax of £12,500 in the 2019/20 tax year.

Your financial planning must take these into account, together with your need requirements, attitude to risk, the size of the investment funds, the need for diversification, and your personal circumstances. For example, too much income could affect your age allowances. The income limit for age-related allowances is £29,600 in 2019/20. Income earned in excess of this figure reduces it £1 for every £2 by which income exceeds the income limit until the age allowance is reduced to the normal allowance. The personal allowance is reduced before the married couple's allowance of £8,910 (the allowance is 10% of this – £891), with a minimum of £3,450 (MCA).

Planning may involve taking income up to a certain level and then capital gains within the CGT personal allowances thereafter.

Whatever your personal objectives and need requirements, a super-charged investment fund can be built for you. It will take into account all available investments that provide income or capital gains, suitability and diversification aspects, and be bespoke to yourself. Returns of cash plus 1-2% (average inflation) is a common benchmark. This keeps pace with inflation and should be achievable.

What if you make too much income?

Making too much income can be a problem. For example, suppose you have retired and have no debts and the house is paid off. You have an income from pension funds and also a discounted gift trust investment bond. Excess income being provided (as you cannot reduce the bond income if related to a discounted gift trust) should be gifted to say your grandchildren as surplus to your requirements under the gifts out of normal expenditure rule. Otherwise excess income adds to your taxable estate and will be lost to inheritance taxes at 40%.

You could also recycle this excess income into a life assurance policy in trust as premiums to pay for IHT liabilities.

What if you have a non-performing investment portfolio?

This is quite common where proper asset allocation has not been done or the investments are viewed against the wrong benchmarks. For example, to be linked to a tracker index is great when the stock markets are booming, but not so good when in decline as the tracker will track downwards and lose you money. Your investment portfolio should be reviewed on a regular basis, and checked for effectiveness and market averages on performance. If not performing switch to better performers. Asset allocation will ensure balance. Do not be afraid to take your capital gains as part of your investment strategy for income.

Unless terribly risk averse, there is no reason why cautious investment portfolios in 2019/20 should not be performing in late single figures for investment growth at say 7%+, and 2.5% for income. If not happy about an investment portfolio of single stocks and shares, try a collective one of unit trusts, OEICs and investment trusts.

There are many options available to you. There is no single solution. However, some investments lock you in for lengthy periods and may be inflexible; others are far more manageable. Use your NISA allowances of £20,000 each, which can go into shares or a cash or a combination of these.

Getting in for reduced charges

Product providers will offer reduced charges and higher allocation amounts to your investment. The average fees are usually 2-3% plus an annual trail of 0.5%, but can be double that figure. Some internet providers charge a fee and take no commission, as do financial advisers who are fee-based. From 2012 all investment products became fee only, with no commissions payable, so get used to the idea of paying fees.

Protecting your capital

There are capital protected investments as well as those that offer a guarantee on your capital if stock markets fall. Generally, there is a trade-off between investment performance and the protection of your capital. In other words, there is a cost to capital protection. Your stock market gains may be locked in and also be protected. Products with guaranteed capital investments do this.

No investment is without risk. However you are at risk of not making money if you do not make full use of your allowances and exemptions, and being in the correct product or investment mix for you at any given time.

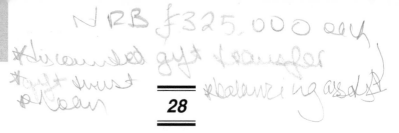

28

The 15 Biggest Inheritance Tax Mistakes

Learn how not to fall into the worst IHT traps and avoid the costly mistakes experienced by others. Regular concerns over IHT and how to overcome them.

Not dealing with IHT issues and how they affect you can be a costly exercise in the long run. You could lose the family home and certainly see the value of other assets in your estate being decimated through taxes after death. Planning strategies can mitigate much of your IHT liabilities, or at the very least, provide for IHT payments to be met without having to sell assets. However, there are IHT tax traps and mistakes that could cost you dearly. The most important ones are given below.

1. Failure to plan

The rate of Inheritance tax is 40%. It is payable on certain gifts chargeable during your lifetime at the lifetime rate of 20%, and on your death at 40%, if over the nil rate band and with no further exemptions applying. Whilst the use of the spouse exemption if married or in a civil partnership, gives 100% IHT relief on the first death, there will be the loss of one nil rate band, currently worth £325,000 in 2019/20. By incorporating the bequest of assets to a nil rate band trust, savings of £130,000 (40% x £325,000) can be made in the estate of the last to die, or make use of transferable NRBs for married couples and civil partners. Often the position is that one spouse or civil partner has most of the assets in his or her name, while the other partner has fewer assets. By 'equalising' the estates of both parties, through gifting assets to the spouse or civil partner with fewer assets, more IHT savings can be made for both spouses and their estates. If, in the final analysis, it was the intention for spouses or parties to inherit from each other, it will be preferable to provide the means for each spouse to make use of all available exemptions whilst alive, and then on death. For example, two spouses using the discounted gift trust or gift trust and loan route will each have nil rate band exemptions to use to better effect, thus saving IHT. The same applies for annual gifts to reduce your estates and other exemptions. However, you must have the cash in the first place to do gift away. One spouse or civil partner can give it to the other spouse to do so.

If the parties are cohabitees, and not spouses or civil partners, then no spouse exemption applies at death. If the relationship is genuinely long-term and as if they were married, then early planning is essential as the seven-year PET rule will apply on gifts made, where you must survive for seven years for the gift to be out of your estate. Be careful not to reserve any benefit on the gift made. In other words, you cannot derive any benefit from it whilst alive, otherwise it will fall back into your estate and be taxed. On death, both parties immediately have their own nil rate band exemptions, currently worth £325,000 in 2019/20. The balance is subject to IHT in the deceased's estate. Estate equalisation for the unmarried, or so-called 'common law' spouses (which has no legal significance), can be an important planning tool.

2. Not planning around the family

In its entirety, financial planning should encompass those you will inherit from and those to whom you wish to pass assets on your death. It could be that you already have a significant IHT problem and passing further assets to you will make your position worse. Granted there are 'deaths in quick succession' taper reliefs that may exempt some of the tax already paid (so as not to pay IHT twice too soon); however, although you may have planned properly, those above you – your parents or grandparents – by leaving assets to you will have achieved nothing other than increased inheritance taxes.

Generation planning is therefore an important aspect. For example, suppose that the grandparents have a taxable estate and wish to reduce it through making gifts and utilising their available exemptions. You are paying thousands of pounds in school fees annually. The grandparents could make gifts out of 'normal expenditure' as well as their annual allowances to assist with the school fees, thus reducing their estates and saving your after-tax money, that can now go into pension funding or reducing your mortgage. Alternatively, the grandparents could set up a discounted gift trust investment bond and secure an immediate IHT deduction for themselves. The beneficiaries could be their grandchildren, thus bypassing your estate. These strategies could save you thousands.

Going the other way, your adult children could have taxable estates, and inheriting from you could make their positions worse. Similar strategies could be applied to bypass their estates for the benefits of their children.

Financial family planning going up and down the generations is therefore important and too few financial planners go this far. Insist on an open discussion with family members if wealth creation and preservation for the whole family unit is important. Remember also that younger family members are cheaper (and possibly healthier) to insure for IHT liabilities and it is better from a cash-flow point of view to do this as early as possible. For the humorous amongst us, family planning with IHT contraception is no bad thing!

You can also make use of the unused portion of the first-dying's nil rate band in the second estate if a married couple or civil partner, as well as your RNRB where the family home is left to direct descendants, currently £150,000 in2019/20.

3. Not enough liquidity in the estate

If sufficient estate liquidity is available to cover death duties and other liabilities (cash available in or to the estate), this means that valuable assets such as the family home or investment portfolio do not need to be sold. Many people have life assurance to cover these costs, but may be in the wrong types of policies, or the policies are not underwritten in trust, so that the policies themselves become IHT taxable.

When doing the IHT liquidity review, ensure that sufficient cash is available to cover your liabilities and bequests and legacies. This is one of the biggest mistakes made by people who are asset-rich but cash-poor – and assets that have to be sold are often sold at 'fire sale' values or when the investment markets are down and losses are made. In other words, by not having sufficient cash available when you need it, you could create a situation where in order to produce the cash, assets may be sold at undervalue, purely to enable probate to happen faster. No one can benefit from your estate until the IHT is paid. There are reliefs available to pay IHT in instalments, but this only applies in certain instances.

4. Gifts made with reservation

If you make a gift and reserve a benefit, the value of the gift made will fall back into your estate at full value on your death. It will be as if the gift had not been made. This has happened where you gift your house to your children and continue to live there rent free. The Government will now allow you to reverse this situation by either paying a market rent to your children or suffering an income tax under the pre-owned assets tax rules (POAT). You can still live rent free, but must declare that the asset will now be liable to IHT. The same would apply if you gifted an investment to someone and continued to derive an income from it. There are exemptions for certain kinds of investments, such as a discounted gift trust, where you gift the investment to beneficiaries and derive an income from it, so make sure you are in the correct type of investment to start with.

Gifts to spouses must not be conditional on you receiving any benefits from the gift, or HMRC could have the value of the asset fall back into your estate. Gifts to trusts where you are the settlor and derive a benefit from the trust as a beneficiary will be taxable in your hands, and depending on the trust, will usually be out of your estate if within the nil rate band at death, as well as the growth on the trust asset. Always check to ensure that the GWR (gift with reservation rules) do not apply to you.

5. Out of date or non-existent wills and trusts

Your will directs to whom you wish to leave assets on your death and gives instructions to your personal representatives, executors and administrators, as well as wide investment and other powers. You either have one or you do not. Even if you have a will it may be out of date or your circumstances may have changed. For example, you die and your spouse has died before you, and you have not changed your will; or you get divorced, and your 'spouse' is now your 'ex spouse', not your spouse, and will not inherit from you – even if you intended your 'ex spouse' to benefit from you. You may now not intend certain beneficiaries to inherit from you, or the disposable assets may no longer exist, although referred to in the will.

There are many reasons why wills should be reviewed at least every two years, and are easily changeable, by adding a codicil to the will with your new wishes, if required. If you do not have a will, then no one knows what your wishes are. Similarly if you do have a will and it cannot be found at your death, you will die intestate, as if you did not have a will.

The order of succession if you die without a will is defined by statute, and the limits have recently been increased. The previous position was that a surviving spouse with no surviving children shared the estate with the deceased's relatives (parents, brothers and sisters and others) where the estate value was greater than £450,000. Under the revised rules, the spouse could inherit the whole deceased estate without sharing it.

Previously, where the deceased left a spouse and children, the estate was shared with him or her and the children. For estates larger than £250,000 the survivor received £250,000 as a statutory legacy and a life interest in 50% of the residue – children being entitled to the remaining 50% on attaining the age of 18. From 1 October 2014 the surviving spouse receives 50% of the residue outright, not only the income. If no spouse, children or relatives, everything goes to the Crown, the Duchy of Lancaster (the Queen) or the Duchy of Cornwall (Prince Charles).

At present, though, if you die with a spouse surviving you and issue, after the first £250,000 worth of assets passing to that spouse or civil partner, your spouse shares in your estate with your children, which may not be exactly what you want. It could be that brothers and sisters, grandparents and remoter issue may inherit from you, which is not really what you want either. The will lies at the end of the estate planning process and even if you have few assets, at least it will supply some direction as to your wishes.

Even if you have a will, if all adult beneficiaries agree (and other criteria), after your death, your will can be modified through a 'deed of variation' and dispositions may be re-directed. The deed of variation may also be used on intestacy to direct your assets. On both occasions this must be done within a two-year period. The most common reason for a variation though is to make use of the nil late band trust to bypass a generation for IHT purposes. The 2015 Budget introduced consultation on deeds of variation as tax avoidance vehicles. It is important to have your will in order, as well as trusts to not fall foul of any impending legislation in this regard.

There have also been significant changes to the law on interest-in-possession trusts, more commonly where a surviving spouse has the use of assets during their lifetime, and with the assets passing on death to children, or other parties. The will should be checked to ensure that you have correct arrangements to provide for trust income to a surviving spouse or partner.

The past two years have seen significant changes to trust law and who may benefit from trusts and when. Apart from bare or absolute trusts and certain other exempt trusts, all trusts now fall under the discretionary trust rules and taxation, whether made whilst alive, or whether coming into existence on your death. It is therefore crucial that you do not make the mistake of assuming that existing wills and trusts are still correct and sufficient for your needs, and these should be reviewed immediately.

On the question of wills, a surprising number of people seem to feel that the making of a will could somehow hasten their demise, and so they don't. This is a big mistake as many estate and financial planning exemptions are lost, especially if one party makes a will and the other doesn't. The spouse exemption at 100% only applies to those assets left to the spouse. If, by default under intestacy rules, assets pass to third parties, the amount over the nil rate band exemption will be fully subject to IHT at 40%.

Then there is the issue of relying on others to clear up your unprepared estate after you have gone. This is not only costly, but takes up much time, and leaves those who follow you having to deal with issues that could have been settled before and not after your death.

6. Losing the house

With many families falling into the IHT net, where the house is a major asset in the estate due to rising house prices in the future, and where the nil rate band has not kept pace with house inflation, the possibility of losing the house on death to pay inheritance taxes is a major concern for many. Even if not sold, it may have to be remortgaged or loans taken against it to pay for IHT. In the South and South East it is of greater concern as houses are more expensive, and possibly as much as 50% of all houses will fall into the IHT net. The value of the nil rate band is £325,000 in 2019/20, and if your house is worth more than that, it could become inheritance taxable. Planning around the house is of major importance, as families still need to live somewhere, even if other assets may be sold to cover death duties. The new transferable NRB will take more homes out of the IHT regime.

There are strategies dealing with the house, and these are covered elsewhere.

Planning around the house includes planning for long-term care, equity release planning to augment retirement income and other issues. A big mistake is not to recognise that the house, for most people, is their principal fixed asset and store of value. Yet extra consideration is required, because no one can afford to lose their family home through planning strategies that may or may not work.

The main issue is one of liquidity at death and ensuring enough cash is available to cover inheritance taxes. This is usually met though life assurance, which is a small price to pay to cover IHT and mortgage debt at that time. If you die with a liability, such as a mortgage or loan secured against your house, this will reduce the value of the property for IHT purposes and the equity release market is booming in this regard. Planning around the house requires long-term flexibility for many and decisions are not that easily made. It may be that strategies have previously been undertaken that now have to be rectified with changes in legislation.

If you own the house as joint tenants, then on your death, your ownership automatically passes to the survivor. If you own as tenants in common, then you can direct to whom your share of the house will pass. If you wish to become a tenant in common, then you need to sever the joint tenancy, which can done by a solicitor. By having tenants in common, your share of the house can be passed to a nil rate band discretionary trust on your death, for the benefit of your children, enabling you to stay in the house until your death, but more importantly utilising a nil rate band as well as the spouse exemption, if married or in a civil partnership. A solicitor can advise you on these aspects, as well as the importance of a lasting power of attorney (LPA), which should be done at the same time as your wills, if possible. This will enable someone to deal with your financial affairs should you become mentally incapable of doing so yourself.

7. Believing you have protection when you do not

Assume you have an inheritance tax problem. You have an amount to invest and you require income from the investment for the rest of your life. On death, the investment will pass to your children or grandchildren. If you merely invest, say, into an investment bond, it will provide you with an income at say 5% that is tax deferred. On death, the value of the investment bond will fall into your estate and be taxed at 40%, the balance passing to your heirs.

Had you 'wrapped' the investment for IHT mitigation purposes and made it into a discounted gift trust (DGT), immediately a percentage is out of your taxable estate and the balance and growth on it is out of your estate after a period of seven years. You could save 40% in inheritance taxes, and still have the income. However, your flexibility in dealing with the investment has gone. You can still decide on where the bond investments go, but you cannot change the income once taken, with the DGT arrangement.

Assume your share portfolio consists entirely of FTSE shares. On death, you lose 40% of its value in inheritance tax. If you had diversified into a qualifying EIS portfolio (that may include AIM stocks), and survived for only two years, the value of the qualifying shares will be out of your estate for IHT purposes, a saving of 40%. There could be other savings such as on capital gains tax and income tax investing into qualifying shares.

You decide to invest into a commercial property. On death, 40% of the investment falls into your estate for IHT. Had you decided to invest into woodlands then agricultural and business property reliefs may apply and the investments may be 100% out of your estate. There are income tax, capital gains tax and also special IHT reliefs for growing timber passing on death.

There are therefore investment opportunities to make use of that are exempt from IHT. These include investing into businesses for business property and agricultural property reliefs at up to 100%. If you have an IHT problem, investment diversification can mitigate and reduce your IHT liability, and should be planned for as part of your overall asset allocation and tax savings plans.

Many have built up substantial ISA portfolios and their value falls fully into your estate for IHT. Gifting of assets can also save on IHT, as long as you survive for seven years and derive no benefit from the gift made.

8. Not consulting professional advisers

A big mistake is to think that you will cover all of the IHT mitigation and reduction bases yourself. If you do this you take on all of the risk. By using professional advisers, you pass some of the risk on to them. They deal with these issues all the time and should be able to respond to your changing circumstances faster. Also, they will have PI cover; should you be misadvised or missold anything, you can claim against them. Where you have been advised, you have additional protections offered through regulatory authorities, including the investors' compensation fund. Whilst you may make short-term savings in costs and commissions by not taking advice, the peace of mind from obtaining regulated advice cannot be under-estimated.

Professional advisers specialise in different aspects of financial planning and usually adopt a team approach to ensure that you get best overall coverage and advice on those aspects that concern your financial planning. Begin shifting the risk now.

9. Not having life policies in trust

If a life policy is not underwritten into trust, on your death, 40% of the proceeds of the policy could be subject to inheritance taxes. It is estimated that less than 20% of all life policies are in trust. For most estates well under the nil rate band, this does not matter, however, for those over the nil rate band, 40% of your premiums are funding the Government take of your policy premiums. Life assurance companies offer trusts at no extra charge, or your solicitor can draw up a trust deed for you. It is possible to put your policies into trust after the event, and this may save you thousands of pounds in the long term.

Policies underwritten in trust also mean that the proceeds do not have to pass through probate and the money is available before probate. The beneficiaries of the trust, or the trustees, use the proceeds to pay the IHT liabilities and other liabilities, and to provide for bequests. Check all your policies to see if underwritten under trust, as by not doing so and amending your position will cost your estate thousands of pounds in inheritance taxes.

10. Not planning pension funds properly

Although much less with regard to amount, after recent pension reforms, unfortunately today, tax and other charges may occur on your death, and the passing of your pension fund to another. If it passes on first death to your spouse or civil partner or dependants, there is no IHT payable, although there may be other tax charges depending on what stage of the retirement cycle you are in (see Chapter 15). Pension funds passing to third parties who are not charities, will be taxable in your estate. Pension annuities, after their terms have expired, will cease on death and not fall into your estate, and will therefore not be taxed.

Pension reduction strategies are covered elsewhere, for example, drawing out maximum allowable income drawdown and gifting the excess, or investing it into other IHT savings areas.

As pension assets can be huge, this is an important area of financial planning. Part of your strategy may be to provide retirement funding from assets that are protected from IHT, and not from pension funding itself. This is a complex area and you will certainly need advice on it. Some pension funds may be 'ported' abroad with HMRC permission, and may then fall out of your estate altogether. However, this will no doubt be seen to be a loophole that will not endure for very long.

11. Thinking you are exempt through living abroad

If you do not live in the UK now but previously did so and have moved abroad without changing your domicile, perhaps to retire, even if you say you have no intention of returning to the UK, the facts of your case may mean that you are deemed domicile and all of your assets worldwide will be subject to UK inheritance taxes. You may have kept a holiday home in the UK, have bank accounts here and still educate your children in the UK; you may regularly visit relatives, retain membership of clubs and sporting associations or take out UK medical insurance to cover you abroad. All of these things may be factors in determining deemed domicile. To be truly non-domiciled and to escape IHT in the UK, you must sever all obvious ties with the UK. You may have been a non-domicile to begin with, having moved to the UK with the intention of eventually retiring abroad. After seventeen years of continuously living in the UK, you will be deemed domicile there, whatever your intention. If, after seventeen years have passed, you then leave the UK, you will still retain your domicile in the UK and your worldwide assets could be subject to IHT. This is a complex planning area, and expert advice may be required. See chapter 9 for the new proposals on non-domicilliaries, announced in Budget 2015.

12. Not reducing your estate when you could

I have a client Harry who did all of the right things. He took out a discounted gift trust investment bond and achieved an immediate IHT reduction. The balance of his investment was out of his estate after seven years, and he draws an income from his plan. However, he is retired and in advanced years, and together with his wife has a large investment portfolio, his house is unencumbered and he has no liabilities. His problem is having too much income. The income generated by his IHT reduction investment policy is too much to spend and is being added to his estate, where as further investments are made, it will be subject to IHT when he dies. Well, you may say he has been too clever in his planning and whilst he has moved assets out of his taxable estate on the one hand, they are slowly creeping back in, adding to his wealth. This is correct.

As a result, Harry required alternative planning, and now regularly makes gifts out of income to his grandchildren to help pay their mortgages. Not only is he helping them when they most need the money – now – but for every pound he gives to them, he saves 40 pence that will not be taxable in his estate.

You may make gifts to individuals and bare trusts (and certain other trusts) that will be within the PET rules – if you survive for seven years, the value of the gift and any growth on it will be out of your estate. Gifts made to spouses or civil partners will immediately be out of your estate as the gift is not potential, but absolute and not dependant on the seven-year survival rules. Because of the PET rules, you need to plan well in advance with regard to depleting your estate through donations to others.

This is an area requiring careful attention as you may live longer than you thought and may have unnecessarily deprived yourself of capital needed in the future; the gifting is irrevocable – once made you cannot normally ask for it back – if you do, the chargeable rules may apply. If you make it conditional on receiving an income from it or other benefit then the GWR (gift with reservation) rules apply and the value falls back into your estate.

Gifting of capital and income is a simple process to reduce your estate and can be planned for in the correct manner.

13. Making gifts in the wrong order

If you get the order of gift-making wrong, it can be costly. This assumes that gifts to be made may either chargeable, for example made to a trust, or exempt, such as those made to other persons under the PET rules.

First, fully exempt gifts should be made, then loans to trusts, then chargeable lifetime transfers (CLTs), and finally potentially exempt transfers (PETs). It is important that CLTs are made to discretionary trusts before PETs, as the ten-year periodic charge on the discretionary trust will depend on what other CLTs were made in the seven years before the discretionary trust was established.

Had the client made a PET within the seven-year period and died within the seven years, the now failed PET becomes a CLT and will be included in the calculation at the ten-year anniversary for the discretionary trust. If the PET was made after the CLT then, on failing within the seven-year period, it cannot be included in the calculation, thus reducing the tax bill.

Getting the order wrong could result in higher IHT bills. Getting it right could save a massive amount in IHT. If a gift of £325,000 was made in the 2019/20 tax year to a discretionary trust, and treated as a CLT, and the same amount to a bare trust (treated as a PET), then the estate could be reduced by £650,000 without any IHT consequences.

14. Not planning around the business

The business can be useful as an investment that gains 100% IHT business property reliefs; it can create income to pay for insurance premiums and could offer you cheaper benefits than if you paid for them yourself. For example, life cover on a group scheme basis, or medical cover on a group scheme basis spreads the risk and the costs are cheaper. Also, if you are uninsurable, there may be a possibility of being included for cover under a group scheme, whereas you may be refused cover if attempted individually. That is because the business cover may have higher 'free of evidence of health' clauses, whereas personal covers do not. Granted the range of cover will cease when you retire, but some schemes have a continuation option to cover you in retirement and you should check this out.

A firm of solicitors engaged in succession planning found that three out of eleven partners were uninsurable. However, by combining all employees (121 in this case), we were able to include the partners for cover at 4 times their taxable earnings. In another case, the director's loan account in the business was £150,000 (the business owed the director the money which was used for working capital) and BPR on death would not apply to it, thus losing some 40%, or £60,000. The loan account was taken out of the business and invested into an IHT mitigation plan; the loan account money was replaced with bank finance and the interest on the bank money was tax deductible.

The business comprises a valuable asset and should be included in all estate and IHT planning. One area of prime importance is where there are partners or shareholders who want cash for their shares on death. The partners or shareholders can insure themselves for their share values under a double option agreement and in trust, so that cash is paid for their share of the business at the time when required. This cash is free of IHT. The business can pay the premiums, but they will be taxable in your hands as well as NICs being payable, as a benefit in kind. Even so, to you personally this represents a cash-flow advantage.

Gifts of business shares are not treated as a reservation of benefit under the GWR rules, and if shares are gifted to a family member who earns dividends, these will not be taxed in your hands (unless the gift is by a parent to a minor age under the age of 18).

There are many planning opportunities with businesses that are not considered, and are therefore lost. If you can get your personal assets subject to the business or agricultural relief rules, then this is a major IHT mitigation planning device. After your death, where shares pass to another, the BPR passes with it, under current legislation. When the shares are sold, there may be capital gains tax issues, but reliefs may also apply in this area.

15. Wrong advisers

It is most important that you only deal with advisers able and competent to advise you properly and across a broad range of issues. IHT and estate planning encompasses planning around your investments and tax, your business, your house, trusts, wills, your domicile, pensions, generations above and below you, your gifting strategy, and your personal circumstances and objectives. Some financial advisers are only trained in selling tax-relievable investments, others can manage a far wider scenario in advising you. Check out their qualifications and expertise and make it known what the planning parameters are going to be.

The above will give you a flavour of the areas to be aware of in IHT mitigation and reduction planning. Don't fall into the IHT trap of doing nothing about your circumstances. Always get a professional opinion on what you should and should not be doing to achieve a successful outcome.

29

Going From Retirement Into Long-Term Care

*Releasing equity to provide for care fees and costs.
Preserving your estate and passing your wealth on to heirs,
or spending the kids' inheritance? Protecting your assets for
future generations.*

The next stage on from retirement would be long-term care for around 20-25% of people aged over 85, not to mention those who enter care before this date. In a typical year, some 70,000 people are forced to sell their homes to provide for care and this is consistent with the 40,000 homes lost each year to pay for care costs.

Fidelity International (Five Pitfalls on the Road to Financial Security in Retirement – October 2006) mentions the five pitfalls as living too long and relying on income sources that are not guaranteed; the insidious effect of inflation reducing an investment portfolio – a rise in 2% inflation would see £50,000 worth of annual income fall to £25,000 in just 25 years; poor asset allocation being unable to provide sustainable incomes as you live longer; drawing income from a portfolio at too high a level, thus depleting it too soon; and allocating no or too little money to cover the huge financial impact of long-term and serious illness in later life. All of this means you could run out of money before you die, but the more so if you have to pay for increasing long-term care costs.

Average home care fees have risen by 51.5% in the last five years, the state pension by 60% less over the same period, meaning that more and more capital assets may need to be committed to paying for long-term care.

From April 2005, the State will meet the full cost of care where all of your assets are less than the lower limit, and proportionately where assets are between the two bands below:

	Lower	Upper
England	£14,250	£23,250
Wales	£0	£40,000
Scotland	£16,500	£26,500
Northern Ireland	£14,250	£23,250

If you have assets available valued at over £23,250 (England, and Northern Ireland), £26,500 (Scotland) and £40,000 (Wales), then you are liable for full care fees. Your home is not included in the means test if a spouse, civil partner or partner resides in the property; any relative aged over 60 or is disabled resides in the property; a child under age 16 lives in the property; you are in the first 12 weeks of needing permanent care; or if the care is being provided on a temporary basis.

The Government wishes to promote a greater level of 'social inclusion', requiring more people to fund for their care costs. There is a new Treasury Public Service Agreement target to help a larger number of people to live independently at home.

However recently published statistics show that 69% of people have no plans to earmark savings for long-term care; 25% do not set aside money for long-term care; and generally 74% of women and 66% of men do not intend to set aside money for care funding (source: Legal Support Services website). The message is that people actually do not care and see long-term care as more of a remote possibility. Yet it could decimate your savings and income to pay for care if you need it and will affect how you wish to deal with assets in the future and whether after paying for long-term care, there is anything left for your heirs to inherit from you.

The fact is that few of those actually going into care do any planning. This has to be done for them, usually by adult children, and is a very time-consuming and costly process, and for those who have had to do it, extremely stressful.

The main estate planning issues are:

- personal assets and income are usually above the low thresholds to qualify for free care, which is means tested
- the State wants you to take on the risk of providing for care at home, rather than being institutionalised, where the costs are greater
- we have an aging population – there are more people aged over the age of 65 than those over the age of 16
- coping with severe illnesses such as strokes or heart attacks, Parkinsons etc
- choice of care
- financial independence
- worry about using up all of your capital
- desire to leave the house to the children (not the Government or local councils who can dispossess it to pay for care costs)
- planning by the next generation for the older generation
- dealing with the options of investing capital, taking out a care fees policy to meet the care costs; moving to a cheaper care home; dealing with these issues and others that may arise
- not being a burden on the family

- flexibility for care fees increases
- leaving an inheritance
- peace of mind
- investment planning to meet monthly care costs averaging around £2,500 per month, which can only increase in the future – over 20 million people in the UK are over the age of 65.

The problem is that as the needs of the long-term care market are increasing with greater longevity, the product providers of long-term care policies have become greatly reduced over the years, with 2-3 main players in the market place. There are policies available that provide for a single premium payment to take care of regular monthly payments for as long as the care is required, and these benefits can be indexed to provide for inflation. If paid to a care home, the benefit payments are tax free, but taxable if paid to the policyholder.

The single premium investment can be up to £250,000, but the average is £55,392 (*AXA PPP LifetimeCare statistics 2006*).

Whilst on the one hand, the costs of going into LTC, or providing for it, will deplete your estate for IHT purposes, on the other hand, it may seriously deplete your retirement income, carefully planned for your old age. Part of your investment planning should be to consider a LTC policy, which can be effected when you go into care, and need not be taken out earlier. This will pass most of the funding risk onto the care product provider and reduce your overall investment risk exposure. Capital can be protected or not protected and you have many flexible options.

Dealing with the house – a contentious issue

For means testing, the home may be disregarded if a spouse or unmarried partner still resides in the dwelling, or if a relative aged over 60 resides in the dwelling, or a relative with incapacity, a dependant child under the age of 16 resides in a dwelling and for the first 12 weeks after entering a care home. There are issues with equity release and home reversion plans where equity has been released to provide for care at home and subsequently you go into care accommodation that is not your home, but most scheme providers, including providers of the Equity Release Council – formerly Safe Home Income Plans (SHIP), will offer a negative equity guarantee and are familiar with these issues, so you would not necessarily lose your home.

If you have an IHT problem and are planning around the home and wish to leave assets on death to your dependants then careful planning is required around the home. These may include equity release lifetime mortgages or home reversion plans (where you sell part of your home for capital but remain there for life for you and your spouse or partner), as they will immediately reduce the value of your home on death. If investing into an immediate annuity that is not capital protected for long-term care fees, this should end on your death and be out of your estate for IHT planning.

Over the past ten years plans have been developed for those going into long-term care, where the local authorities pay for your care, and on your death dispossesses your home to sell it to reimburse it for the care fees expended on you. One of your choices may be to sell your home in advance and invest the proceeds into an investment that provides for a high level of non-taxable income, and returns the investment capital to your heirs, thus ensuring an inheritance.

There are therefore many financial planning options available in dealing with long-term care issues, and they cannot be ignored. Preserving your estate for future generations, whilst ensuring you receive the best care available should be a major personal objective for most people.

30

IHT Mitigation

The essential ingredients. What you need to do. Your own checklist – this deals with your requirements and allows your financial planner to help you do the things you want to do – in a safe environment.

Your IHT liability can be mitigated, reduced or provided for, depending on your objectives and personal circumstances. Some may do no other planning than to provide sufficient cash to pay the IHT liability, usually through life assurance or 'free assets'. Free assets are assets easily turned into cash and available to pay for liabilities.

Mitigation procedures

Reducing your IHT or doing away with it altogether can be accomplished through qualifying investments or tax strategies. These will include the following:

• Qualifying investments such as EIS and those qualifying for APR and BPR reliefs at up to 100%. The waiting period is usually two years to be out of your estate. An example is Woodlands, which is treated as a business for IHT purposes and qualifies for business property relief at 100%.
• Discounted gift (and loan) trust investments (DGTs). These have an immediate IHT discount and also a deferred relief if you survive for at least seven years.
• Life assurance policies underwritten in trust. These are not subject to inheritance tax.
• Making gifts up to allowable exempt limits; using your annual exemptions of £3,000 per annum (£6,000 if you have not made a gift in the preceding year)
• Making gifts under the PET (Potentially Exempt Transfer) rules. Such gifts are out of your estate after seven years, and taper reliefs apply if you die between three and seven years after making the gift.

- Equalising estate assets so that a spouse or civil partner may make gifts or utilise IHT exemptions.
- Full IHT relief for all estates, after allowable deductions, that are within the nil rate band, currently £325,000 in 2019/20. Also the RNRB of £150,000 in 2019/20 for leaving the main residence to direct descendants. Plan for chargeable gifts that fall within the nil rate band allowance.
- Check transferable nil rate band amounts.
- Small gifts of £250 to any person; gifts made in the contemplation of marriage up to certain limits. These are £5,000 from any parent, £2,500 from a grandparent or remoter ancestor, £1,000 by others.
- Excess income over normal expenditure that is gifted.
- Gifts to charities and political parties; gifts of heritage property.
- Gifts between spouses and civil partners (but limited to £325,000 if the recipient spouse is domiciled outside the UK).
- Pension funds passing to a spouse or a civil partner.
- Pension annuities ceasing on death.
- On death, assets passing to a spouse or civil partner (100% spouse exemption).
- On second death, to use the unused portion of the first-dying's nil rate band if a married couple or civil partner.
- On death, using a bypass trust for the amount of the nil rate band, where the spouse exemption has been used. This will bypass IHT in the second spouse dying.
- If domiciled outside the UK, reliefs on non-UK assets. There are specific IHT rules affecting domicile.
- If domiciled outside the UK, reliefs on UK authorised unit trusts or OEICs. These are exempt (otherwise all UK assets held by a non-UK domiciled individual are subject to IHT).
- Foreign currency accounts of those dying not domiciled, resident or ordinarily resident in the UK. Certain of these are exempt.
- From 6 April 2017 there is an additional nil rate band (family allowance) starting at £100,000 and rising to £175,000 by 2020 if the family home is left to direct descendants such as children and grandchildren.

Further measures that reduce your estate

You can further reduce your estate through the following actions. Estate reduction will mean that less value is available for inheritance tax purposes. However, you may not achieve your objective if by reducing the estate on the one hand, you add to it through your actions. For example, you take a loan against your home and invest that loan amount for income. The loan will reduce your estate, but the investment made, if not protected, will increase it by the same amount.

- Increasing your liabilities will reduce your estate. However, debts do not usually die with you and this gives rise to estate liability issues. Life assurance in trust is the most effective funding mechanism, as the life assurance in trust does not add to your estate.
- Mortgages and remortgages.
- Equity release through lifetime mortgages.
- Equity release through home reversion.
- Genuine IOUs properly recorded could be a debt against your estate but do take into account the ramifications of the recent Phizackerley case affecting the use of IOUs (see page 137).
- Owning assets through a company, such as a holiday property abroad (relief was announced in the March 2007 budget and was included in the *Finance Act 2007*).
- Make use of wills planning and set up bypass trusts.

The above are examples of some financial planning measures. Tax advisers will have many more. Most planning in this area is longer term by its nature. Often cash is provided for IHT reduction or 'wrap' investments by releasing equity from the family home. However, there are risks, and if interest payments are payable and these are not met, you could lose your house. Increasing income could also affect areas such as pension credits and council tax reliefs and checks should be made in these areas before proceeding with any actions.

Planning actions

- Educate yourself in financial and estate planning, so that you can have a meaningful discussion around your requirements.
- Set your objectives – what do you hope to achieve in the short, medium and long term?
- Prioritise your objectives in order of importance to you. An example on how to do this is included in the chapter on the role of the financial adviser.
- What must be provided for in respect of future income and capital requirements, and when? Who must be provided for?
- Consider your attitude to investment risk and your investment likes and dislikes; your need for flexibility in the future and contingency planning.
- Take into account your personal circumstances and how you feel about things. You may only require simple solutions, but you have a need to know what the overall picture may look like. You will need options to consider before making up your mind on what course of action to follow.
- Have a financial plan completed for you by a qualified financial planner.
- Consider the recommendations made to you and take action to implement your plan.

- Review your actions.
- Monitor your plan and test effectiveness against your objectives.

The above checklist is not exhaustive, but will give you a fair idea of how to instruct your financial planner and other advisers to help shape your financial plan and recommend future courses of action to you. To have a track to run on, you will need a financial plan and a written report as a starting point. You may need to take legal advice as well as tax advice on certain aspects, depending on your circumstances. Your financial planner can co-ordinate these aspects for you. Once the financial and estate plan is completed, the next stage is a visit to your solicitor to tie up wills and trusts aspects, as well as enduring powers of attorney, so that decisions can be taken if you become mentally incapable. Your planning can be flexible and will change as your circumstances change, or your attitude to risk changes.

31

More Information and Help With Your Decision-Making

What to do next. Having a track to run on with a plan of action. What to do if things go wrong ? The people best equipped to help you.

In previous chapters we looked at IHT mitigation procedures and the need for a financial report detailing your objectives, prioritising them, your attitude to risk profiling and other concepts. All of these are subjective, depending on how you feel about things and what you would like to happen in any given situation. You need options to consider, and by providing you with these options, the financial planner will also be educating you in the various strategies, products and services available to you and your business.

Previously, it was found that planning in isolation may be inappropriate and that often estate planning and IHT mitigation planning needed to be around the extended family, including generations above you and below you, as their decisions and need requirements may impact on your planning.

Changing circumstances

Your financial plan will give you a snapshot of your present position and required actions going forward to achieve your objectives. It will give you a much-needed track to run on. You may not be able to fulfil all of your needs requirements, but at least you will know what can be done and what cannot be done. However, what if your circumstances change? Can your plan change? Do you need new advisers? What if the complex arrangements put into place for you are affected by new legislation? One thing is certain. Over the years there will be changes and keeping up to date and being informed is an important part of the financial planning process.

There could be a death in the family, a divorce, a marriage of a child to someone you do not like, children who are unable to handle large sums of money such as inheritances, new and better IHT investment plans in the market place; retirement from your business; the choice of pension options and income in retirement; having to cope with long-term care issues and a plethora of other events that may make you feel your planning is inadequate or not fit for purpose.

Reviews

The ongoing review process in financial planning is important, as is the regular review of your wills and trusts, as well as your investments. Let the financial planner do the work for you and report back on your new options and actions. Have the review at least once a year. The more detailed your plan the better. Even financial advisers do not live forever and someone familiar with your affairs today may not be around tomorrow.

What if things go wrong?

You have taken various actions based on advice that you worry may turn out not to be sound. You should immediately take a second opinion to confirm your fears, if in any doubt. Previous actions could be changed; however, some investment actions could be irrevocable. For example, suppose you entered into a discounted gift trust bond (DGT) arrangement to save immediate IHT, which gives you income for life. However, your business has run into serious difficulty and you need to inject cash urgently into it and your only investment is the DGT. Unfortunately you cannot encash it as you no longer own it (the trust does), and this investment source is not available to you. A different structure using a gift and loan trust would have been more accessible to you as the loan element is immediately repayable on demand. You have purchased EIS qualifying shares that give you 100% IHT relief after holding them for two years. You have also claimed income tax relief on the investment, and it has to be held for at least three years to qualify for that relief. After two years, you have an urgent need for cash and decide to cash in the shares. This you can do, but will lose the potential IHT reliefs, and the tax reduction claimed for income tax will be reclaimed from you. If you made a loss on the sale of the shares, that loss is relievable against either income or capital gains. The EIS investment is therefore more flexible to exit than the DGT, and flexibility options may be what you required in the first place.

There are usually consequences when your planning needs and objectives change, and you should be made aware of them at the financial reporting stage, before you take any action.

Who can help you?

This will depend on the type of advice required and why. If you require a second opinion then a qualified financial planner, solicitor or accountant should be your first port of call. If you feel you have been missold a product or been given the wrong advice, you can sue the person who gave you that advice, and may have a claim against that firm, or against the Financial Services Compensation Scheme, if the advice was authorised. All authorised advisers must have PI cover to cover their actions, although there are exclusions. Tax planning is generally a non-authorised activity, so always ensure the tax planner giving the advice has PI cover for his or her actions. There is also the Financial Services Ombudsman who can adjudicate on matters between you and the financial adviser, and who is able to make awards, but you must register a complaint against the advice-giver first before proceeding down this route. The Financial Conduct Authority (FCA) is easily accessible at **www.fca. org.uk** and further details can be obtained from their website.

32

Role of the Financial Adviser and Estate Planner

Financial advisers come in many shapes and sizes and perform different functions. I am often asked whether a particular financial adviser has advised properly or has covered all the bases, or whether a second opinion is required. The whole regime relating to financial planning is vast and there are many specialist functions undertaken. As a result, no single person has all the answers. For example, a solicitor may draft perfectly good wills, but has to defer to a financial adviser to find the correct financial planning products available to be implemented to achieve the client's objectives.

It is probably a good idea to have a certified, chartered or qualified financial planner manage your estate planning process for you. The planner will then interact with your accountant, solicitor, tax advisers and other parties in order to ensure that the process is complete.

The financial planning process brings together your advisers. Either you co-ordinate them, or the financial planner does so.

Estate and inheritance tax planning is undertaken on an individual, family or trust basis, and can include the business and business assets.

Those who specialise in this area will be accountants, solicitors, independent financial advisers and chartered financial planners. They will have a variety of qualifications. Generally though, the financial adviser should have at least the CII's advanced financial planning certificate (AFPC) or the Institute of Financial Planning's CFP (certified financial planner) certificate (now merged with the CISI), or have chartered status with the Personal Financial Society (PFS), or equivalent. Solicitors and others dealing with trusts are usually members of Society of Trust and Estate Practitioners (STEP).

If the financial adviser is advising on post-retirement issues, they should be qualified to advise on equity release schemes, home reversions and long-term care.

Information organisations will have details of specialist advisers in most areas, as will the Law Society and Institute of Chartered Accountants. Their details appear in the contact pages that follow.

The Role of the estate and IHT financial planner

Understanding of your total picture plays a major part in advising you. If all the facts are not to hand, then the advice spectrum is much narrower. The financial planner will collect all relevant information, as well as your goals and objectives. A typical objectives scenario is as follows for a wealthy client with a young family:

Life objectives

Your core objectives are given as follows. These can be added to and changed as your circumstances change.

Financial objectives (on a scale of 1-4 where one is most important)
- Family Protection '1'
- Income protection '2'
- Critical Illness Cover '1'
- Private medical insurance '1'
- Long Term care '4'
- Mortgage/loan arrangements '4'
- Regular savings '2'
- Planning for retirement '1'
- Inheritance tax planning '1'
- Lump sum investment for growth '1'
- School and university fees planning '1'
- Reduce income tax '1'
- Use of ISA allowances for 2019/20 '1'
- Financial Track to run on '1' with investment ideas
- To have a financial plan '1'

Lifestyle planning objectives
- Provide for the school fees funding issues
- Best for the family and family security and protection
- A decent retirement – early, if possible
- Financial security
- To be healthy and active
- Using money most efficiently – including the investment of future lump sums received or generated

In particular, you wish the financial planning process to include the following:
- To keep track of investments and investment management
- Keep cash in a high interest account for access
- Advice on capital gains tax
- General capital gains tax savings and saving income tax

- Children's savings and to achieve £50,000 at the age of 23
- School and education fees planning
- Planning around wills and inheritance taxes
- Reduce the risk of IHT for your life policies, through trusts
- You can invest up to £1,000 per month for savings
- You have £100,000 for capital gains tax payments
- For investments, you are interested in IHT and CGT wrappers and may be interested in geared funds and non-correlated investments

An **older** client approaching retirement at the age of 65 may have the following objectives:

Financial objectives (on a scale of 1-4 where one is most important)
- Family Protection '1'
- Income protection '4'
- Critical Illness Cover '4'
- Private medical insurance '1'
- Long Term care '2-3'
- Mortgage/loan arrangements '4'
- Regular savings '4'
- Planning for retirement '1'
- Inheritance tax planning '1'
- Lump sum investment for income and growth '1'
- Reduce income tax '2'
- Use of ISA allowances for 2019/20 '1'
- Financial Track to run on '1' with investment ideas
- To have a financial plan '1'

In terms of lifestyle planning, the following are your objectives:
- Best for the family and family security and protection
- A financially secure retirement
- Financial security
- To be healthy and active
- Using money most efficiently – including the investment of pension lump sums

In particular, you wish the financial planning process to include the following:
- The best retirement options
- Maximise income with least risk
- To keep track of investments and investment management
- Planning around wills and reducing future inheritance taxes

Once the initial fact-finding and planning has been completed, including your attitude to investment risk, and, most of all, what you want your financial plan to do for you, the financial planner will compile a report with his findings, possible solutions and recommendations. This is also an educational process. If you do not understand what is being discussed, now is the time to find out and do not be afraid to ask questions. Financial planning is all about attitudes: your attitude towards a particular issue or problem, your attitude to investment risk, your attitude to the proposals that have been formulated for you. If you don't like them, or they do not sit comfortably with you, inertia will set in and you will do nothing. If the results spring off the page at you, you will be more motivated to do something about it.

Prepare to pay a fee for advice and a report. Usual fee rates are between £150 and £200 +VAT per hour (but could be higher in London), and you could save hundreds of thousands of pounds.

Advisers can also advise trustees of trusts, and are engaged in inheritance tax and estate planning. These are known as Nominated Advisers.

The role of the nominated adviser in trusts

A 'nominated adviser' can be one of a variety of different professionals: for example, a stockbroker accepting instructions to buy or sell shares or gilts; or an independent financial adviser constructing an investment portfolio, or making a bond investment; a fund manager managing a portfolio or investments; or a banker taking instructions for a trust fixed interest investment.

The nominated adviser acts through the delegated powers of the trustees to make investments and advise on them, following instructions contained in the Policy Statement and Guidelines for the trust.

If an IFA is acting, a financial plan is constructed on the proposed investments to be made, following the Guidelines as outlined to the IFA; or a portfolio may be constructed. The actions taken by the IFA are not only subject to the *Trustee Act 2000* but also to the complex rules and regulations of the Financial Services Authority and the *Financial Services Markets Act 2000* and certain EU laws and directives.

Whatever the professional capacity, a nominated adviser *must* report back to the trustees at regular intervals and undertake *systematic* reviews of the investments and financial planning processes.

The statutory duty of care laid down in the *Trustee Act 2000* does not apply to agents, only to trustees. An agent is subject to a contractual duty of care. An agent is subject to the same restrictions as would apply to trustees who are carrying out the functions themselves. If an agent is authorised under *section 11* of the Act, then the agent must act in accordance with the provisions of *section 4* of the Act in exercising a 'general investment power'. This section lays down the standard investment rules which include a requirement to review the investments, to consider their suitability and to consider diversification.

Where a breach of the duty of care set out in the Act is alleged, the trustees may have recourse against the nominated adviser, acting under their delegated investment powers; however, the trustees are ultimately responsible for the 'health' of the trust(s) and for any and all actions taken in relation to investment decisions, management and compliance.

The role of the client

The client has the most important role. The client must supply all available information and describe his attitude to risk and his objectives. He must agree beforehand to the terms of business and fee agreement with the financial adviser before any work can commence, and should be consulted on a regular basis with regard to the proposals being made for him. The client should also be brought up to speed on the mechanics of the proposals and how products and tax planning work. This is an important part of consumer education and understanding of how the financial processes work, so that the correct courses of action are undertaken. The financial adviser has a duty of care to the client, and must treat the client fairly, and is under an obligation to do so. The client should therefore prepare himself with as much knowledge and understanding as possible, and be fully aware of what he is undertaking.

Many client complaints stem from not understanding the proposed recommendations and thereafter being in products and strategies that are not suitable for them. The main problems arise from the client being placed in unsuitable products and investments. Much has to do with risk-rating of products and strategies and the client's understanding of risk. There are many different definitions of risk, some relating to the client's attitude to risk, others relating to risk-rating of products and strategies, so that these can be aligned with the client's attitude to risk. The risk-rating spectrum of the financial adviser is wide, and covers all investment possibilities. The risk-rating perception of the client may be narrower, depending on his understanding of risk as it applies to him at that time. His perceptions may change in the future.

For example, before retirement, a client with some time to go to retirement may be less risk averse and put more investment assets at risk with the hope of increased returns. After retirement, the same client cannot afford to lose capital and his risk profile may change substantially. Terminology used is therefore important and must be understood. Your perception of a balanced investment portfolio may be 50% in the building society and 50% in National Savings – however, the financial planner's perception is a mix of fixed interest investments and equities and bonds to give you a balanced return.

There are substantial inheritance tax savings to be made through proper planning – you may save thousands of pounds (though you will not be round to experience it at the end of the day!), and should be prepared to pay a fee for advice to achieve your objectives. As they say, a good financial planner is worth his or her weight in gold; a poor one may cost you dearly.

Epilogue

Inheritance Tax Simplified has been produced as a guide to take you through the maze of complex tax and other legislation which may affect you. One thing is certain – there will always be change, and such change may even be retrospective. This does not mean that you stop planning – in fact the reverse, as plans need to be constantly reviewed to ensure that they are updated and meet your changing needs and circumstances. Inheritance tax will affect people directly and indirectly. Government-quoted assertions that IHT only affects the very rich are unreliable, as I have shown. Around one in five households will feel the impact of IHT over the coming years. IHT liabilities up the line will mean that those down the line will get less. This applies equally to your house, your investments and your pensions. The knock-on effect of reducing your wealth by at least 40% on death affects what is available for your dependants, and your heirs.

There are further planning opportunities using transferable NRBs – however, good planners will already have taken these into account and many estates will in all likelihood not be affected by these changes. Certainly, unmarried couples and single and divorced people will not be.

You therefore need to 'box clever' on this one. On the one hand there are ground rules laid down by the Government on what you can and cannot do; on the other, experienced financial planners and tax strategists will work within these rules to get the best possible advantage for you.

Whilst house values generally are increasing in 2015 and mortgage rates remain low, IHT remains an ever-present factor. The introduction from April 2017 of the Additional nil rate band (Family Allowance) for home owners. announced in Budget 2015 only applies where the home is left to children or grandchildren (it begins at £100,000 in 2017 and rises to £175,000 by 2020), and many will be left out of this new allowance. Also, if the total estate value exceeds £2 million, the new NRB tapers significantly.

Whilst appeasing homeowners, the Government is still looking to obtain over £6bn from taxpayers over the next two years in inheritance taxes – so plan as early as possible.

Major recent changes have been that pension funds are no longer subject to IHT (in certain circumstances they still are though); the nil rate band remains at £325,000 until at least 2021 where it should be increased by the CPI for inflation (there have no inflationary increases since 2009) thus causing further devaluation of your estate. The Government continues to seek ways to punish non domicilliaries with penal taxation and removal of the non-dom status wherever possible.

There is a new statutory residency test (announced in FA 2013); a reduced IHT rate of 36% will apply if you leave at least 10% of assets to charity from 5

April 2012. The attack on life assurance policies and restricting premiums to £3,600 per annum and the closing of the excluded property trust loophole to escape IHT was announced. The Government attack on trusts has continued unabated with the proposed new regime for a single nil rate band for each person, as opposed to each trust, however this has been temporarily shelved following consultation. It would have increased periodic costs for those falling over the NRB limit. The calculation of periodic and exit charges from trusts will be simplified, as the present calculations are onerous. There will now be a fixed flat rate of 6% after any nil rate band is taken into account. There has also been an attack on deeds of variation – a much used estate planning tool used after death – as this is seen as tax avoidance, and the current system is open to consultation. Lastly, the intestacy rules have been modified, which is to be welcomed.

I cannot over-emphasise the need to plan effectively, if only to get your financial affairs in order for when you die. Often when I am asked to advise on estates after the death of a loved one I find that more could have been done not only to mitigate or reduce IHT, but also to ensure effective passage of estate assets to where they should be going. To give yourself a track to run on, and to make it less onerous for those coming after you, it is better to be organised now with effective planning, rather than to be remembered as someone who did nothing.

This book will help you to think about your own situation and to plan a way forward. You will be better prepared to answer the questions of the financial planner, and will have a better overall understanding of what is required and how to go about ensuring a successful outcome.

Abbreviations

A-Day	Start of pensions reform on 6th April 2006
AIM	Alternative Investment Market
A&M	Accumulation-and-maintenance trust
APR	Agricultural property relief
ASP	Alternatively secured pension from the age of 75/77
BPR	Business property relief
CFP	Chartered financial planner
CGT	Capital gains tax
CGTA	Capital Gains Taxes Act
CII	Chartered Insurance Institute
CLT	Chargeable lifetime transfer
CPI	Consumer prices index
DGT	Discounted gift trust
EIS	Enterprise Investment Scheme
FLAT	Funded life assurance trust
FCA	Financial Conduct Authority
FSB	Federation of Small Businesses
FTSE	Main UK stock exchange
FURBS	Funded unapproved retirement benefit scheme
GWR	Gifts with reservation
HMRC	Her Majesty's Revenue and Customs
IFAP	IFA Promotion Ltd
IFP	Institute of Financial Planning
IHT	Inheritance tax
IHTA	Inheritance Tax Act 1984
IIP	Interest in possession
IOU	'I owe you' – a debt undertaking
ISA	Individual Savings Account
LPA	Lasting Power of Attorney
MIR	Minimum income requirement (for flexible drawdown)
NI	National Insurance
NEST	National Employment Savings Trust
NPSS	National Pension Savings Scheme
NRB	Nil rate band

OEIC	Open-ended investment company
PET	Potentially exempt transfer
PFS	Personal Finance Society
POAT	Pre-owned assets tax
RNRB	Residential nil rate band
RPI	Retail prices index
SEIS	Seed EIS
SHIP	Safe Home Income Plan provider
SLA	Standard Lifetime Allowance
TA	Trustee Act 2000
TFC	Tax-free cash or pension commencement lump sum
USP	Unsecured pension to the age of 75
VCT	Venture capital trust

References

Tolley's Practical Tax Newsletters

Tolleys Tax Planning (Lexis Nexis)

Tolleys Tax Guide (Lexis Nexis)

Personal Financial Planning Manual (Tottel Publishing)

Pensions Simplified (Management Books 2000)

Long-Term Care Simplified (Management Books 2000)

Tax Planning for Family and Owner-Managed Companies (Tottel Publishing)

Clerical Medical Financial Planning Bulletin 'The Knowledge'

Skandia Informer

Zurich Technical Focus, Trust Literature, Product Literature

Aviva technical

Canada Life technical

Friends Provident technical

Prudential technical

Articles from: National and Trade Press; Money Marketing, Financial Adviser, Professional Adviser, New Model Adviser, Tax Insider, The Times, The Financial Times, Sunday Times; briefings from City Wire, Investment Week

Useful Addresses and Contacts

Personal Investment Management & Financial Advice Association (PIMFA)
22 City Road,
Finsbury Square,
London
EC1Y 2AJ
+44 (0) 20 7448 710
info@pimfa.co.uk

CISI
Chartered Institute for Securities and Investment
20 Fenchurch Street
London, EC3
customersupport@cisi.org
 +44 20 7645 0600

IFA Promotion Ltd
IFA Promotion can found at **www.unbiased.co.uk** or by phoning 0800 085 3251.

www.unbiased.co.uk and **www.impartial.co.uk**
for lists of IFAs and their competencies in your area

IFS School of Finance
Now the London Institute of Banking and Finance
409 Burgate lane
Canterbury
Kent
CT1 2XJ
Tel: 01227 818680

Law Society
Tel: 0207 242 1222 - general enquiries.
www.lawsociety.org.uk (England and Wales)
www.lawscot.org.uk (Scotland)
www.lawsoc-ni.org (Northern Ireland)

Institute of Chartered Accountants
Tel: 0207 920 8620

www.icaew.co.uk (England and Wales)
www.ifac.org (Scotland)
www.icai.ie (Ireland and Northern Ireland)

Institute of Financial Planning (IFP)
now merged with the Chartered Institute for Securities and Investment
www.financialplanning.org.uk

Personal Financial Society
42-48 High Road
South Woodford
London E18 2JP
Customer.serv@thepfs.org
Tel: 0208 5300852
www.thepfs.org

Chartered Insurance Institute (CII)
1st Floor, 21 Lombard Street, London, EC3V 9AH
Tel: 0208 9898464
www.cii.co.uk

STEP
Society of Trust and Estate Practitioners
26 Grosvenor Gardens
London
SW1W OGT
Tel: 0207 8384890

FCA
25 The North Colonnade
Canary Wharf
London
E14 5HS
Tel: 02070661000
www.fca.org.uk

Tony Granger
tonygranger@hotmail.com
07968 451854

Index

For further confidential information on inheritance tax, estate planning, or trusts, or to attend a seminar in your area:

- email the author at tonygranger@hotmail.com

- call 07968 451854, or

- send this page to:
  Tony Granger
  IHT Planning
  11 Melbourne Rise
  Bicton Heath
  Shrewsbury
  SY3 5DA

| Name: |
| Address: |
| |
| Postcode: |
| Telephone: |
| Email: |
| Nature of your enquiry: |
| |

Please photocopy this page to avoid spoiling your book.

www.elysium50plus.co.uk
tonygranger@hotmail.com
Tel: 01743 360827   Mob: 07968 451854